# RUSSIAN WRITERS AND SOCIETY IN THE SECOND HALF OF THE NINETEENTH CENTURY

# Russian Writers and Society in the Second Half of the Nineteenth Century

Joe Andrew
*Lecturer in Russian Studies*
*University of Keele*

*First published 1982 by*
THE MACMILLAN PRESS LTD
*London and Basingstoke*
*Companies and representatives*
*throughout the world*

ISBN 0 333 25911 4

*Typeset in Great Britain by*
Activity, Teffont, Salisbury, Wilts
*and printed in Hong Kong*

For My Parents

# Contents

# Acknowledgements

I would like to thank very warmly all those who have in any way assisted me in the writing of this book: Sir Isaiah Berlin whom I consulted at an early stage of research and whose own writings on the period have proved of immense assistance; and Professor Eugenie Lampert, who first suggested that I take on this work and whose studies of the social and intellectual background have proved consistently stimulating and helpful; and all the other members of the Russian Studies Department at Keele, whom I have consulted and who have offered me great service in reading the manuscript and offering invaluable suggestions — Roger Bartlett, Chris Pike, Bob Service and Valentina Polukhina. I would particularly like to mention Katia Lampert, whose advice, assistance and encouragement were always most important. Finally I would like to thank Mrs Joan Heath who typed it.

*Keele, 1979*                                                               *Joe Andrew*

# Introduction

It is almost exactly one hundred years since Ivan Turgenev received an honorary doctorate of civil law at Oxford, in 1879. He was the first Russian writer to be known outside his homeland, the first translation of his work having appeared as early as 1855. Oxford's honouring of Turgenev was simply official recognition of his already established international fame and his works enjoyed a great vogue in the last quarter of the nineteenth century, on the European continent and in America, as well as in Britain. Conrad, Galsworthy, Henry James, Virginia Woolf and many others all attached what now seems an exaggerated importance to his work. In 1911 Ford Madox Ford declared: 'Shakespeare, if he had taken time to think upon these matters, would have been as great an artist as Tourgénieff.' But Turgenev was only the first to capture a foreign readership. Dostoevsky and Tolstoy, and to a lesser extent Chekhov, became very popular towards the end of the last century, and their popularity has hardly diminished today. Not only are these authors still widely read: many of them have had a major impact on twentieth-century literature and culture. Chekhov is rightly seen as one of the greatest influences on contemporary theatre and the short story, Dostoevsky is regarded as the forerunner of many important aspects of twentieth-century thinking, while Tolstoy's extra-literary activities had (and perhaps still have) great significance in the wider, political world, not least through one of his principal followers, Mahatma Gandhi.

It is an impossible task to explain fully why Russian writers have attained this position. To say that they are 'great writers' is clearly insufficient, and myths about the 'Russian soul' do not lead us very far. However, if one particular factor can be highlighted, it might well be the *intensity* of the writers' involvement with their contemporary society which so appeals to foreign as well as indigenous audiences. Writing towards the end of the eighteenth century, Alexandr Radishchev comments at the opening of his celebrated *A Journey from St Petersburg to Moscow*: 'I looked around — and my soul was wounded by the sufferings of man. I turned my gaze inward — and saw that the disasters of man proceed from man, and often because of the single fact that he does not look directly at the objects which surround him.' It was Radishchev's aim to turn a ruthlessly direct gaze at his society, to accuse it and to correct it. The whole work is inspired by disgust and indignation on the one hand, and self-lacerating compassion on the other — notes which were, in turn, to inspire many writers and thinkers who were to follow him in the nineteenth century. In his work, Radishchev brought to a culmination the eighteenth-century themes of civic criticism and established the tradition of a second voice in Russian society, the 'alternative government' which much of nineteenth-century literature was to form, and whose dominant notes were to be intense compassion and civic involvement.

During the first half of the nineteenth century most of the major writers and thinkers implicitly followed the direction mapped out by Radishchev — the early Pushkin, Lermontov, the Decembrist writers and, in particular, the men of the 'remarkable decade', such as Herzen, Bakunin and Belinsky. Literature and the criticism of it became almost the only available forum for political discussion. Both opposition and government viewed literature as a kind of 'alternative government', a second voice which was able, if only indirectly, to offer some kind of challenge to established ideas and behaviour when more obvious political methods were virtually impossible. It was the aim of an earlier study by the present author, *Writers and Society during the Rise of Russian Realism*, to trace the development of this 'alternative government', particularly during the reign of Nicholas I. The present work continues this discussion, in an attempt to see how the four great realists of the second half of nineteenth-century Russia, Turgenev, Dostoevsky, Tolstoy and Chekhov, developed the tradition inaugurated by Radishchev and built upon by Pushkin, Lermontov, Gogol and Belinsky.

As in the previous work, the four writers concerned will be discussed in terms of their involvement with their contemporary society, and the method used will largely follow the one I employed earlier. The link between writers and their society is an exceedingly complex one, and the problem will be approached from a number of different points of view. The first priority is to establish the authors' original position in society, that is, their class origins and the implications these may have in their particular society. What impact does belonging to a declining or rising class have on a writer's self-perception? And if writers are alienated from their own class, to what extent can they join or identify themselves with another? How important is education and the general spirit of the age of their early years in modifying their social origins?

Perhaps the single most important result of the social position of writers is their financial situation and the impact this inevitably has on their work. Financial independence protects any artist against the demands of the market, and financially insecure artists, who have to live off their literary income, for example, are faced with a difficult struggle if they are not to succumb to extraneous influences. Some writers obviously, then, regard their work primarily as a much-needed source of income, but the motives for artistic creation are clearly much more complicated. Do they write for a specific readership, and if so, for which one — the established, conventional market, or do they attempt to lead, to set new patterns, establish new genres, express new or oppositional views? Most important of all is the extent to which writing is to be considered a private or a public activity. That writers can ever create entirely for themselves, without even a notional readership in view, is an extremely dubious proposition. And whatever may be the ostensible integration of any artist into his society, or a specific audience within it, it is also important to consider his self-perception. What value, that is, can artists place on their work, what purpose do they see it serving, what aims do they have when they write?

The social function of art can also be considered within a narrower field, since artistic change is almost always closely linked with social change. New genres and forms usually spring from new patterns of behaviour, the rise to power of a new class or the emergence of a new ideology. And so a study of writers' relationships to the art that immediately precedes them is no mere formalistic exercise: on the contrary, an examination of innovatory techniques will give new insights on the changing role of art in any society. A prominent instance of this is Dostoevsky's attempt to to put an end to 'landowners' literature' with his new 'higher realism'.

It is also important to consider the writers' own views of art, to discuss what demands from society they accept or reject in principle, as well as in practice. Do they consider that art should be useful, or do they regard it as serving its own ends? In either case writers generally regard art as having a meaningful function, although the precise meaning varies greatly even within the development of a single writer, or in a given period. The most striking example of this diversity of viewpoint in the present work is the bitter polemics between the 'fathers', particularly Turgenev, Tolstoy and Dostoevsky and the 'sons', Chernyshevsky and Dobrolyubov, at the end of the 1850s, precisely over the issue of the social function of art. Closely linked with this issue is the way in which a writer chooses to depict society. Many writers in nineteenth-century Russia followed Radishchev and turned a ruthless gaze at their relatively backward country; the tension between writer and publicist can be seen particularly in Tolstoy. Others attempted to depict 'the body and pressure of time', as Turgenev quoted Shakespeare, but even in the least utilitarian of authors, such as Chekhov and Turgenev himself, there was a strong undercurrent of moralism. No writer can ever really be a mere 'mirror' held up to nature.

Just as an artistic work inevitably has a social value and function — whatever its creator's intentions — so too a writer can often be more usefully viewed as a member of a particular group or society rather than as an isolated being. Accordingly a consideration of the writers' relationships with their society will play a central part in the ensuing discussion. Usually writers participate in a literary or intellectual grouping whose opinions they deliberately or unwittingly express, and their changing relationships with their intellectual peers tell us much about both their own artistic development and the meaning of their art, as well as about the shifting currents of opinion in society. This applies even more so to the critical reaction to a writer's work, especially in Russia, where after 1830 almost all literary criticism was implicitly or explicitly ideological — and usually the latter. The importance of critical opinion in nineteenth-century Russian literature, particularly after Belinsky, cannot be overstated, and we cannot fully understand the role of literature in the period without careful consideration of how and why certain books were acclaimed or vilified.

Similarly, an artist's popularity tells us much about both the aims of a writer and about the changing demands of society. We need to look at who read a particular work, and why, in an attempt to understand whether a writer was catering for known demands or striving to create new ones, to invoke fresh responses from the public. Innovatory works, it should be noted, generally fare badly with both the critics and the public. Despite this a great writer will occasionally succeed in changing public taste, and will create new perceptions of reality. Indeed, it can be argued that the sign of great writers is precisely their ability to force the wider society to reconsider, and even change its accepted view of reality.

A rather different problem is the degree of the writer's integration within more specific sections of society, that is, oppositional, even revolutionary forces on the one hand, and the government or 'establishment' on the other. Superficially, these relationships may seem to have little to do with a writer's art, but in nineteenth-century Russia the opposite was usually the case. Some of the writers considered here not only experienced censorship difficulties, but found themselves suspect to and in conflict with the ruling authorities, and some of them, at some stage in their lives, were associated with radical groups.

All the above questions concern the writer's relationship with society. We cannot, though, fully understand this, our central concern, without taking into account what particular writers thought of the world that surrounded them — both in their artistic writings and elsewhere. Writers' explicit political and philosophical views are often interesting in themselves and can tell us much about their artistic writing. They also usually play an important part in shaping their actual relationships with society, and in turn are changed by their experience of the world. What is rather more problematical is the view of the world expressed in their artistic writings. While any work of art will inevitably embody a certain world-view many questions arise. Can one find a coherent viewpoint in all, or most, of an artist's creations, and is this the artist's own or that of a social group or class? To what extent can art best be viewed as visionary — as propagating an *alternative* reality rather than the reality which actually surrounds the artist? In other words, can we best view art as a *challenge* to reality as it is perceived by other members of society? Such questions are particularly important in the period that concerns us. The nineteenth century in Russia saw immense social change, bringing with it the final destruction of

a semi-feudal society. Industrialisation, the rise of capitalism
and the bourgeoisie, increased secularisation — all this was
carried through alongside the disintegration of old values and
beliefs. It was a century of conflict and dissension culminating
in the establishment of an unprecedented political order. The
role of literature in such a society was inevitably markedly
different from its function in a more stable period and the
demands placed on literature were rather idiosyncratic. And so
we find that literature came to play a part that is always latent
within any art. It came, that is, to work for society, by working
against it; it challenged old beliefs and sought new ones; it acted
as the forum for political discussion when more obvious channels
were closed. From a purely aesthetic point of view, art may have
suffered, but in many other ways its peculiar function as an
'alternative government' enormously enriched it. And for this
reason nineteenth-century Russian literature remains a remarkable social as well as artistic monument to those who involun-
tarily, or wholeheartedly, followed Radishchev from St Petersburg to Moscow.

A couple of technical points should be mentioned. All trans-
lations in the text and notes are my own unless otherwise stated.
The transliteration is that used in *The Slavonic and East European
Review*.

# Chronology

| | |
|---|---|
| 1790 | Publication of Radishchev's *A Journey from St Petersburg to Moscow* |
| 1796 | Accession of Paul I |
| 1799 | Birth of Pushkin |
| 1801 | Accession of Alexander I |
| 1809 | Birth of Gogol |
| 1811 | Birth of Belinsky |
| 1812 | French invasion of Russia, followed by Russian entry in Western Europe and occupation of Paris |
| | Birth of Herzen |
| 1814 | Birth of Lermontov |
| 1818 | Birth of Turgenev |
| 1821 | Birth of Dostoevsky |
| 1825 | Accession of Nicholas I |
| | Decembrist uprising |
| 1826 | Trial, exile and execution of Decembrists |
| | Third Section set up |
| 1828 | Birth of Tolstoy |
| | Birth of Chernyshevsky |
| 1830–1 | Polish uprising; abrogation of Polish Constitution |
| 1836 | Publication of Chaadaev's *First Philosophical Letter* |
| | Birth of Dobrolyubov |
| 1837 | Death of Pushkin |
| 1841 | Death of Lermontov |
| 1848 | European revolutions |
| | Death of Belinsky |
| 1849 | Petrashevsky 'conspirators' arrested |
| 1852 | Death of Gogol |
| 1853–6 | Crimean War |
| 1855 | Accession of Alexander II |
| 1860 | Birth of Chekhov |
| 1861 | Emancipation of serfs |

|          | Death of Dobrolyubov |
|----------|----------------------|
| 1863     | Polish uprising |
| 1864     | Court reform |
|          | Introduction of *zemstvo* and city self-government |
| 1866     | First assassination attempt on Alexander II, by Karakozov |
| 1868     | Birth of Maxim Gorky |
| 1870     | Death of Herzen |
| 1871     | Paris Commune |
| 1874     | First 'going to the people' movement |
| 1877–8   | Trials of '50' and '193' |
| 1878     | Vera Zasulich shoots St Petersburg police chief |
|          | Series of anti-terrorist measures |
| 1880     | Terrorists succeed in planting bomb in Winter Palace |
|          | Third Section abolished; establishment of new department of State Police |
| 1881     | Assassination of Alexander II |
|          | Death of Dostoevsky |
|          | Accession of Alexander III |
| 1883     | Death of Turgenev |
| 1889     | Death of Chernyshevsky |
| 1892–1903 | Witte revolutionises industry, commerce and transport |
| 1894     | Accession of Nicholas II |
| 1897     | Foundation of Moscow Arts Theatre |
| 1898     | Foundation of Marxist R.S.D.L.P. (Social Democratic Labour Party) |
| 1903     | Lenin splits Social Democratic Party into Bolshevik and Menshevik wings |
|          | Kishinyov pogrom |
| 1904     | Assassination of V. I. Plehve (Minister of Interior) |
| 1905     | End of Russo-Japanese War |
|          | Bloody Sunday (9 January) |
|          | Assassination of Grand Duke Sergei |
|          | Abortive revolution |
|          | State Duma conceded |
| 1906–11  | Stolypin era. Successive dumas |
|          | Revolutionary agricultural reforms |
|          | Rasputin gains ascendancy over Tsaritsa and Tsar |
| 1910     | Death of Tolstoy |

| | |
|---|---|
| 1911 | Assassination of Stolypin |
| 1914–1917 | War with Germany and Austria |
| 1916 | Rasputin murdered |
| 1917 | Nicholas abdicates (February) |
| | The Provisional Government |
| | October 26: October Revolution |

# 1 Ivan Turgenev

Turgenev was the first important political novelist in nineteenth-century Russian literature. No other novelist of the period was able to combine to the same extent insight into contemporary political developments with artistic achievement. It was Turgenev's aim to deal with such developments, and it was this element which was the most important to his contemporaries. He was no preacher but he was as concerned as any other writer of the period with the 'accursed questions', in particular the future destiny of Russia,[1] and brought his own type of commitment to bear on his treatment of contemporary issues. Given that his writing career began under the direct influence of Belinsky, such commitment is hardly surprising, even if it was underplayed by many contemporary and later critics. Turgenev was much maligned for apparent lack of conviction, and today he may seem pallid in comparison with Tolstoy and Dostoevsky, but both these views pay scant justice to his art and deeply-held beliefs.

Turgenev's background is typical of most Russian writers and intellectuals in the nineteenth century; it was rich and aristocratic with private tutors, expensive education and high personal income in later life. Turgenev's circumstances were particularly affluent — his mother owned five thousand serfs.[2] Yet the emotional ethos of Turgenev's early years at the hands of a tyrannical mother left many negative impressions: he lived in an atmosphere of *samodurstvo*, that is, extremely backward, provincial behaviour and thinking.[3] Turgenev claimed to have not a single happy memory from his childhood. On the other hand, however, he became well acquainted with provincial life, in particular that of the peasants, which provided him with abundant material for his early stories, such as *A Sportsman's Sketches* (1847–52). Even more important were the social convictions formed in these years, which were to remain central to his beliefs in later life. Turgenev frequently argued with his mother about

1

her treatment of the peasants,[4] and he probably developed at this time the social conscience of the 'repentant nobleman' — that is, a feeling of guilt and shame before his oppressed brothers, whose lot he felt obliged to ameliorate.

It is also important to consider the background to Turgenev's early years in a more general framework, for the period of his maturation (roughly 1830–55) saw crucial changes in the intellectual life of Russia which were to have far-reaching consequences. The era was distinguished by two closely related phenomena: a highly repressive and reactionary regime and an intellectual withdrawal from political concerns into the realms of abstract thought. As Granjard puts it, Stankevich had eclipsed Pestel and Ryleev,[5] and the intelligentsia was more concerned with Schellingian Idealism and problems of universal dimensions than with the grim reality which surrounded them.[6] After Chaadaev's *Letter* of 1836 the situation changed, even if not immediately. The principal question he raised — that of Russia's destiny — was of course an old one, and had been discussed in the eighteenth century as well as by the Romantic writers and critics in their search for *narodnost'*, but after 1836 the question had greater immediacy and by 1840 the intellectual circles had begun to move from their Idealism to a greater concern with socio-political questions.

In the 1840s, then, Russian intellectual thought became radicalised, and Belinsky, Herzen, Bakunin and many others came under the influence of the French Utopian Socialists,[7] and the German materialist thinker Feuerbach. The system as a whole was attacked even if there were few specific plans for rebellion. This was partly because oppositional thought was much less coherent, and less radical than in the latter part of the century, but also because the possibility of any revolution was too remote. The State was too strong and the mass of the people too politically naive and ignorant. Moreover, of course, political parties did not exist and there were not even any organised political groups of a smaller nature, at least until the 1860s, although the Petrashevtsy 'conspiracy' in the later 1840s was the first sign of radical thought becoming radical action.

Similar charges occurred in literature: from the late 1830s there was a growing demand for greater realism and criticism of contemporary reality. A new role emerged for the writer. He could no longer stand apart from society on his aloof, Romantic heights; now he had responsibility towards his society. At the same time, specific intellectual groupings arose – the Slavophils and Westernisers. Their differences are well known, but they were also united by a common hatred of the regime and by a concern with the dominant question of the 1840s – the emancipation of the peasants. The discovery of this unknown people originated perhaps with Rousseau and by the 1840s had become a pan-European phenomenon.[8] The first response on the part of intellectual circles, especially the Westernisers, was to stand aloof,[9] but this position soon became untenable, and the question then was, as it was for Turgenev in his childhood, what can one do to help? By 1845–50 there was a consensus that the peasants should be liberated, if only for economic reasons.[10] Even the government by now was aware that something had to be done, and in the late 1830s and 1840s a series of reform commissions were set up in response to an increase in peasant uprisings and a worsening economic situation.[11] The Slavophils, while idealising the spiritual value of the peasantry, were also opposed to serfdom. Khomyakov wrote in 1839: 'This execrable legal slavery which is crippling for us in all respects, from the material point of view as much as the legal, ought to be quickly extirpated by general and efficacious measures.'[12] The Westernisers now agreed, even if from a variety of viewpoints.[13] It was this common climate of opinion, of reason, pity and conscience, that gave birth to the 'repentent noblemen' and to Turgenev's first major work, *A Sportsman's Sketches,* which in turn greatly advanced this climate of opinion.

The year after the first of these sketches appeared, 1848, was the year of revolutions in Europe, which in turn engendered even deeper reaction in Russia. The year 1849 saw the arrest of the Petrashevtsy,[14] as well as the radical writer Saltykov-Shchedrin and of the leading Slavophils Samarin and Ivan Aksakov – the last three all for trivial offences. The chief censor, Buturlin, declared that he would ban the Gospels if he could, because they contained so many democratic ideas![15] Censorship became even stricter and secret committees were set up to detect any 'unsoundness' in material that was actually published. For the next seven years almost all forms of political and social criticism were stifled, there was no glimmering of liberal thought. Indeed, the regime seemed hostile to thought as such. Count Uspensky noted: 'One could not move, one could not even

dream; it was dangerous to give any sign of thought – of the
fact that you were not afraid'.[16] In these years Belinsky and
Gogol died, Dostoevsky was exiled, Herzen emigrated never to
return, and Turgenev himself was exiled to his estate.

Such, then, were the dark years of Turgenev's maturation.
Equally important were his own education and the influences
on him. As a child Turgenev was passionately interested in literature and began writing poetry at the age of eight. In 1827, he
moved to Moscow where he attended first a preparatory school
and then the Lazarevsky Institute, a select boarding-school. In
1833 he went to Moscow University before moving to St Petersburg University a year later. All this was a mere preparation for
his move in 1838 to Berlin, the centre of Hegelianism. Turgenev's
early interests were various: he read enthusiastically the Enlightenment writers, especially Voltaire and Diderot, and took a keen
interest in the ideas and personalities of 1789.[17] However, the
crucial period of his education were the years in Berlin where
Turgenev, like many others, plunged into the 'German Sea' –
and even considered becoming a lecturer in philosophy, taking
an M.A. at St Petersburg in 1842, as well as applying (unsuccess-
fully) for a job there. (His dissertation shows the obvious influence of Hegel.)[18] It was also in Berlin, and shortly afterwards,
that Turgenev came into contact with the personalities who
were to exert a decisive influence on his life – Stankevich,
Bakunin and, above all, Belinksy.[19]

All these personalities had a common impact on Turgenev:
each displayed passion and idealism, which Turgenev admired
even if lacking them himself. Turgenev met Stankevich in Berlin
in 1838, and immediately fell under the sway of the religious,
philosophical Idealism to which Stankevich had devoted his
life.[20] Stankevich had almost no interest in politics: instead he
placed his emphasis on the need for the self-perfection of each
individual before society could be regenerated. Stankevich had a
profound impact on Turgenev, and Turgenev felt it as a great
blow when Stankevich died in 1840. The influence was lasting:
although Turgenev later became interested in political developments, he took almost no active part in politics, and personalism
was to remain an essential feature of his liberalism.

Two months after Stankevich's death Turgenev entered an
equally intense friendship with Bakunin. The later anarchist was
at this time as uninterested in politics as were Stankevich and

Turgenev, and he led Turgenev even further away from socio-political realities (as he had done three years before to Belinsky). Only when Turgenev became close friends with Belinsky in 1843 did he come to see the ludicrousness of such a position in the Russia of the 1840s. It was Belinsky (who had come to similar conclusions in 1841) who established him firmly on the path of social realism and social responsibility. Turgenev's work in the 1840s reflects the developing influence of Belinksy. Indeed, some of the most important stories of the *Sketches,* such as *The Bailiff,* were written or conceived of in Salzbrunn where Turgenev was with the dying Belinsky.[21] But the legacy lasted long after the critic's death and remained the central influence. He learned from him that a writer must, at the very least, bear witness to the truth, that one has a profound responsibility as a *citizen* to one's fellow-countrymen.[22] Turgenev's favourite hero, Bazarov, has certain parallels with Belinsky, while Rudin's thought clearly echoes the critic's. Turgenev also derived inspiration from Belinsky's life and writing for many of his central beliefs: his love of Russia with an equal regard for Western culture, a belief in the individual and his inalienable rights. Turgenev clearly remembered his mentor dearly: thirty years later he proposed a toast to his friend at a banquet in St Petersburg and spoke of him with warm, intense feeling.[23]

Given Turgenev's aristocratic background it may seem surprising that he had such a close friendship with Belinsky. It does, indeed, say much for Turgenev's ability to overcome the prejudices of his class. In many ways, however, he remained true to his class origin. His life in the 1840s was typical of that of a young man of good family — he was only vaguely interested in the Civil Service career he reluctantly began in 1842 and took a dilettante interest in the arts. He found the intense atmosphere of the circles oppressive, and affected the manners of a young man of society.[24] Indeed, when he did begin to take his writing career more seriously, his mother was most indignant. Her position is revealing of the prevailing attitude to literature among the conservative nobility. 'Is that the business of a nobleman?' she cried. 'In my opinion, écrivain ou gratte-papier, c'est tout un. Both daub paper for money.'[25] She insisted that he should enter the Civil Service, rise a few ranks, get married — and then he would be worthy of his name. When Turgenev showed her Belinksy's favourable review of *Parasha,* hoping to appease her, his mother became even more furious, shouting that now any *popovich* (i.e. a village priest's son) could criticise him — *him* a nobleman![26]

Such was the aristocratic milieu with which Turgenev partially identified. And his manners and habits remained those of the born aristocrat — and they were later to precipitate conflicts with both Dostoevsky and the 'new men'.[27] Some of Turgenev's attitudes also stem from his class background. His depiction of the peasants, however sympathetic, is essentially that of the philanthropic squire, and he remained a nobleman in his dealings with them, even if a repentent nobleman. Gilbert Phelps puts it well, when comparing Turgenev to Galsworthy:

> They were both gentlemen with inheritances, they were both expensively educated, cultured, fond of travel and of sport. They both found themselves out of step with their own class, critical of its traditions and conventions, but still rooted in it. . . . . They were both sensitive to the injustices inflicted on the victims of the social system, but were both unable to throw themselves whole-heartedly into a cause.[28]

But Turgenev was not completely identified with his class. Of all elements in Russian society, he was most critical of the 'fathers', his own class and generation. Both *Fathers and Sons* (1862) and *Virgin Soil* (1876), while sympathetic to the elder liberals, stand as condemnations of the aristocracy and their position as the ruling class in Russia. At all times Turgenev, if he was on anyone's side, was on the side of the 'sons' — the rising, non-aristocratic intelligentsia. Like Stendhal and Balzac before him, Turgenev was able to see beyond his own class, as in the sympathetic portraits of the revolutionary Insarov in *On the Eve* (1859) and the 'nihilist' Bazarov in *Fathers and Sons*. P. F. Yakubovich describes Turgenev's imaginative 'altruism' well: 'A gentleman by birth, an aristocrat by upbringing and character, a gradualist by conviction, Turgenev, perhaps without knowing it himself . . . sympathised with and even served the Russian revolution.'[29]

Turgenev's origins obviously afforded him many advantages: in particular, it allowed him great freedom from the exigencies of the market. This freedom was almost always his. In his early adulthood he was able to live as extravagantly as he liked, always supported by his mother. However, relations between them worsened in the 1840s. She disliked his attitude to the Civil Service, they argued over the serfs, and his liaison with Pauline Viardot also displeased her. Accordingly, she cut down his allowance, and in 1848 cut off his financial supply altogether (although she relented in 1850 and sent him sufficient money to pay off his debts).[30] For a short time Turgenev was forced to live off his own resources, which he managed by borrowing from his friends, Viardot and his servants.[31] At the time, though, he was directly dependent on his literary income which, of course, was not large: Annenkov in 1847 described him as 'very poor'[32] and Turgenev claimed that the 200R he received as literary fees saved him from starvation. Turgenev's relative hardship contributed to the worsening of relations with the *Contemporary* group. Twice in the 1840s he received advances from the journal and failed to deliver the promised material: in 1850 he even sold a story to *Notes of the Fatherland*, after promising it to *The Contemporary*.[33]

Turgenev's salvation came the following year when his mother died, leaving him the master of eleven estates, and an annual income of about 25,000R.[34] In addition, with increasing literary fame, he became, along with Tolstoy, the best-paid writer of his day. In 1857 an edition of his stories brought him 7,500R, while *On the Eve* realised 4,000R. By 1882 he was receiving 60,000R per annum from his literary income. In later years the security afforded by his personal fortune was slightly diminished by some financial worries — his uncle Nicholas seems to have swindled him of 50,000R[35] and his son-in-law went bankrupt in the 1870s — but generally after 1851 Turgenev was never faced with any need to publish. Moreover, he was able to allow himself the luxury of costly agricultural experiments after 1861,[36] as well as to be famous for his generosity to other writers and causes. In the 1850s he bailed Tolstoy out after the latter had lost all his money gambling; he helped Bakunin in the 1860s, and supported Flaubert after he had settled in Paris in the 1870s. Turgenev's generosity became a by-word and he became a kind of unofficial Russian ambassador, whose door and purse were open to almost any petitioner — especially young writers and emigré radicals. In particular, Turgenev contributed regularly to the funds of the radical populist journal, *Forward!*

Because of his wealth, Turgenev could take a fairly relaxed
view of literature: he did not regard it as a chosen career until
the mid-1840s. When he first went to St Petersburg he made
no attempt to acquaint himself with the literary milieu: Gogol,
Pushkin and Lermontov were observed only from a distance.
Academic studies appealed to him more – Greek and Latin, and
then abstract philosophy. In the early 1840s the Civil Service
became his career, and he took some genuine interest in it, submitting a Memorandum on serfdom in 1842 – of which nothing
came. None the less, he continued writing and in 1843 published
*Parasha*: Belinsky wrote well of it, the two became friends and
thereafter Turgenev's mind was made up. For some time, in fact,
he had been looking for his true métier: academic work and the
Civil Service had led nowhere, he did not feel committed to
being a landowner and he felt oppressed by the intellectual
circles.[37] Now writing became the most important element in
his life. He wrote, not because he had to, but to create objects
of beauty and to describe and comment on the changing aspect
of Russian society. Although there were periods in which he
wrote little, as for Lermontov before him, art lent meaning to
his life, and indeed, gave meaning to a world which seemed
increasingly meaningless.

The change was not, however, immediate. He may have decided to devote himself to literature, but he was still very unreliable in his vocation. Indeed for the rest of his life, he was never
entirely sure of himself as a writer. Constantly he was beset by
doubts about his talent, constantly he threatened to abandon
writing. These doubts occurred first in the mid-1850s and
deepened after his popularity declined. In 1869, after the controversy over *Fathers and Sons* and the failure of *Smoke* (1867),
he seriously thought of abandoning literature and did not publish another novel for seven years. In tune with his general pessimism of this time he thought that his work was no longer
needed or read, he was out of touch.[38] These thoughts continued
throughout the 1870s and account in large part for Turgenev's
delight at the rapturous reception he received in 1879.[39]

Belinsky's memory remained an inspiration when doubts
assailed Turgenev: he also engendered his fundamental conceptions of the role of art in society. Turgenev's early ideas stem
from his immersion in German Idealist philosophy: i.e. art was
'disinterested', the artist was a seer or prophet, aloof from the

everyday world.[40] This élitism crumbled in the late 1830s and the high moral responsibility that the Romantic conception of art implied took on a social dimension. Whereas Pushkin and Lermontov had consistently despised the 'mob', Turgenev sought, through his art, to elevate them to the level of the educated élite and to ameliorate their condition in general. And although Turgenev never became a teacher he was also never able to stand aloof from society. Thus, when he was attacked and vilified in the 1860s he never abnegated his responsibility as an artist and constantly sought to justify himself in the eyes of the public.[41]

Indeed, under the influence of Belinsky Turgenev came close to being a writer engagé. Certain of his works of the 1840s and early 1850s — *The Landowner, Mumu* and, of course *A Sportsman's Sketches* — while not explicit in their condemnation of the landowning class, are very clear as to their general intention. Turgenev attacked, almost caricatured, the masters (see in particular *The Landlord*) while giving a rather idealised, neo-sentimentalist view of the peasantry.[42] At the same time, however, Turgenev's social views, which inspired these works, suffered a serious setback with the collapse of the revolutions of 1848, and after the 'radicalism' of his art in these early works he sought to express his social commitment in more oblique ways. That is, he would never present reality in such relatively black and white tones again, with rare exceptions. He continued to write social works (all six of his novels), and to be critical of many facets of society, but he modified his views of the degree of social commitment of the artist considerably.

This proved particularly true when he came into contact with the followers of Belinsky in the 1850s. While he agreed that art should have a directly social role he could not accept that social considerations should take precedence over aesthetic considerations. Chernyshevsky's dissertation was published in 1855 and when Turgenev read it he was horrified, referring to it as a 'false and harmful book'.[43] Chernyshevsky's advocacy of purely utilitarian art, art that should act virtually as propaganda of a particular (i.e. radical) cause, was for Turgenev a negation of art as such. Even his own most directly polemical works of the 1840s had at least retained the appearance of objectivity. He attacked the critic Dobrolyubov as well, primarily for lacking Belinsky's aesthetic sensibilities, but as Nekrasov pointed out to him, times had changed and 'aesthetic' art, even with a strong civic commitment, was no longer sufficient.[44]

Nevertheless, for the rest of his life Turgenev remained adamant that the first duty of the artist was to present the truth (as he saw it) as faithfully as possible, with the minimum of tendentiousness. Throughout his correspondence with the conservative poet Fet in the 1860s he kept returning to this point: 'An artist who is incapable of seeing the white *and* the black, of looking both to the right and to the left, already stands on the brink of disaster.'[45] Nekrasov had argued that it was more important to be a citizen than an artist: except perhaps in the late 1840s Turgenev would have put this proposition in reverse — that is, like Pushkin, he attempted to look at reality 'with a Shakespearean gaze'. In the 1860s and 1870s in France he became closely associated with Flaubert and the Goncourt brothers and generally agreed with their proposition that 'the only duty of a novel was to be well written'.[46] Turgenev gave the clearest expression of his view of the artist's role in 1880 in *A Foreword to the Novels*. Here, significantly, he quotes Shakespeare. He had, he maintained, attempted: 'to depict honestly and impartially . . . "the body and pressure of time", and the rapidly changing face of cultured Russians'. Art, he insists — continuing and giving his last word on the polemics of the 1850s — must *not* serve extraneous ends: and he concludes with a very thinly disguised attack on Chernyshevsky: 'Only those who can do no other, no better, can subordinate themselves to a given theme or carry through a programme.'

There was another reason for Turgenev's refusal to accept utilitarian art. For him it destroyed the essence of art — the beautiful — and this was doubly tragic for him in that beauty was the most important value in his life, higher even than justice or freedom. He derived this appreciation originally from his Idealist days, but it was to remain with him all his life. In 1850 he wrote to Pauline Viardot: ' . . . You ask me what "The Beautiful" is. It is, despite the action of time which destroys the form in which it is expressed, always here . . . because Beauty is the only Imperishable thing, and so long as even the smallest remnant of its material form exists, its immortality is ensured.'[47] Art for Turgenev was the only immortality to which man could aspire; art remained higher than nature. He believed that only a work of beauty could transcend reality — and thereby overcome the awful nothingness that increasingly seemed to him to lie beneath the surface of life. And Beauty was to remain more important than social commitment.

Turgenev's representation of reality also played a part in the conflict with the 'sons'. After an adolescent flirtation with subjective, Lermontovian Romanticism, Turgenev began his public writing career in line with the two main tenets of the 'natural' school: he attempted to give a simple depiction of ordinary, everyday life, and to attack the negative aspects of his life. The very title of his first published work, *Parasha* – a 'lowly' peasant name – immediately indicated a break with his own Romantic past: we know immediately that this will be a drama of ordinary 'little' folk, and throughout the poem Turgenev consistently emphasises the typical and unexceptional. The language is deliberately prosaic: Parasha's mother has a 'face remarkably like a pie'. Parasha is a simple, sunburnt peasant girl and is not sentimentalised in the way that Karamzin's *Poor Liza* or Radishchev's virginal peasant girls were. The ending of the poem, with its prosaic anti-climax of a dull marriage – instead of tragic suicide – emphasises the implicit polemic.[48] Turgenev's 'naturalist' approach continued in later works of the 1840s, in particular *The Landowner,* whose 'Flemish scenes' (as Pushkin referred to similar details in his own work) of prosaic dullness continued the tradition of *Count Nulin* and parts of *Yevgeny Onegin.* Here the emphasis is firmly on the vulgar, the *poshlost'* of Russian life. It is the negative sides of country life that Turgenev describes here – the mediocre, hypocritical pretentiousness and the stupidity of all the characters – in suitably precise *details,* a technique Turgenev borrowed from Gogol.

This 'naturalism' should not disguise the fact that in these years Turgenev was far from being a totally objective artist. In accordance with the second main tenet of the 'natural' school, he emphasised and attacked the negative aspects of the reality he apparently 'faithfully' recorded, an approach which delighted the radicals and antagonised both the conservative critics and the government. *The Landowner* was probably the most tendentious work of the early period, with its virulent attack on the Slavophil landowner; it is an exposé, and with the possible exception of *Smoke* Turgenev was never to be so unambivalent again. *A Sportsman's Sketches,* while gentler in tone, were no less tendentious. Turgenev humanises the peasants, represents them as noble, proud and independent – despite their awful conditions – and shows the masters, for all their education and luxury, as being at best ignorant and inefficient and at worst cruel and despotic.[49] We have Turgenev's answer to Herzen's novel of 1844, *Who is Guilty?* The message may be discreet but Turgenev's propaganda is clear. *Mumu* continued this diadic approach: the ill-treated deaf-mute Gerassim attains almost heroic proportions in his fortitude and love of his dog, while the depiction of the cruel mistress is one of unalleviated cruelty and despotism. Both this story and the earlier ones make a very tendentious point and in a tone which often approaches indignant outrage: there is something very obviously wrong with the whole system of serfdom if such human, even heroic characters can be treated as mere chattels by incompetent masters.

Closely linked to this committed treatment of the serf–master relationship is Turgenev's account of his own class: the idealist 'Hamlets' or 'superfluous men' who, despite (or because of) their excellent education in abstract philosophy, are unequipped to deal with the realities of Russian life. *Rudin* is the fullest treatment of the type – for all his fine words on duty and self-sacrifice he is unable *to act*, to respond to the spontaneous love he awakens in Natalya – but all the earlier portraits conform to Turgenev's essentially critical approach. In *Parasha* the 'hero' is a clear descendent of Onegin, indifferent, bored and unable to act, to respond to genuine feeling. *The Conversation* (1845) continues the treatment of this type of egoistical 'spiritual invalid',[50] which at this stage is an impassioned, even vehement dismissal of the men who are of no value to society. As in the peasant stories, Turgenev's message is clear and the blame is directly placed on the individuals themselves for their own failings and failure.

However, by the late 1840s Turgenev was beginning to take a more genuinely objective approach to the world. *Hamlet of Shchigrov Province* (1849) marks a significant switch: Turgenev begins to see both 'the white and the black' of the situation, and this applies *a fortiori* to Turgenev's treatment of Rudin. Increasingly Turgenev came to see wider social forces as 'extenuating circumstances': he *gradually* came, that is, to the 'Shakesperean view' that he was later to see as the *conditio sine qua non* of the true artist. Rudin's failure is, then, as much a con-

demnation of society as of the individual. Noble thoughts may
no longer be enough for Russian society, new approaches may
be required, but Rudin himself cannot be held entirely responsible for what his education and society in general have made
him.

And so the early 1850s marked a reassessment of Turgenev's
representation of reality. From early commitment, even tendentiousness, he 'retreated' to a more all-round, objective view of
reality. This is not to say that his approach ceased to be personal. For example, his depiction of the liberals and idealists
remained consistently critical, as in *Fathers and Sons*, or in the
character of Sipyagin in *Virgin Soil*. Equally, he remained at
least partially committed in his depiction of the 'new men'. For
all his personal differences with them he consistently depicted
the Bazarov types not merely objectively, but with great sympathy. In *Fathers and Sons* Bazarov himself is the most admirable character in the novel. Turgenev later claimed that he
shared all his views, apart from those on art. In almost all his
novels, in fact, Turgenev remained committed, and almost
always on the side of the rising generation, as in *On the Eve*
where Insarov and Yelena are the most heroic of the characters,
or in *Virgin Soil* where once again his depiction of the revolutionary forces is much more sympathetic than that of the faded,
ineffectual liberals.

The radical critic Pisarev was almost alone in accepting Turgenev as a sympathetic 'fellow-traveller': indeed he insisted that
Turgenev's depiction of Bazarov was *impartial*. While this is on
the whole true and supports the general thesis that Turgenev
after 1850 was an objective chronicler of Russia (Granjard calls
him the Pimen of his age),[51] it is also true that on another level
Turgenev was never objective nor, in fact, did he ever really
want to be, for all his claims to impartiality. For as Gershenzon,[52] and others note, in all Turgenev's accounts of contemporary reality there is an essential, underlying moralism, however well disguised. From *Parasha* onwards, and especially after
*Rudin*, Turgenev's characters are assessed in terms of what
Russia needs. To put it crudely, Rudin, the Kirsanovs (in *Fathers
and Sons*), Panshin (in *A Nest of Gentlefolk*), Sipyagin and
many others are criticised, because they are no longer socially
beneficial to Russia, while Yelena, Bazarov, Marianna (in *Virgin
Soil*) are presented more positively because, in Turgenev's

opinion, they *are* what Russia and her future is desperately in need of. His whole work then, stands not merely as a chronicle of the 'body and pressure' of his times, but as a very discreet series of cautious suggestions of what Russia probably needs, even if he refuses to give a definite answer.[53]

That Turgenev was so sympathetic to progressive movements is something of a paradox, given his almost totally pessimistic view of the world. From the late 1840s the implication of almost all his writing is that man is born merely to die, death is the only certainty in life, happiness is impossible and any hope to the contrary is a cruel illusion. For a brief period, however, in his early work, the colours are a little brighter. The peasants, in particular, are generally presented as a positive contrast to the tortured intellectuals and corrupt masters. This picture of the peasants and the generally more positive, confident tone of the 1840s changes after 1848, when Turgenev's optimistic views were all but shattered by the events of that year. Man in general is now seen as out of harmony with the *wholeness* of nature. Thereafter, Turgenev's writing represents a quest, almost always a futile quest, for this lost harmony and integration and a search for some sort of faith or ideal. But the ideals prove to be false, or else brief happiness and fulfilment are swept away by death or 'Fate'.

The chief focus of Turgenev's pessimism up to about 1856 was his critical treatment of his own generation of 'spiritual invalids'. In particular he reproached them for their 'disease' of introspection, their inability to act. As he moved from a somewhat schematic, Rousseauesque contrast between the intellectuals and the peasants he reappraised the role of the Hamlet type in general. That is, he came to ask to what extent are personal and general happiness compatible. What is the role of the individual in society, and in a hostile universe? Should one be a self-centred egoist and search for personal happiness, or should one abandon self and devote one's life to the amelioration of others' lives? By the mid-1850s, that is, he had come to see not only the tragedy, but also the value of Hamletism. Criticism and negation *are* necessary, because without them the truth cannot be discovered — they are an inevitable component of any highly developed intellect. Yet at the same time, the ultimate result of reflection is the agonising consciousness of death, of the absurdity of life.

But the qualities for real admiration lay elsewhere: in the Don Quixote type.[54] The essential features of the type are an ability to believe, and therefore to act, to serve others fearlessly, to sacrifice oneself. While the Hamlets may be necessary in that their analytical doubt and scepticism lead to the truth, they are of little value to society, and bring little happiness to themselves. Yet the question remains: are those who sacrifice themselves, those who reconcile duty and desire, any happier? Is happiness indeed possible in Turgenev's world? Liza (in *A Nest of Gentlefolk*) does appear to achieve some sort of fulfilment as her conception of duty is also what she desires, but her happiness lies within the walls of a convent, in *resignation* to Divine Will, to what she sees as her ordained lot. Those who seek happiness in more egoistical terms never achieve it and it is Turgenev's view that personal happiness is quite simply impossible. Either happiness is at hand, but then is arbitrarily snatched away by 'death the fisherman', as in *On the Eve*, or else personal happiness is shrouded by guilt. *A Nest of Gentlefolk* is the most extreme statement of Turgenev's view that personal happiness in impossible. Lavretsky and Liza fall in love, commit themselves to each other — only for Lavretsky's wife, Varvara, who was thought to be dead, to return and crush their hopes. Even before the appearance of this rather grotesque *dea ex machina*, Liza had felt intensely guilty about her love, her happiness, and had thought that she did not have the right to be happy. Being alive in Turgenev's world means to be guilty, and both Lavretsky and Liza are punished simply for wanting to be happy. Erotic love in Turgenev's world leads not life and fulfilment, but to guilt or to death.[55]

However, even if Turgenev occasionally offers some slim chance of happiness in this world, he immediately removes it by his more general view of the world. Happiness, essentially, could not be achieved because for Turgenev the world was absurd and meaningless. To be fulfilled for Turgenev was to find a meaning in life, whether it be in love, or in a revolutionary cause, but because he conceived of the universe as lacking meaning, both these enterprises were doomed to failure. Life would just go on its same pitiless way as before. Such a conception of the world is implicit in much of the work of the 1840s and 1850s, but in becomes explicit only in the 1860s and finds fullest expression in *Enough* (1865) and *Smoke*. The former work (subtitled *An*

*Extract from the Notes of a Dead Artist*) acts as a total denial
of all the values advocated elsewhere and for which civilisation
stands. Art, beauty, love, the achievements of man, are comforting words, but they too are eventually swept away, revealing
the dark chaos that they had merely obscured. Life will always
go on, the writer argues, whether man is good or bad, whether
anything is achieved or nor, because nothing lasts, nothing –
not even Art – can conquer death. He refers to Shakespeare and
asks: 'Nationalism, justice, freedom, humanity, art' (all the
words which Rudin champions and which Turgenev himself
championed throughout his life), do they mean nothing? Unfortunately, they do mean nothing and if Shakespeare returned
now, he would find exactly the same futile picture: 'The same
credulity and cruelty, the same lust for blood, for gold and dirt,
the same vulgar enjoyments, the same senseless sufferings in the
name of . . . well, even in the name of the same rubbish which
Aristophanes mocked two thousand  years ago.' Man can do
nothing to change this gruesome charade, progress is an illusion
and one can only submit to this grim eternal law. *Smoke* continues Turgenev's bitter denial of all he himself, held dear,
because, however much he wanted to believe in the values of
European culture and civilisation, he remained totally sceptical
about its ultimate achievements: these too would disappear,
they were just as much smoke as everything else. Towards the
end of the novel Litvinov muses on the train leaving Baden-
Baden, in words which could well be Turgenev's own:

> 'Smoke, smoke', – he repeated several times; and suddenly
> everything seemed to be smoke, everything, his own life,
> Russian life – everything human, especially everything
> Russian. Everything is smoke and steam, he thought; every-
> thing seemed to change constantly, everywhere there were
> new images, events followed by events, but in essence every-
> thing was just the same; everything hurried, rushed somewhere
> – and everything disappeared, achieving nothing; another
> wind blew – and everything was thrown in the opposite
> direction, and there too was the same ceaseless, restless,
> unnecessary game.

Man would keep striving to win this game, as Rudin, Lavretsky,
Insarov and Yelena and Bazarov had tried, and as Nezhdanov

later would, but no one would succeed. Life cannot be changed, and death is inevitable. In the 1870s Turgenev regained some faint optimism, and Marianna and Solomin in *Virgin Soil* have all the vitality and hope of Yelena and Insarov, but as *Senilia* (1878-82) show, Turgenev's gloomy view of man's lot remained essentially the same for the rest of his life. In this sense, Liza is something of an ideal for Turgenev in that she resigns herself to her fate and achieves some sort of fulfilment thereby, and for Turgenev this is the only way. (A later, more extreme version is Pul'kheriya in *Living Relics* (1874), who overcomes her physical paralysis by religious contemplation and attains happiness thereby.)

Almost the only consistent element (apart from death) in Turgenev's world was nature. But after the Rousseauism of the 1840s, nature offered scant comfort: on the contrary, Turgenev's pessimism was very closely linked with the *indifference* of nature to man and his aspirations. Nature increasingly was seen as a predatory force, which devoured man as incessantly and pitilessly as death itself. Man was alone in a hostile universe and did not even have the consolation of being a favoured being: he was as insignificant as a butterfly, a blade of grass or a speck of dirt. Ultimately the universe was profoundly amoral because nature was blind and indifferent to the concerns of man. *Enough* again presents a clear picture of Turgenev's grim vision:

Unconsciously and unswervingly obedient to laws, she [Nature] knows nothing of art, as she knows nothing of freedom; moving from the ages, she tolerates nothing immortal, nothing unchanging. . . . Man is her child; but what is human — and artificial — is hostile to her, precisely because mankind strives to be immortal and unchanging. Man is the child of nature; but she is the mother of all, and has no preferences: everything that exists has arisen at the expense of something else and must in its own time cede its place to something else — she creates by destroying, and everything is the same to her.

In the face of nature, in the face of death, there is no hope for man in an irrational universe and all hopes inevitably turn to dust, and man, devoid in Turgenev's eyes of free-will, can do nothing. In all his works the tragedy of political or personal failure is always deepened by this underlying darkness and chaos.

Remarkably enough, Turgenev's political views remained progressive. In the 1830s and 1840s they were at their most radical (he bore the nickname of 'The American'). In his *Memoirs* (1868) he recalls his feelings of the period: 'Almost everything I saw around myself evoked in me feelings of embarrassment, indignation — even revulsion.' At the same time he developed a hatred of the repressive Tsarist autocracy which was to last all his life. In his novels, and elsewhere, these forces were always the object of his most bitter reproach and satire, as in *Smoke*, where although Turgenev attacks almost all aspects of contemporary Russia, his greatest loathing is reserved for the official conservatives. But not only did Turgenev reject and despise the autocracy, he also questioned the validity of the social position of the aristocracy, as we have seen. As *Fathers and Sons* in particular indicates, but as *Hamlet of Shchigrov Province* or *Virgin Soil* and many other works also imply, the aristocracy is a burned-out class which no longer deserves to be the ruling class of Russia. Equally clear is his sympathy for the oppressed classes. This was essentially Westernist in inclination in that Turgenev was concerned with practical economic reform and did not simply wish to recognise the suffering masses as his 'brothers'.[56] Turgenev did not wish merely to tinker with the system: until 1861, when Emancipation was achieved, his chief social aim was abolition of the whole system of serfdom. *A Sportsman's Sketches* was written to this end, and many foreigners in fact thought that the peasants had been liberated mainly because Turgenev had written his famous collection![57] In his *Memoirs* Turgenev argues that this was his chief motive force at the time, to rid society of the 'enemy': 'In my eyes this enemy had a clearly-defined form, bore a well-known name: this enemy was — serfdom. In this name I gathered together and concentrated everything against which I was determined to struggle to the end, which which I vowed never to be reconciled. . . . This was my Hannibal's oath.' If Turgenev rather exaggerates his singlemindedness with the benefit of hindsight, the general picture is true enough. He did not call for — nor did he want — a peasant rebellion but the establishment of clearly defined and universally accepted legal rights. Serfdom was morally, economically and legally wrong, and no progress in Russia could be achieved while this barbaric institution remained.

Closely related to his attack on the political position of the aristocracy was a critique of the liberal intelligentsia, of his own type and class — the idealists, the Hamlets of the forties, which has already been discussed.[58] However, after the disappointments of 1848 Turgenev began to be increasingly pessimistic about the very fundamentals of democratic Westernism. At the same time he became wary of superficial Westernism, the snobbish adulation of all things Western, simply because they were Western and therefore fashionable — as in the near caricature of Panshin in *A Nest of Gentlefolk*. Indeed, all characters in this novel who disdain the national, indigenous traditions are antipathetic, and in the end, Lavretsky overcomes his false Westernism and returns to his estate to till the soil. This distrust of Westernism both explains Turgenev's flirtation with Slavophilism in the 1850s, and indeed, was reinforced by it. As we know, Turgenev in the 1840s was radically opposed to the Slavophils (as in *The Landowner*), but by the later stories of *A Sportsman's Sketches* he had come to a certain extent under their influence. His reappraisal of the Westernist idealists, 1848 and the consequent need for a new 'faith', largely explain this change of direction. His relations with the *Contemporary* group were approaching a crisis and he was subjected to profound doubts about his artistic talents. Accordingly, he turned to the national heritage, his roots, for some sort of consolation. This flirtation lasted until about 1857, when the consistent points of friction finally drew Turgenev and the group apart — their unrelenting hostility to Belinsky and their idealised picture of Russia, especially the peasantry, in particular caused the break. None the less, Turgenev derived some important beliefs from them, as *A Nest of Gentlefolk* reveals — Turgenev's most Slavophil work even though it was written after they had gone their separate ways. Liza, in particular, is very close to the Slavophil ideal. She, almost alone in the novel, is unaffected by foreign influences and finds her consolation in religion. In later years Turgenev was to return to his critical approach to Slavophilism, but this close contact with their ideas helped him not only to overcome his personal depression and sense of isolation, but also to rediscover his faith in Russia, his essential patriotism.

This flirtation with Slavophilism can be further explained by Turgenev's need to find ideas and types which were socially useful. The central theme of the novels of this period is this question of patriotism, of social usefulness, with a series of debates between Westernism and Slavophilism, egoism and altruism idealist contemplation and revolutionary action. The time for pure thought, discussion and debate is finished, what Russia now needs, above all else, is *action*. This is implicit at the end of *A Nest of Gentlefolk* as Lavretsky sits watching the young people around him and realises — just as Turgenev realised at the same time — that the future of Russia lay not in his hands, but in theirs. *On the Eve* recognises this all the more so: it is the young, restless Yelena, with her longing to serve others, who represents the best in Russian life: this is the type now needed by Russia. (Similarly, the essay on Hamlet and Don Quixote is no abstract discussion on universal character types, but carries a topical immediacy.) The novel is a clear reflection of the rising hopes of Turgenev, and of Russia in general, on the eve of Emancipation, with the improved political climate and the generally reforming tendencies of the period.[59] 'When will the real day come?' Dobrolyubov asked in the title of his review. Turgenev did not know, of course, but he was responsive enough to the changing political climate, as he always was, to know it was at hand, and that something urgent had to be done to prepare for it. In this sense the novel is a *call* to action, as indeed all his novels can be seen as a demand for change in Russia, a demand for patriotic service.[60]

Turgenev was aware of the need for action in his own life too. Indeed, as early as 1851 he had introduced some relatively far-reaching changes on his estates, freeing all the domestic serfs.[61] When the news appeared in 1858 that Emancipation was planned, Turgenev was delighted and began to organise reforms on his own estate, which are closely paralleled by the measures taken by Nikolay Kirsanov in *Fathers and Sons*. He ceded almost half of his land to the peasants, and cultivated his own land by hired labour. In general, Turgenev was much more progressive than most landowners in his methods.[62] When Emancipation finally came, the overjoyed Turgenev shed tears at the commemorative service — albeit in Paris! He was later bitterly disappointed that the Reforms had brought so little real change, but maintained an active, very *practical* interest in the possibility of further changes. In 1862 he organised a project for the setting-up of peasant schools, in the belief that universal literacy was central to progress, and sent plans to Herzen, Ogarev, Druzhinin, Nekrasov, Chernyshevsky, Fet and others, but in the end nothing came of the rather poorly conceived scheme.[63] In the 1870s Turgenev took a very keen interest in the new courts,[64] and throughout his later years he constantly tried to keep in touch with change and reform, and to encourage and help it whenever he could.

But, to return to the later 1850s: as Turgenev came to realise the need for immediate action, he turned his gaze to those most likely to initiate this action: the young, the radicals. Turgenev's first really sympathetic treatment of the 'sons' was, of course, Bazarov. The real radicals were not so sure of Turgenev's intentions, and this particularly distressed him, as he had attempted to show Bazarov as the best character in the book. None the less, with the exception of *Smoke*, Turgenev maintained his sympathy for the young radicals, both in his art and in his life. In his political scepticism, he may never quite have believed in the future of the Bazarovs, but objectively he could see that they were the best force in Russian life and deeply admired their strength and commitment. Later portraits, such as Marianna and the girl in *The Threshold*, are consistently sympathetic.

The memoirs of Lavrov reveal quite clearly Turgenev's sympathetic appreciation of their work. Turgenev realised the vital, progressive role they played, published articles in their defence, contributed money to their cause.[65] In 1881, he records Turgenev as declaring: 'Before I believed in reforms from above, but now I'm completely disillusioned in this; I would gladly join the youth movement myself, if I were not so old and believed in the possibility of movement from below.'[66] The last remark is particularly revealing of Turgenev's lasting scepticism; but the general intent of his declaration is highly significant. Another populist friend of Turgenev's, G. A. Lopatin, asserted that Turgenev was even partially sympathetic to socialism: 'Turgenev passionately and sincerely loved our simple people, our peasantry, and willingly dreamed of better days for it in the future, which he conceived of in a fairly humanitarian, semi-socialistic, semi-fantastic form.'[67] Later Lopatin withdrew this claim as rather exaggerated (which it probably was), but, again, the depths of Turgenev's rapport with the radicals is quite evident.

For all that, Turgenev was never fully in sympathy with them, primarily because of their methods. True to his essentially liberal principles he could at no time tolerate violence, still less, organised terrorism. As early as 1848, in Paris, these feelings became apparent: he was sympathetic to the democratic aims expressed, but shrank — and literally ran away from! — violence and destruction as a means of bringing about this new order. With the sharpening conflicts in society in the early 1860s following the Reforms, Turgenev dissociated himself from the 'revolutionary democrats'. He saw terrorist activities as leading to increased repression, and was horrified by the attempted assassination of Alexander II by Karakozov in 1866.[68] Russian society became increasingly polarised. Turgenev no longer felt at home in Russia, and withdrew to Baden-Baden, thinking he might never return. Turgenev the liberal was furious, and saw their methods as destroying all the good work liberal reform had done. He was not, of course, against action — which he himself had called for — but against the wrong sort of action. Like Dostoevsky, in fact, he admired the strength and conviction of the revolutionaries, but feared their violence and above all else their irresponsibility.[69] Turgenev's later response to terrorist violence remained the same, and in 1879 he described himself as a 'principled opponent of revolution, to say nothing of the recent atrocities',[70] referring, of course, to the rising wave of terrorism at the time. He was fond of quoting Pushkin on the subject: 'May God preserve us from seeing a Russian uprising, senseless and merciless.'[71]

Moreover, Turgenev remained out of sympathy with the young radicals in their *ultimate* aims. He shared their desire for a more progressive humanitarian form of society, but at no time — *pace* Lopatin — did he believe in socialism, populism or any of the other left-wing causes which he lived to witness. To him, as Berlin points out,[72] they were mere fantasies, but fantasies for which unfortunately the Russians seemed to have a peculiar penchant. *Smoke* in particular attacks the populist 'idolatry' of the peasantry, the advocacy of the commune as a form of primitive socialism which could form the foundation of a future, regenerated society (a belief which stems from Slavophil teaching). Even in the 1840s, Turgenev had advocated the abolition of the commune, as he saw it as the main obstacle to agrarian reform, and his views were merely reinforced by the left's adoption of this institution. Indeed, despite Turgenev's compassion for the peasants, he was deeply distrustful of them as a progressive force. Like Belinsky before him he regarded them as deeply conservative. In the 1860s he wrote to Herzen, who was moving towards a form of revolutionary populism:

> The masses whom you worship are conservative *par excellence*
> and carry within themselves an embryonic middle class,
> wearing a tanned sheepskin, living in a stuffy, dirty hut, fill-
> ing its belly to the point of heartburn, and loathing all civic
> responsibility and activity — such a middle class as will beat
> hollow the Western bourgeoisie which you characterised so
> aptly in your letters.[73]

*Virgin Soil*, although much more sympathetic to the left, is
equally critical of the continuing obsession with the 'people'.
Part of the reason Nezhdanov and the others fail is that they
simply do not understand the peasants properly and, in their
ideological fervour, ignore the essential — even if understand-
able — brutality and inertia of the *muzhiks*.

Turgenev's attitude to the young radicals in the end was a
form of tolerant scepticism. He could never fully support any
cause or party, particularly after the renewed hopes of 1861
had been crushed even more decisively than those of 1848, and
the political events of the 1860s merely confirmed his scepticism. Even when the liberals began to emerge as a cohesive political force in the 1870s, Turgenev was no more sanguine about
them, as Lavrov records.[74] They may have demanded liberty
and so on, but Turgenev was well aware that they would sacrifice nothing for this. He allowed himself to be used by them as
a kind of figurehead during his tumultuous visit to Russia in
1879, but was never fooled — he was convinced that they were
too weak and afraid to emerge as a genuine political force. They
were too soft and tolerant: he knew himself well enough to
know that a party of Turgenevs would not get very far in the
Russia of the 1880s.

Caught, then, between two opposing forces, Turgenev smiled
benignly at the political machinations around him, attacked the
right and sympathised with the left, but remained uncommitted. Yet this should not suggest that he had no political convictions. Indeed, his political views remained more or less constant
from his Westernist days of the 1840s. However much he was
accused of weakness in his day and since, he remained remarkably firm, even courageous in holding to what he believed to be
true. These views were those of nineteenth-century liberalism —

of the 'English, dynastic' type, as Turgenev himself referred to them. He was a pragmatist, always prepared to cooperate with the government, however timid their overtures might be, to assist the revolutionaries when he could. He was a gradualist, desiring, even seeking reform, but slowly, and through the proper, legally constituted authorities. He believed above all else in the power of reason, to teach man social responsibility, tolerance and disinterestedness. He valued above all else personal liberty. He looked for, in the long run, some form of constitutional government. The major medium of change was to be education – only by enlightenment and persuasion could society be changed, while preserving the essential liberties he valued. In a more specifically Russian context, Turgenev remained a thorough going liberal Westerniser decades after the original grouping had disintegrated. All his life he believed that the only possible source of progress for Russia was greater Europeanisation. Whenever he returned to Russia from abroad he was appalled by the immense gulf he perceived between the West and Russia, and devoted his life to narrowing the gap, and all his life he proudly, even defiantly, termed himself a 'European'.

Almost all writers on Turgenev stress this tolerant liberalism, yet despite this – or in a peculiar way, because of it – he succeeded in quarrelling seriously with almost every other writer of significance of the period. In trying to please everyone, Turgenev ended up by pleasing almost no one. However, until the early 1860s, Turgenev was a popular figure in literary circles. Whenever he visited Moscow or St Petersburg in the 1850s his house was always full of visitors – Nekrasov, Panaev, Druzhinin, Grigorovich, Tolstoy, Goncharov and many others. The first group with which he was associated was, of course, the *Contemporary* circle. Turgenev in fact had been one of the first to offer Belinsky help in setting up a new journal after the latter's break with *Notes of the Fatherland* in 1846, and he was one of the most active contributors in the first few months.[75] For some years relations continued to be generally good, despite Turgenev's rather irresponsible attitude to the journal. In 1854 a dinner was held in his honour by the journal, and when Nekrasov visited Paris in 1856 he was shown round by Turgenev who had rushed there to meet him. Two years later Turgenev was still on relatively good terms with Nekrasov – reading *A Nest of Gentlefolk* to him before deciding to publish it. But the split was coming, based essentially on the ideological quarrel, to which we can return in our consideration of Turgenev's relationships with oppositional forces.

The next major quarrel in Turgenev's literary life was with Tolstoy, a quarrel which was to last until the late 1870s (as was also the case with Nekrasov). The two writers never got on particularly well. They met in the mid-1850s when Tolstoy, 'the troglodyte', as Turgenev referred to him, had just returned from the Crimean War. Turgenev admired his talent, but their personalities were antithetical. Turgenev was sceptical, rational and 'soft', while Tolstoy was passionate and fond of gambling. They were both aristocrats, but this merely emphasised their differences. Tolstoy simply could not believe that Turgenev's democratic ideas were sincere − how could an aristocrat advocate major changes which were against his own class interests, and he accused Turgenev of merely 'waggling his democratic haunches' at him![76] Turgenev admired Tolstoy, but from a distance − he liked his boldness and independence, but found him impossible to live with. Dostoevsky, or indeed Tolstoy himself, confronted with such an *enfant terrible*, would have washed his hands of him, but Turgenev, in his inimitable blend of magnanimity and desire to be liked by all, constantly tried to patch things up, writing him letters of encouragement, generally acting as his good genius. Eventually, however, on 27 May 1861, when both were visiting their neighbour Fet, they had a ridiculous quarrel over Turgenev's liberal education of his illegitimate daughter, which almost ended in a duel, and severed their relationship for seventeen years. Despite the acrimony surrounding the event, Turgenev bore no grudge. Throughout the 1860s and 1870s as Tolstoy's major works appeared Turgenev praised them lavishly (though he disliked the philosophising in *War and Peace* and in general abhorred Tolstoy's moralising) and acted almost as Tolstoy's literary ambassador abroad.

Turgenev's progressive views also caused a breach with the conservative poet Fet. According to a familiar pattern, when the two writers first became acquainted in the mid-1850s Turgenev went out of his way to assist the younger writer, getting him work on *The Contemporary* and acting as a populariser of his work. In 1856 a collection of Fet's poetry appeared, for which Turgenev wrote the introduction.[77] However, in the 1860s their relations rapidly deteriorated, principally because of Fet's openly reactionary views, as is evident from Fet's own memoirs. He records his amazement at Turgenev's acquaintance with the radical Ukrainian poet Shevchenko, and even more so, with Saltykov-Shchedrin, to whom Fet virtually refused to speak.[78] Eventually, an open break came in 1874, and although the two writers resumed relationships in 1878, the former intimacy had gone.

The most bitter quarrel of all though was undoubtedly with Dostoevsky. Here too there was a mix of personal and ideological reasons. When Turgenev and Dostoevsky first met in 1845, Turgenev, according to Dostoevsky, seemed almost to have fallen in love with the emerging writer.[79] For a time their relations were excellent, but a few months later Turgenev and Nekrasov wrote a vicious lampoon of Dostoevsky's morbid vanity and pride, which the latter was never to forget. When Dostoevsky returned from Siberia in 1859, the two men resumed their acquaintance, although it never became friendship. Dostoevsky was launching a new journal, *Time*, and persuaded Turgenev to contribute to it, which Turgenev was glad to do as he was looking for a relatively moderate journal after his break with *The Contemporary*. When *Time* was closed, Dostoevsky began a new journal, *Epoch*, and again importuned Turgenev to publish in it – sending him hypocritical praise for Turgenev's story *Phantoms* which he had not even read. In 1864 Turgenev lent Dostoevsky some money and it was this unpaid debt which led to their disastrous quarrel in 1867 in Baden-Baden. The issues at stake were partly their deep antipathy but also their views. Dostoevsky accused Turgenev of slandering Russia (in *Smoke*), he hated his aristocratic manners, was jealous of his financial security, loathed his democratic opinions and his lack of religious beliefs, as well as his deterministic view of man. Their stormy meeting lasted one and a half hours and although Turgenev attempted to remain calm, when the two met accidentally at the station a month later they did not even greet each other.

Four years later Dostoevsky published his own vicious lampoon, in *The Devils*, in the caricature of Karamazinov. Turgenev at first was relatively indifferent to the matter, commenting that 'it would have been just a libel if Dostoevsky had not been a madman – which I do not doubt he is'. When he read the novel he realised the maliciousness of Dostoevsky's attack, but disdained to reply to it, at least in public. Relations thenceforth were severed. They were to meet again, however, during the Pushkin celebrations. At the time Turgenev was enthusiastic about Dostoevsky's overrated and hysterical speech, but later noted that it was 'the same intolerable pride under the mask of humility'. Turgenev's final verdict came in letters to Saltykov-Shchedrin and Annenkov sixteen months after Dostoevsky's death when he compared him to de Sade. He refused to write an obituary but − typically! − contributed fifty roubles to a memorial fund.[80] At best, Turgenev merely tolerated Dostoevsky but never had any liking for him − his Slavophilism and reactionary views, his dogmatism, his morbid, pathological religious art were the antithesis of everything he himself stood for. Turgenev was tolerant of almost everyone, but ultimately not of Dostoevsky.

In general, the limits of Turgenev's tolerance were precisely of this kind. In his desire for progress he abhorred all those who stood in the way of this, in particular the government. Turgenev did not suffer at the hands of the government as much as many nineteenth-century writers did, but he had his difficulties all the same. He experienced most of the difficulties with the censor in the 1840s and 1850s. His play *The Parasite* (1848) was banned on the grounds of its 'utter immorality' and its attacks against the Russian nobility, while *A Month in the Country* (1849) received the same treatment and was not performed until 1872[81] *The Diary of a Superfluous Man* (1850) was also heavily censored, but the first and most important clash with the government arose two years later, ostensibly over his obituary of Gogol, but at least as much over the first complete edition of *A Sportsman's Sketches*. Of course, Turgenev could not be arrested for the latter work, not indeed could it be reasonably banned, as all the stories had already been published separately. And so his obituary of Gogol, published in fact without his knowledge, and in which he had the temerity to call Gogol a 'great writer', was seized on. It was a time of severe repression − four days after Turgenev's arrest, the conservative Slavophil Pogodin had to report to the police for publishing his journal with a black border out of respect for Gogol[82] − and Turgenev was merely the latest thorn in Nicholas' side. Writers in particular were seen as hostile forces by the regime. On Turgenev's arrest Dubel't commented to Orlov: 'At the present time writers are the *dramatis personae* in all the troubles of the government and is is essential that we pay strict attention to them.'[83] Turgenev was even regarded as an 'ardent and enterprising man' (*sic!*) and Nicholas himself ordered severe punishment for 'blatant disobedience'.[84] (All mention of Gogol had been banned.) Public reactions among conservative elements were equally hostile, although they were well aware that the true cause of the arrest was *A Sportsman's Sketches*. Countess Rostopchina, an influential pillar of the establishment, referred to it as 'un livre incendiaire',[85] while the Minister of Education saw it as dangerous and likely to cause disrespect to the rightful masters among the lower classes.[86]

Turgenev did not, in fact, suffer unduly. His few days in prison were pleasant enough, and he was eventually exiled to his estates, and finally released in October 1853, although Nicholas I ordered that he should be kept under strict surveillance, which he was, until the amnesty of 1856. Turgenev was clearly unabashed, for two years after his arrest he published *Mumu*. (The censor who passed it was severely reprimanded.)[87]

Despite this major conflict and his general hostility to the regime, Turgenev remained pragmatic in his dealings with it. In 1856 he used his friendship with Countess Lambert to obtain a passport to travel abroad,[88] and then in the period of Emancipation he supported the government plans. But his continuing attempts to steer a middle course were to cause him further trouble in 1862, in the 'Affair of the 32'. Bakunin had mentioned in a letter to his sisters that Turgenev was prepared to help him financially (specifically to help move Bakunin's wife from Siberia), and the letter, as well as some of Herzen's, came to the notice of the authorities. In January 1863 Turgenev was summoned to appear before the Senate to answer charges of complicity with émigré radicals. Turgenev was more than a little concerned – he had been threatened with confiscation of all his property if he did not appear. After a time it became apparent that the charges brought against him were entirely innocuous and in January 1864 he appeared before the Senate, admitted that he had offered to help Bakunin, an old friend, but had nothing to do with his politics, which was true enough, and he was cleared.[89]

His release put him in a situation he did not like: he was no revolutionary, but he did not wish to appear pro-government. He need not really have worried too much, for the conservatives

remained consistently hostile. Indeed, contemporary conservative opinion, for the most part, tarred Turgenev with the same
brush as the radicals. *On the Eve*, for example, had so offended
Countess Lambert that Turgenev had almost burned it,[90] while
the reaction to his negative portrayal of officialdom in *Smoke*
so incensed the generals of the English Club that they wrote a
letter to Turgenev excluding him from the club[91] – which
delighted Turgenev, who always liked to appear in such a light.
The conservative reaction to *Father and Sons* was rather more
mixed, but in general Turgenev was for once praised by this section of society for (or so they thought) attacking the nihilists. A
secret police report noted that the novel had 'a beneficient
influence on the public mind . . . to the surprise of the younger
generation, which had recently been applauding him, with this
work Turgenev branded our underage revolutionaries with the
biting name of "Nihilist" and shook the doctrine of materialism
and its representatives.'[92]

Turgenev's relations with Katkov are indicative of his general
loathing for the right-wing elements in Russian society. Katkov
had criticised Turgenev over *Fathers and Sons*, in which he saw
Turgenev as kow-towing to the radicals, but Turgenev continued
to publish in his journal *The Russian Herald* (mainly because of
the lack of a more suitable outlet). After *Smoke* and the conservative response to it, Turgenev broke finally with Katkov,
which engendered the latter's implacable hostility. Turgenev
returned it fully: in 1874 he wrote to Fet: 'All that remains of
my hatred and contempt is directed against Katkov, the vilest
and most dangerous man in Russia.'[93] When he met him again
during the Pushkin celebrations he twice refused to clink glasses
with Katkov – a small gesture perhaps, but given the general
euphoria of the occasion, a significant one. It is another indica-
tion of the new 'radicalism' of Turgenev in the last decade of his
life. In turn, the conservative elements grew to dislike and suspect him to an extent only equalled by their opinion of him in
the early 1850s. *Virgin Soil* displeased them intensely, while
even the French police kept him under close surveillance because
of his open fraternising with émigré radicals.[94] During Turgenev's visit to Russia in 1879 when he received a tumultuous
reception, particularly from the students, he was closely
watched; indeed, he was not allowed to meet students in St
Petersburg, and was 'advised' to leave. Alexander II – the 'Tsar

Liberator' — had by this time come to remark of Turgenev: 'C'est ma bête noire', but, of course, the government did not dare to touch a writer who by this time had such an international reputation.[95] Turgenev visited Russia again in 1881, shortly after the assassination of Alexander, and was again 'advised', this time in person by Pobedonostsev, procurator of the Holy Synod, not to stay in St Petersburg, and Turgenev admitted that he did not feel safe in the capital.[96] On another occasion he gave Lavrov two tickets for a Russian official charity concert in Paris, for which he was reported and investigated.[97] Finally, when Turgenev's body was returned to St Petersburg in 1883, to be buried next to Belinsky's, the greatest precautions were taken for fear of demonstrations, exactly as had happened forty-six years previously when Pushkin was buried.

If the government was glad to be rid of Turgenev, his funeral took on the character of a national mourning for all but the most reactionary sections of society, for, with the exception of the 1860s, Turgenev had proved to be one of the most popular writers in Russia's history. Public acclaim was first achieved with the publication of *A Sportsman's Sketches* in 1852, which proved to be an instantaneous success.[98] The success of the collection proved to be lasting and widespread: in 1874 Turgenev was met by two young artisans at a station near Moscow and was thanked 'in the name of the Russian people' for his book.[99] *Rudin*, also a great triumph, established his reputation, which was finally certain two years later with the publication of *A Nest of Gentlefolk*. It proved to be his most popular book: by 1858 he had become the foremost writer of his day. The novel had greater success than his other works mainly because of the quasi-Slavophil views implicit in the fates of Lavretsky and Liza, which widened his appeal. Meanwhile, his earlier works continued to be popular: the previous year a collection of his stories had been published in the large edition of five thousand copies, and had sold well.[100]

However, this popularity was not to be repeated. *On the Eve* marked the turning-point in Turgenev's relationship with his public. The liberal tone pleased the young, students, academics and writers, while high society (witness Countess Lambert's reaction) was shocked and frightened.[101] But the real tumult was reserved for *Fathers and Sons*. On one level, the novel was a great success, because of its immense topicality. Contemporaries such as Strakhov noted that the work aroused more excitement and controversy than any previous work in Russian literature.[102] It was read by people who had not looked at a book since school, while the word 'nihilist' passed immediately into everyday use. Opinions, of course, varied immensely, but the entire literate population, it seemed, was in a state of uproar, and Turgenev even received anonymous letters and threats.[103] But the novel also inaugurated a rapid decline in his reputation, particularly among the young, which was exacerbated by Turgenev's bitter response in *Smoke*. None the less, it too was read eagerly.[104] Even if the young distrusted him, Turgenev's novels were still of vital, topical interest.

The year 1871 marked a resurgence of Turgenev's popularity, with the publication of *Spring Torrents*. Turgenev deliberately avoided topical issues here, but it proved to be an immense success. The journal in which it was published immediately went into a second printing, an unprecedented event.[105] In general, Turgenev's works of the 1870s were well received by the public, culminating in his *annus mirabilis* of 1879 when he returned in triumph to Russia. All was forgiven: after the bitter quarrels of the 1860s a wider perspective could now be taken, and he was appreciated for what he really was. Wherever he went he was met by public acclaim, carried shoulder-high by students, cheered and applauded. Dinners were held in his honour,Turgenev gave public readings and speeches and all were a tremendous success. He was welcomed as a great writer, and as a leading liberal, a fact for which Turgenev was deeply grateful. Rather naively he saw his reception as a sign of reconciliation between the old and young, the liberals and radicals, which would lead to new harmony and progress in Russia. Two years later, Alexander II was assassinated and renewed repression and terrorism ensued. . . .

The critical reception of Turgenev's work matched his general popularity only in the early period. At first, the radical sections of society met his work favourably. Belinsky praised *Parasha* highly for its simplicity and realism and welcomed the 'naturalism' of the first of *A Sportsman's Sketches*.[106] Other radicals were equally impressed by most of Turgenev's early work, in particular *A Sportsman's Sketches*: Herzen, Nekrasov and Saltykov-Shchedrin all praised the stories highly.[107] The Slavo-

phils also liked the stories, as well as *Mumu*, because of Turgenev's picture of the essential goodness and moral purity of the
peasants. Turgenev's first novel *Rudin*, although a popular success, received rather a cool reception in the press, although
somewhat surprisingly, the conservative Senkovsky wrote a
most favourable review.[108] After the success of Turgenev's next
novel, *A Nest of Gentlefolk*, *On the Eve* marked a dramatic
change with attacks coming from both extremes: the conservatives saw it as dangerous and immoral, while the radicals (in particular Dobrolyubov) considered that Turgenev had written an
unfair portrayal of the revolutionary Insarov.

In general, in the late 1850s Turgenev began to fall out of
favour with the radical critics, a tendency which was conditioned
by their demands for greater commitment by the writer, and by
the worsening personal relationships between Turgenev and the
younger elements of the *Contemporary* group. Moreover, as
Turgenev's pessimistic, quasi-deterministic philosophy began to
emerge the radicals began to oppose Turgenev's whole view and
presentation of the world. While they called for strong men of
action to people Russian fiction, Turgenev showed man doomed
to die, as unable to reconcile duty and desire. Among the first
major attacks was Dobrolyubov's *When Will the Real Day Come?*
(1860), a highly critical and tendentious review of *On the Eve*.
The critique is plainly and unashamedly ideological – indeed
for Dobrolyubov and his group the time for 'pure' literary criticism had long since passed. He was not interested in 'art', but in
the social value of art, and Turgenev's novel is approached
almost entirely on this basis.

This review begins with disarming praise for the positive elements in the novel. Turgenev has succeeded here because of his
chief gift as a novelist, his responsiveness to contemporary currents and his ability continually to raise new, relevant social
questions. *On the Eve* is particularly successful because Turgenev has realised the need for a new path, the need for action.
Dobrolyubov goes on to praise the truthful characterisation of
Yelena, and later accords Turgenev merit for the character of
Insarov, in particular his selfless dedication to his revolutionary
task. However, the main thrust of his attack then centres on
Insarov. He argues that Insarov, for all his positive qualities, is
simply a veiled slander on Young Russia. Insarov is a Bulgarian
and the implication, therefore, is that such types do not yet exist

in Russia. Moreover, Insarov is neither very endearing nor convincing as a character (which is true enough): he is rather abstract, and worst of all, somewhat ridiculous. Finally, in returning to Yelena, Dobrolyubov argues that she has to leave Russia to fulfil her heroic potential. The overall implication, then, is that there are no heroic men in Russia, and the revolutionary type as such is comic and unconvincing. All that Russia has to offer are more pusillanimous intellectuals like Shubin and his academic friend Bersenev. Dobrolyubov does scant justice to Turgenev's novel, but the important point is that he refuses to appreciate Turgenev's very honest attempt to come to terms with the new problems of Russia.

Both this and Chernyshevsky's similar review of Turgenev's lyrical novella *Asya* – *The Russian at the Rendezvous* (1859) can be read as deliberate attempts to discredit Turgenev in the eyes of the young. If anything, Chernyshevsky's article is even more abusive and has even fewer pretensions to literary criticism. The article attacks the weakness and vacillations of Turgenev's hero, and at the same time dismisses all Turgenev's heroes, as well as Turgenev himself and his whole generation. As Turgenev himself realised (a fact which Chernyshevsky overlooks or chooses to ignore) their time is over, and new men are required and, as Dobrolyubov was to a year later, Chernyshevsky reproaches Turgenev principally for failing to depict these new men.

Given this open hostility from the left, and the simmering anger of the right, *Fathers and Sons* can be seen as a *reply* to an ongoing polemic as much as an initiator of controversy. Turgenev was aware of the storm it would create. Friends advised him to burn it and, given the troubled background, he thought of postponing publication. In the end, he went ahead, and, if he had expected criticism, his fears were more than justified. Quite simply, it created the greatest critical storm before or since. There were five principal reactions to it,[109] and both extremes were divided. On the right, some were critical of Turgenev's 'subservience' to the radicals: even before publication Katkov had complained to Turgenev of this,[110] and his reaction remained the same even after publication (in his own journal!). He accused Turgenev of being 'too fair' and of showing Bazarov in the best possible light and turned his review into an attack on the 'nihilists' themselves who, he claimed, were 'no better than the ignorant, benighted Russian priesthood from whose ranks they mostly spring, and far more dangerous'.[111] Other conservatives, however, praised Turgenev for his successful exposé of precisely this danger to society, and he even received grateful letters on the subejct.[112] Turgenev was upset by these new 'friends' and their praise, but it was the abusive response of the majority of the left wing that wounded him most deeply, given that he had done his best to portray Bazarov sympathetically. Antonovich, a mediocre successor to Dobrolyubov, in his vicious review accused Turgenev of slander and caricature in his portrayal of Bazarov, and claimed that he had shown his true colours − that of a black reactionary.[113] Antonovich was not alone in his attacks and his views probably expressed the general consensus of the editorial board and perhaps of the majority of young radicals.[114] Turgenev summed up this remarkable cacophony of opinions in *On the Subject of 'Fathers and Sons'* (1868-9):

> While some were accusing me of insulting the younger generation, of backwardness and obscurantism, informing me that 'my photographs were being burnt amid derisive laughter', others indignantly reproached me with kow-towing to this very same younger generation. 'You're crawling at Bazarov's feet!' − one correspondent exclaimed − 'you only pretend to judge him; in reality you're fawning on him and wait for one careless smile as if for a favour.'

One sane voice was heard on the left, that of Pisarev who defended Turgenev's position and proudly identified himself with Bazarov. His review of 1862 hailed Turgenev as one of the best elements of the older generation. Turgenev, he admits, could never be a Bazarov himself, but he has depicted him fairly, even generously − and much better than any of the younger generation could do. Pisarev sees, quite correctly, that Turgenev *was* on their side. Bazarov is not a caricature, but indeed, is shown to be superior to all around him, the finest flower of his generation. The whole review is extremely favourable, and Pisarev accepts not only the character of Bazarov, but Turgenev's whole treatment of him. The truth, then, could still be spoken by a committed critic, and Turgenev was grateful for it.

The fifth reaction was that of the non-partisan literary critics who attempted to assess the work on its own merits. Such critics as Annenkov and Herzen saw Turgenev at odds with himself, unsure which side he was on,[115] while the liberal conservative Strakhov saw Turgenev as on nobody's side, but merely attempting to tell the truth. He agreed with Pisarev that Bazarov towered above all other characters, and ultimately praised the novel extremely highly, especially Turgenev's objectivity and lack of ulterior motive.[116] (Dostoevsky, incidentally, also praised the novel.)

Such reactions, and in particular Pisarev's, comforted Turgenev, but his response remained one of profound shock. Above all he felt that he had been totally misunderstood in his intentions, and that he had been placed in a false position *vis-à-vis* the party he most sympathised with, the young radicals.[117] *Smoke* came as his caustic response to this climate of opinion, and as he anticipated, it was attacked on all sides, and he was dismissed as an embittered émigré who no longer understood his country. Dostoevsky's views on the novel are well known: they are more extremely expressed, but remain typical of the general critical feeling. The novel merely served to widen the gap between Turgenev and contemporary critial opinion. Turgenev affected to be indifferent to this, but none the less sent a copy to Pisarev, asking for his opinions. Pisarev was not impressed: in particular he disliked Turgenev's omission of the Bazarov character.[118] Even Strakhov wrote a very poor review of *Smoke*. Turgenev's own negative feelings were too apparent, he said, and weakened the artistic merit of the work. Moreover, his polemical caricature and obvious dislike of most contemporary tendencies reduced his work almost to the level of a satire.[119]

Over these years Turgenev turned away from the present, drawing on the past, the supernatural or the lightweight for his material, returning only nine years later in *Virgin Soil* to justify and explain his true political position. This effort was no more successful. The fatalism that infects Nezhdanov who cannot 'simplify himself' sufficiently to fit into the rough revolutionary world (and who ultimately commits suicide), was condemned by the left, while Turgenev's generally sympathetic treatment of the revolutionaries evoked the wrath of Katkov once more. Condemnation was again unanimous.

Turgenev's relationship with oppositional groups follows a similar, fluctuating pattern. Belinsky first introduced Turgenev to the radical, oppositional groups in Russian society and to their ideas. At this time Turgenev was uninterested in politics as such and kept apart from the intellectual circles. But he was encouraged by Belinsky's review of *Parasha* and became intimate with him and the whole *Contemporary* group. This closeness lasted until the mid-1850s, when relations slowly deteriorated, centring principally on the differences between Turgenev and Chernyshevsky and Dobrolyubov. A number of underlying ideological and social issues shaped the conflict. By the mid-1850s the composition of the Russian intelligentsia had significantly altered. Whereas Belinsky had been an exception among the largely aristocratic intelligentsia, the *raznochintsy* were now rapidly becoming the dominant element: by about 1855, for example, there were as many *raznochintsy* as nobles at Moscow university.[120] Chernyshevsky, the son of a village priest, became their spiritual leader and the utilitarian aesthetic stance which he advanced, and which became the position of his whole group, played the most significant part in the ideological conflict that was to ensue. Panaeva records a conversation between Turgenev and her husband on this specific issue which conveys Turgenev's principled objections to their view of art: 'With their insolence they want to wipe from the face of the earth poetry, the fine arts, all aesthetic pleasures and introduce their own coarse seminarist principles. They are literary Robespierres.'[121]

Another powerful contributory factor was Turgenev's pessimistic world-view, the deterministic fatalism which was absolutely rejected by Chernyshevsky and Dobrolyubov. Finally, Turgenev at all times found it difficult to get on well with them precisely because of their different social origins. Turgenev was ultimately an aristocrat whose cultured sensibilities were more than a little insulted by their toughness and ill-mannered arrogance (as he saw it). Despite this unfavourable background, however, the two 'parties' attempted for a while to work together, and there was, in fact, much that bound them. Chernyshevsky and Dobrolyubov valued Turgenev as a writer. He was, after all, the author of *A Sportsman's Sketches*, a close friend of Belinsky, and a leader of post-Gogolian 'naturalism'. Turgenev for his part, although he was horrified by some of Chernyshevsky's ideas, saw him as a worthy follower of Belinsky and the best critic of his day. He was also fascinated by the fervour and intensity of the two seminarists and for some time attempted to like them, or at least to work harmoniously for the same journal. Neither side wanted a break, recognising that it could only be detrimental for all concerned. As the ideological conflict emerged – essentially between the men of the 1840s and the new generation – Turgenev first sided with the latter, defending Chernyshevsky against the outraged attacks of such as Druzhinin and Tolstoy.[122]

But the underlying ideological, class and personal antagonisms were not slow to emerge. The first real sign of a break was Turgenev's decision to publish *On the Eve* in Katkov's *Russian Herald*, although Nekrasov had tried to acquire the novel for *The Contemporary*. Dobrolyubov's scathing review followed and this, together with Chernyshevsky's attack on Turgenev in his review of *Asya*, made the rift public. The late 1850s was, of course, a period of sharpening political tensions in Russian society, and the break between Turgenev and *The Contemporary* reflects the struggle for power within the intelligentsia, between the aristocratic liberals and social democrats and the radicals. Turgenev was the chief victim of this struggle, but not the only one: ultimately he was forced out, along with most of the old guard, Annenkov, Botkin, Grigorovich and others, while Nekrasov stayed on, siding with the victorious seminarists, who by 1859 were in control of the journal. There was, indeed, something of a concerted campaign against the 'fathers'. The two reviews of Turgenev's work were clear attempts to discredit the generation of 'superfluous men', while Dobrolyubov's *What is Oblomovism?* (1859) was a more general critique of the ineffectual, passive idealists who had dominated Russian literature and intellectual life for the past thirty years. Onegin, Pechorin, Rudin, Herzen's Beltov (in *Who Is Guilty?*) and Goncharov's Oblomov are all brutally axed in Dobrolyubov's vitriolic polemic.

The conflicts sharpened after Dobrolyubov's review of *On the Eve* which Turgenev took as an attack on his literary authority. He insisted to Nekrasov that the latter choose between Dobrolyubov and Turgenev himself, and although neither side wanted a break, Turgenev had broken faith (as he had so often before) by working for Katkov, and in the end Dobrolyubov was more important to the journal.[123] By 1860 a final break was inevitable and one of the last contributory factors was Turgenev's new ending for *Rudin*, an epilogue in which the hero dies on the 1848 barricades. Chernyshevsky saw this as a 'vicious caricature' against Bakunin, just as he was later to see Bazarov as a 'pasquille' against Dobrolyubov.[124] Turgenev, according to Annenkov, was particularly offended by Chernyshevsky's claim that this supposed caricature was to please Turgenev's rich friends.[125] Nekrasov did his best to heal the breach, but Turgenev insisted that he could no longer work for *The Contemporary*, and *Hamlet and Don Quixote* (which, of course, did nothing to defuse the issue) was the last work Turgenev published for the journal. Given the lasting bitterness engendered by the quarrel (Chernyshevsky's memoirs in which he made these allegations were dictated in 1884), it is remarkable that Turgenev in *Fathers and Sons* was so fair to them.

Shortly afterwards Turgenev's long-standing friendship with Herzen suffered a similar fate. Although Herzen was six years Turgenev's senior, the two men had much in common in terms of background and education. Herzen had always been much more radical than Turgenev, but they shared a similar Westernist outlook. The year 1848 had proved a severe shock for both men, though for Herzen it was much more profound. Herzen remained abroad for the rest of his life but Turgenev kept in close touch, and despite their political differences Turgenev was happy to help Herzen and his journal *The Bell* with information and documents from within Russia. As with the younger radicals, relations began to be strained in the period immediately before and after the Emancipation. Turgenev, as we have seen, supported the official plans, while Herzen, although he had long hoped for reform from above, joined the younger radicals in criticising them. The rift rapidly widened: Turgenev remained true to his old liberalism, while Herzen moved rapidly to the left in the early sixties. Events of the next few years reinforced this polarisation. Herzen had by now adopted a position of quasi-Slavophil radical populism which horrified Turgenev. From July 1862 to January 1863 Herzen published eight letters in *The Bell, Endings and Beginnings,* which were in part an attempt to convince Turgenev that bourgeois liberalism and Western civilisation ·in general were rapidly declining to a state in which the trivial mentality of the petty bourgeoisie would be dominant and would cripple all true freedom and spiritual values. Salvation lay with Russia, Herzen argued, and more specifically, the Russian peasant, and the triad of the *zemstvo*, the commune and the artel. Turgenev rejected Herzen's theses absolutely and in a famous letter denouncing Herzen's new idol he wrote: 'You kneel before the Russian sheepskin and you see in it the supreme good, the novelty, the originality of new social forms.' All his other idols had crumbled, Turgenev continued: 'but how can one live without God? So one erects an altar to the sheepskin, this unknown God of whom one knows almost nothing. One can pray again, believe, have expectations.'[126] Turgenev proudly once more called himself a 'European', and clung to the faith of his youth. Herzen's reply was equally angry: 'You have lost faith in Russia, you are a nihilist, a tired, desperate nihilist, not révolté and angry like Chernyshevsky and Dobrolyubov. The proof of this is that you refer to the authority of Schopenhauer, that ideal nihilist, that Buddhist, that corpse.'[127] Despite the absolute despair of *Enough*, written in these years. Turgenev stood in passionate defence of his old liberalism, even if he no longer fully believed in it. He had rejected the revolutionary democracy of *The Contemporary* and now he spurned the quasi-Slavophil, populist socialism of *The Bell*, and remained almost entirely alone with his unfashionable liberal Westernism.

The chance of the 'trial of the 32' merely confirmed the break, although it was not the end of the affair with Herzen and his allies. Herzen suspected Turgenev of treachery in the matter and published a notice in *The Bell* referring to Turgenev as 'a certain grey-haired Magdalene'. Turgenev wrote an indignant letter in reply denying all accusations. Herzen refused to withdraw them and for two years the two men remained completely estranged. In 1867 Turgenev attempted a reconciliation, but correspondence resumed only in 1869, a year before Herzen's death. By this time he too had been outflanked by elements younger, more radical and more plebeian than himself,[128] and he was happy to restore former relations with his old friend.

For a time, then, Turgenev had almost no contact with any of the oppositional groups of Russian society. Relations were only resumed in the 1870s. In these years Turgenev slowly and carefully reconstructed alliances with the radical opposition which had been largely destroyed by the events of the 1860s. Turgenev's position had in no way changed, and the radicals were aware that he was a 'weak' liberal, but this was no longer so important. To Turgenev's surprised delight they accepted him as the willing fellow-traveller he had always been. As before

he remained hostile to their terrorist methods, was cautious not
to compromise himself too much, but was drawn by their generous idealism and self-sacrificial zeal. They and Turgenev were
both on the side of humanity and progress and now the underlying differences could be forgotten. The most outstanding
manifestation of this renewed alliance was the reception of
1879, but the real work was done in Paris throughout the
1870s when Turgenev mixed more or less freely and contributed to the various radical émigré groups. His friendship with
the radical populist Lavrov is particularly important. They had
first met around 1860 but became close only after 1872, when
Lavrov fled to Paris. This relationship with a declared revolutionary and a friend of Engels and Marx demanded a degree of
courage from Turgenev. He was already under surveillance and
had long since compromised himself by his many associations
with émigré groups. Yet he persisted, partly because he wished
to study the revolutionaries more closely for *Virgin Soil*, but
also out of genuine interest in and sympathy for their cause.
Lavrov's wide-ranging education and personality appealed to
him and he agreed with all the main points of his journal *Forward!* to which he became a regular contributor, as well as
actively supporting the revolutionary cause financially.

Lavrov's memoirs show that he had no illusions about Turgenev's political position, but equally he pays great tribute to
Turgenev's courage, generosity and sympathy for the revolutionary cause. He sums up Turgenev's great achievements with
regard to the forces of progress in Russian society:

> It was fitting for Russian revolutionaries to pay their respects
> to a man who, in propagating humanitarian ideas and liberal
> principles, belonged to the great pléiade of writers of the
> forties, who fought against the kingdom of *poshlost*; to the
> pléiade of those who made way for a more concrete pro-
> gramme of opposition in the ensuing twenty-five years, for a
> better future for Russia; to a man who knew, better than
> most of his contemporaries, how to sympathise, and in part,
> work with the new forces.[129]

Although Turgenev may not have entirely agreed with this interpretation of himself as a John the Baptist of the revolution,
it is indisputable that in his friendship with Lavrov, the help he gave

him and many other émigré revolutionaries, such as Prince Kropotkin,[130] Turgenev to the end sided with this section of society more than any other. He could not offer them the answers they sought, and for a time was therefore rejected by them, but he never rejected them, for he saw in them the chief realistic hope of Russia. It is fitting, therefore, that in the end he was once more respected and honoured by the radicals of Russian society. Turgenev has been too often accused of weakness and compromise but the last ten years of his life reveal that he was prepared to support and even fight for what he believed. In more general terms he remained consistently honest, generous and sincere, and his honesty, sincerity and desire for greater civilisation, freedom and progress in Russia stand as a moment of sanity in a turbulent century in Russian literature and society.

# Turgenev: Important Biographical Dates

| | |
|---|---|
| 1818 | Born in Oryol, Central Russia, on 28 October. |
| 1833 | Enters Moscow University. |
| 1834 | Transfers to St Petersburg University. |
| 1837 | Graduates. |
| 1838-41 | Studies and travels in Germany. Friendship with Stankevich and Bakunin. |
| 1843 | Meets Belinsky and Annenkov. *Parasha*. Works in Ministry of Interior. |
| 1845 | Retires from government service. |
| 1846 | Joins *The Contemporary*. |
| 1847 | *Khor and Kalinych* — first story of *A Sportman's Sketches*. |
| 1848 | Witnesses the February Revolution in Paris. |
| 1850 | *A Month in the Country* finished. |
| 1852 | Arrested for obituary on Gogol. Confined to Spasskoye estate. Publication of *A Sportsman's Sketches*. |
| 1853 | Returns to St Petersburg. |
| 1854 | *Mumu*. |
| 1856 | *Rudin*. |
| 1858 | *Asya*. |
| 1859 | *A Nest of Gentlefolk. Hamlet and Don Quixote*. |
| 1860 | *On the Eve*. Break with *The Contemporary*. |
| 1861 | Quarrels with Tolstoy. Breaks relations with Nekrasov. |
| 1862 | *Fathers and Sons*. |
| 1863 | Trial of the 32. Settles in Baden-Baden. |
| 1864 | Acquitted of charges. Break with Herzen. |
| 1865 | *Enough*. |

| | |
|---|---|
| 1867 | *Smoke.* Renews contact with Herzen. Quarrel with Dostoevsky. |
| 1869 | *Reminiscences.* |
| 1871 | *Spring Torrents.* |
| 1876 | *Virgin Soil.* |
| 1878 | Renews relations with Tolstoy, Nekrasov. |
| 1879 | Fêted in Russia. |
| 1880 | Takes part in Pushkin celebrations. |
| 1881 | Last visit to Russia. |
| 1882 | *Senilia.* |
| 1883 | Dies, 3 September. |

# 2  Fyodor Dostoevsky

It is arguable that Dostoevsky is the most complex nineteenth-century Russian writer. Both as a man and as a writer he is, like Gogol, difficult to 'place'; indeed, a comparison with Gogol (one which is frequently made)[1] serves as a useful beginning in a process of demystification of Dostoevsky, an attempt, that is, to solve the mystery of this particular man.[2] Dostoevsky himself was aware of his special relationship with Gogol: the most celebrated apocryphal remark in the history of nineteenth-century Russian literature is that attributed to him: 'We have all come from under Gogol's *Overcoat*.'[3] Dostoevsky may be more 'intellectual' than his predecessor, but there are many parallels between them. In their own lifetimes, and more especially since, they and their works have given rise to a kaleidoscope of conflicting interpretations, and have inspired many individuals and groups in twentieth-century literature directly or indirectly. One implication of their work is a revolutionary critique of contemporary — or, for that matter, any — society. Yet their own confessed views, except for Dostoevsky's early utopian humanism, were deeply conservative, leading them both ultimately to the sanctuary of the Orthodox Church. Both writers belonged to the 'literary proletariat', coming from much lowlier origins than were typical for nineteenth-century Russian littérateurs. Many more parallels could be drawn, but first let us examine the factors in Dostoevsky's background which helped shape his position in society, his view and depiction of it.

Dostoevsky's family derived from the nobility,[4] but by the time he was born it had become impoverished. His father, who himself had received a seminary education, now worked as a hospital doctor and his salary was low. However, their circumstances were not so straitened. In 1831 they were able to buy a small estate, with one hundred serfs, which cost them 42 000R.[5] The family, though, lived for most of the year in Moscow, and Dostoevsky spent his youth not in 'nests of gentlefolk' as

44

Turgenev and Tolstoy did but in state flats, surrounded by a hospital atmosphere, in a close, restricted, and rather severe family circle. The spirit of early life informs the novels of all three writèrs, in very different ways.

For Dostoevsky, then, these first years were rather gloomy. To S. D. Yanovsky in the 1840s, for example, he talked of a 'heavy and joyless youth'. Their existence was monotonous and strict. The family may have been a close one but any spontaneity or boisterousness was precluded – no rough games, no young friends and few outings. Moreover, the parents were very religious, and the children were obliged to be the same. In brief, it was essentially the spirit of a middle-class Victorian household, whose ethos was to reappear in many of Dostoevsky's later ideas.

The other factors of Dostoevsky's background are also of importance. Because of his father's profession, he was able to see *real* suffering, and he was to remain exposed to and fascinated by suffering through imprisonment, illness and death. He grew up mainly in an urban environment, and this affected his whole view of reality, quite apart from the city providing one of the main themes of his work. His childhood, moreover, was rather solitary: from his earliest years he preferred his own company and withdrew into dreams of mystical Romanticism and the 'religion of the heart'.[6] This general picture was heightened by a number of deaths: in 1837 his first literary idol, Pushkin, and then his mother died, and Dostoevsky was deeply upset by both. His father took to drink, and he too was soon to die, in 1839.[7]

Dostoevsky's formal education did little to improve his position, and what he did learn at this time came from his own omnivorous reading. His education began at home, and most of it came from his parents, in particular his rather severe father,[8] who insisted that everything be learned by heart. His real education, though, derived mainly from the regular family readings, both of the classics – Karamzin, Lomonosov, Derzhavin, Zhukovsky and, in particular, Pushkin – and of more recent historical works, especially by Sir Walter Scott. This pattern was repeated at all his educational institutions. In 1834, he entered the private Chermak school, a reasonable school, but Dostoevsky spent much of his time, as always, avidly reading. Dreary reality once more was replaced by poetry and romantic dreams. Eventually,

in 1839, he moved to the military Engineers' School in St Petersburg, where again he led a solitary existence. He found the
strenuous curriculum, strict discipline and generally brutal
atmosphere most uncongenial and mixed little with his fellow-
pupils.[9] Literature again was the main-spring of his existence.
He continued to read widely – the prevailing Romantic pan-
theon, Hoffmann, Balzac, Scott, Dickens, Hugo, Goethe, and
especially Schiller, as well as Pushkin and Gogol profoundly
inspired the 'monkish' Dostoevsky.[10] Life in the academy, and
the subsequent years of his short-lived military career (until
1844) became more agonising every day, except when he could
immerse himself in his reading, and now, writing. Dostoevsky
now resolved that his vocation was to be literature, through
which he would unravel the mystery of man.

The wider implications of Dostoevsky's class origins are also
important. Firstly, the material conditions of his background,
and its later effects, allowed him (as it did Belinsky) to understand the wider problem of poverty much more directly than
most writers. As Arnold Hauser observes,[11] Dostoevsky is 'one
of the few genuine writers on poverty, for he writes not merely
out of sympathy with the poor, like George Sand or Eugène
Sue, or as a result of vague memories like Dickens, but as one
who has spent most of his time in need and has literally starved
from time to time'. This is, indeed, one of Dostoevsky's great
strengths because his work can always be read as the expression
of the revolt of the poor, a defence of the most oppressed
classes of society. In more personal terms, when he entered the
still predominantly aristocratic literary milieu in the 1840s his
relatively lowly social origins proved a considerable handicap,
and, indeed, served to reinforce his own sense of isolation in the
world. He was almost alone among the new literary talents of
the 1840s, in both social and financial terms, and the gulf could
never be bridged. Even before his first great success with *Poor
Folk* (1846), his hypersensitive nature had become acutely aware
of his inferiority among his peers: as before, he kept aloof,
fearing insults and slights. Accordingly, he looked upon *Poor
Folk* as his great hope, which would both relieve his financial
hardship and bring him acceptance from the disdainful literary
elite. For a time he was accepted on his literary merits, and
Dostoevsky in turn became infatuated with this new, glamorous
world.[12] But Dostoevsky's real social position was fundamentally

unchanged, and when on the one hand his writings changed in a direction which displeased Belinsky and, on the other, his affectations and ludicrous vanity became manifest, the aristocratic elite were not slow to mock Dostoevsky most viciously. Dostoevsky was never to forget his rejection by the higher social world, and his lasting bitterness was to form the basis of his later envy of Tolstoy and Turgenev in particular.

In the prison camp too, Dostoevsky took the burden of his class origins with him, even if in a very different way. According to some sources at least (including Dostoevsky himself), class differences led to hostility from the ordinary convicts, who distrusted him not only because he was from the nobility, but also because he had committed no obvious crime.[13] Whether this was the main cause, or whether Dostoevsky's long-standing aloofness occasioned the enmity, it is true that he remained as isolated from his immediate surroundings as he had been before. Yet, he was again able to turn this negative situation to positive account. It was precisely in the camp years that Dostoevsky not only discovered the immense chasm between himself (and the educated elite in general) and the common people, the *narod*, but also came to believe that the truth of life was on their side. In terms of ideology, at least, this was the most profound consequence of Dostoevsky's class origin and the conflicts into which it led him.

In more literary terms it also had very far-reaching effects. With the partial exception of Gogol Dostoevsky represented a new departure in Russian literature in that he was not from the land-owning classes. His art reflects this most closely: it stands as an end to 'landowners' literature'. His art is that of the modern metropolis,[14] where life is hurried, chaotic, full of action. In particular, his writings depict the life of the impoverished bourgeoisie of the city which stands as the exact antithesis of the orderly, harmonious 'nests of gentlefolk' of Turgenev and Tolstoy. Dostoevsky describes a world without rational causation, whose characters are disconnected, with no roots, no home, and where all the traditional values of the family, continuity and harmony, the life of nature, are disrupted or else positively rejected. Many of Dostoevsky's heroes, and in particular the Underground Man and Raskolnikov, struggle against grinding poverty and fight bitterly against the resulting humiliation. They struggle to preserve their honour and essential human dignity and are constantly suspicious and hypersensitive, preferring solitude to the rejection that unceasingly awaits them in society. In class terms, as in many other ways, Dostoevsky's artistic writings are profoundly autobiographical.

These themes first appear in Dostoevsky's pre-exile writings, in particular *Poor Folk* and *The Double* (1846). They were to reappear with renewed intensity after Dostoevsky's own humiliation and suffering in Siberia, and the humiliation of the earlier years is now supplemented by the theme of revenge on society for these sufferings. Raskolnikov is the fullest expression of this type of Dostoevskyan hero. He is, like many others before him, oppressed, insulted by poverty and responds by a desire for both material and ideological power which will deliver him from this humiliating situation. Through him Dostoevsky discusses the three principal paths open to men of his own class. Either they can devote themselves to hard, painstaking work, or they can rise upwards, usually through blood (as Raskolnikov attempts to do), or they can positively accept their poverty. For Dostoevksy and, somewhat unconvincingly, for Raskolnikov in the end, this last course proves the most desirable.

Dostoevsky's class consciousness began to develop in the 1840s, and he became increasingly interested in the social problems occasioned by the rivalry between wealth and poverty. In this sense, Utopian Socialism, which Dostoevsky now encountered, was ideally suited to his new sensibilities and awareness: he moved, that is, into a world much more attuned to his real interests – the *raznochintsy*, the democratic, even socialistic world of the *Petrashevtsy*. And Dostoevsky was to remain the voice of the bourgeoisie and of the lower orders of Russian society: even in his last works there remains an enmity for the nobility, and sympathy for the *raznochintsy* and, above all, faith in the peasantry.

For all this, the major result – and greatest crisis – of his class position was his disastrous financial situation. The basically parlous situation occasioned by his position in society was merely exacerbated at every turn by Dostoevsky's peculiar, almost psychopathic, relationship with money. That is, as Carr wryly notes,[15] like many reckless spendthrifts, Dostoevsky attributed his hardships not to the excesses of his expenditure, but to the inadequacy of his income. His financial difficulties began more or less as soon as he left home. One of his earliest

surviving letters (10 May 1838) is addressed to his father, respectfully asking for help, merely to meet his bare necessities: unfortunately this source was to prove unreliable. Even when
Dostoevsky was drawing a salary in the early 1840s, his position
failed to improve. (These years, though, before he gave up
working in 1844, were rather more secure than any period until
the 1870s.) Even in 1840, Dostoevsky was already 800R in debt
and a request for 1500R from home only brought him a third
of that amount. When Dr A. E. Riesenkampf visited him in St
Petersburg in 1842 he found him living in a four-room flat – but
two were unfurnished and only one was heated![16] Dostoevsky,
as always, was his own worst enemy: everyone 'borrowed' from
him, he lost 1000R playing billiards, and even in 'normal' circumstances got through his 50R monthly allowance in two weeks.
Not surprisingly Dostoevsky was much more interested in the
financial rewards from his first publications, even if he was
gratified by the good reviews. Almost all his letters to his brother
Mikhail in the 1840s which deal with literary matters concern
themselves much more with fame and money than with literature
as such. As early as 1845 there appears what was to be the
constant refrain of the 1860s and even the more comfortable
1870s. That is, Dostoevsky had to rush his work simply to meet
dead-lines, or else to produce something new to earn the necessary money. He could never, he complains, finish anything worthwhile, or polish his work sufficiently. The vicious circle had
already been entered. His later works of the 1840s failed in
both critical and financial terms, and Dostoevsky attributed this
almost exclusively to his working conditions, which he compared
to those of a 'day-labourer'.[17]

Dostoevsky's material position was no better when he finally
returned from exile. Even when still in Siberia he had to borrow
800R to marry, and in the following few years his letters, as in
the 1840s, mainly concern themselves with the financial aspects
of his literary enterprises. He refused to write to order – as he
was always to do – but, as a result, frequently had to divert his
attention from his major schemes to produce pot-boilers. In
1857 he accepted an advance of 500R from Katkov (and Mikhail
received the same on his behalf) even though he had nothing
ready. Dostoevsky had soon spent the money but refused to
rush his work, Shortly thereafter he finished *The Inhabitants of
the Village of Stepanchikovo* (1859), but it was rejected by

Katkov's *Russian Messenger* because it would not pay Dostoevsky the 100R per sheet he demanded. (Turgenev was already being paid 400R per sheet (for *A Nest of Gentlefolk*) and Dostoevsky angrily demanded why the rich Turgenev received so much and he so little.)

Dostoevsky decided to establish a literary journal with Mikhail in the early 1860s, partially in an attempt to earn money. Their first venture, *Time*, which began appearing in 1861, was quite successful, but the success was short-lived: following an apparently inflammatory article by Strakhov in April 1863, 'A Fatal Question', concerning the Polish situation, the journal was suppressed, leaving them both penniless. Dostoevsky had to borrow again — 100R from the Literary Fund for a journey abroad.[18] The two brothers remained undeterred and in 1864 they launched another journal, *Epoch*. This was a disaster from the beginning. It was launched on credit, it was poorly presented and generally rather badly handled by the two. Censorship problems worsened the situation, and soon the subscribers were demanding their money back. A crushing blow was the death of Mikhail in 1864: Dostoevsky generously took not only the burden of the journal's debts, but also responsibility for his brother's dependants. *Epoch* struggled on until February 1865, its sickly condition made even worse by the death of one of its outstanding contributors, Apollon Grigorev, but ultimately Dostoevsky, genuinely threatened by the debtors' prison, was forced to give in, leaving debts of 1500R.[19]

Dosotevsky, as so often, fled abroad, lost what money he had in five days of compulsive gambling, and literally to avoid starvation, borrowed where and what he could. Once more Dostoevsky complained about his impossible writing conditions, and indeed it is quite remarkable that he wrote anything. He wrote to his old friend Wrangel at this time: 'Forced work, work for money has crushed and corroded me.'[20] But Dostoevsky worked on, if only because he had to in order to stay alive. At this time he entered a ludicrous contract with the notorious Stellovsky who would claim all rights to anything that Dostoevsky might later write if he did not deliver a new work to him by late 1866 (it was the writing of *The Gambler* in less than a month, aided by a young stenographer, Anna Smitkina, who shortly afterwards became Dostoevsky's second wife, that saved him from total ruin). For long periods he was unable to work simply because of the interminable and agonising worry over money. He received an advance of 4000R from Katkov for *Crime and Punishment*, but this hardly touched his debts. In 1866 he asked Katkov for another 2000R, as an advance on his next novel – which he had not even begun – but most of it went to his creditors. His own troubles were merely exacerbated by the unscrupulous demands from the dependants he had collected from his first marriage.[21]

Heavy roulette losses did nothing to help. These continued even after his marriage in 1867 (paid for by one of Katkov's advances). Dostoevsky pawned his winter coat, his wife's jewellery, even the wedding ring, to pay for his gambling.[22] 'Loans' continued from all sources, even from detested radicals like Herzen and Ogarev. And so the late 1860s ground on – more advances, more loans, more creditors' demands, more roulette losses. By the time he began writing his next novel, *The Idiot*, in 1867 he had already received 5200R in advances. He was so worried that he could hardly work, and even when he did he laboured eight hours a day to pay his way. In 1868 he had to send off the first part of *The Idiot* for publication, with the rest unfinished. Dostoevsky emerges from the letters of this period almost as a chained slave. Yet he insisted, he would never write *for* money: he took only commissions if he already had the theme for his work.

By 1870 he owed his creditors at least 6000R (letter to his sister Vera, 19 May 1870). Increasingly, and ever more bitterly, he railed against Turgenev, Tolstoy, and Goncharov too; if only he had their means and their leisure, then he could produce something worthwhile. The following year he returned to Russia, with only a few roubles left, awaited by a swarm of creditors. Soon, however his financial situation was to improve dramatically, mainly because of the economic sense of Anna, who had already persuaded him to abandon his gambling. The early 1870s were full of just as much harrassment as in former years, but gradually Dostoevsky's affairs passed under her management. By 1873 she was more or less in control: for the first time Dostoevsky was able to forget about money and concentrate on writing. In 1873 Anna negotiated a very successful deal over the sale of *The Devils* (1872): she personally published it, and made 300R on one morning's work alone, as she proudly relates in her memoirs.

Even so, Dostoevsky still found, despite his enormous popularity and a rapidly expanding market, that he could not live by artistic writing alone. In 1873 he took the editorship of Meshchersky's *The Citizen*, at 3000R per annum, at least partially out of financial necessity. Soon, however, he felt that he had again fallen into a state of bondage, albeit of a different kind. He hated having to write articles on subjects which did not interest him, as well as the pressure of meeting dead-lines: within a year he resigned. Money continued to worry him, and in his usual opportunistic way, he agreed to publish *Raw Youth* (1875) for Nekrasov, because Katkov, who was publishing *Anna Karenina*, did not want another major novel. Dostoevsky's own journal, *Diary of a Writer*, which was an immense success, further eased his burdens, but still for *The Brothers Karamazov* he was obliged to take advances, which continued to be considerably lower than those of Turgenev and Tolstoy — much to his continuing anger and envy. However, even though all debts were not paid off until 1879, for the first time in twenty years he did not face the debtors' prison. Only, in fact, in the year of his death, 1881, did the Dostoevsky family have no financial problems. The contrast between the ease of life for Turgenev and Tolstoy with their large estates and incomes is indeed a striking one. Dostoevsky hardly made matters any simpler but the basic problem arose from his social origins and the social value of literature. Even in the 1870s the writer's life was not an easy one — unless one were an aristocrat.

Literature was central to Dostoevsky's existence not only in financial terms. Again, like Gogol, there were two main motive forces in Dostoevsky's literary creativity. Probably the first stimulus was a desire for fame, which would elevate him above his own lowly social position. When *Poor Folk* was acclaimed by the *Contemporary* group it was essentially the celebrity that Dostoevsky talked of, in terms depressingly similar to those of Gogol's Khlestakov. On 16 November 1845 he wrote to Mikhail: 'Well, brother, I believe that my fame is just now in its fullest flower. Everywhere I meet with the most amazing consideration and enormous interest. I have made the acquaintance of a lot of very important people. Prince Odoevsky begs me for the honour of a visit, and Count Sollogub is tearing his hair in desperation.'[23] The emphasis on titled littérateurs in his account is no accident. So too when Dostoevsky aspired to re-enter the literary scene, he delayed his work as long as he could so that he might re-emerge as brilliantly as he had begun. Once again he discussed his work not so much in terms of its ideas and literary merits but in terms of the name he would acquire. 'I know', he wrote to Mikhail in 1856, 'that I shall make a career for myself and conquer a high place in literature.'[24] Yet increasingly in the post-exile period another theme emerged. Dostoevsky now longed for fame, not only in its own right, but because his characters, ideas, his very representation of reality were so stunningly original that he had to be allowed to present them to the public, which, he felt, now looked to *him* 'with expectant eyes'. But what was this 'new word'? He had in mind not merely his radically new ideas on man's nature and purpose, but a completely new *view* of reality. What, then, is his relationship to existing literature? After all, not every critic agrees with Dostoevsky's own self-assessment. Nabokov, for example, describes Dostoevsky (in 1880) as 'a much overrated, sentimental and Gothic novelist of the time'.[25] However provocative this remark may be, there is a certain truth in it, and in terms of 'placing' Dostoevsky, it is important to indicate his close links with the popular Romantic fiction of his youth. Several strands influenced him, most obvious of which are the fantastic as well as the sentimental and Gothic of which Nabokov speaks. The latter qualities are particularly apparent in Dostoevsky's early concern for the 'poor folk' of society, and continue right through all the later works dealing with the 'humiliated and wronged', especially in the Marmeladov family in *Crime and Punishment*. This influence is, indeed, most apparent in Dostoevsky's cult of suffering, which commences with *Poor Folk*, reaches its apogee in Sonya Marmeladova, and then continues through all the 'meek' heroines of the major novels. In turning to the very obvious fantastic elements in Dostoevsky's fiction, we once again see the influence of the 'école frénétique' of the 1830s, as well as of the darker side of German Romanticism.[26] Perhaps the most striking element here is the theme of the double, which again commences in Dostoevsky's early period (most obviously in *The Double* itself) and continues through a whole series of famous *Doppelgänger* in the major novels.[27] Other aspects of French and German Romanticism lie submerged beneath the topical and philosophical concerns of Dostoevsky's later work — the 'pure prostitutes' such as Sonya, the demonic Byronic heroes such as Raskolnikov and, particularly, Stavrogin (*The Devils*), or the proud heroines — Katerina

Ivanovna (*The Brothers Karamazov*), Dunya Raskolnikova or
Nastasya Filippovna (*The Idiot*). In many ways, then, we can
consider Dostoevsky, to use Mario Praz's phrase, 'a belated manifestation of the Romanticism of 1830'.[28]

Dostoevsky also learned much from Russian literature of the
1830s and 1840s. Significantly, it was the newest elements in
Russian literature from which Dostoevsky borrowed, the emergent 'natural' school, which in turn was closely linked with popular, street literature. (A striking example of this is the fact that
Dostoevsky's first three works deal with 'petty clerks', one of
the central concerns of Gogol and other writers of the school.)
What was to be of lasting significance for Dostoevsky in these
influences was this connection with everyday topical subjects,
which were to form the basis of his own 'new word'. Dostoevsky
gleaned much else in the 1840s. For example, his work on the
*St Petersburg News* brought him into *direct* contact with the
life of the streets, with the lower and middle-class sections of
the city and with the down-and-outs who populate his fiction
both before and after Siberia. It was, *inter alia*, this introduction
to 'serious' literature of the lowly sections of society which
marked the end of 'landowners' literature'.

In the introduction of street literature as source material
Dostoevsky had again been anticipated by his greatest master,
Gogol. It is his relationship with Gogol which highlights Dostoevsky's newness as an artist in both literary and sociological
terms. Like many other writers in the second half of the nineteenth century, Dostoevsky was deeply influenced by Gogol,
but it was never a question of mere imitation. As Rozanov
notes,[29] Russian literature of this period can be seen as a *rejection* of Gogol; an attempt, that is, to resurrect the dead
souls, to breathe life into a world of inanimate mannequins and
homunculi. From his very first work this was to be Dostoevsky's
approach. *Poor Folk* may in some senses be a continuation of
*The Overcoat*, but it is also a polemic against it, an attempt to
humanise the grotesquely pathetic Akaky Akakyevich, as Makar
Devushkin, the hero of *Poor Folk*, is himself aware. Dostoevsky's
overall purpose, then, is to *rethink* Gogol: to use the same themes
and material, but also to humanise them. In later works he
continues this approach. Whether he borrows Gogol's use of the
fantastic, in *The Double*, or his concern with the underside of
life, in *The Humiliated and Wronged* and many later works, the

effect is usually the antithesis to Gogol's. Dostoevsky was horrified by Gogol's impersonal detachment and reacted strongly
against it. The polemic lasted beyond Siberia, and it was only
with the beginning of the major novels that he was able to release himself from his obsession. Indeed, the parody of Gogol in
the character of Foma Opiskin in *Stepanchikovo* can be seen as
a valedictory statement, even if Gogol's direct influence is felt
as late as 1864 in *Notes from the Underground*.[30]

Dostoevsky, then, invalidates old responses and compels new
ones, and forces the reader to reinterpret the world. In this sense
Gogol played a vital part in the foundations of his new word.
But Dostoevsky also added much that was specifically his own.
Gide goes as far as to call him the Columbus of Russian literature.[31] What he had particularly in mind was the discovery, by
Dostoevsky, of new psychological states, the emphasis on man
living *in extremis*, the view that the irrational was as crucial to
man's nature as the rational. As is now well known, Dostoevsky
'discovered' much about man's behaviour that was only fully
appreciated after Freud's more scientific investigations of the
same subjects — the perverse, the cruel, the masochistic. But
Dostoevsky went much further than this in the view of man
which his work presents. For Bakhtin,[32] this is precisely the
nature of Dostoevsky's new word. Dostoevsky's work shows
man not as a finished product, but in a state of *becoming*. He
shows man not only as he is, as he appears to the world, but he
also shows how the world appears to him. His characters, then,
emerge before us not as finished products but as creatures in
conflict. And this conflict too is essential to Dostoevsky's new
word. Gone is the harmonious, ordered, rational world of the
old order, to be replaced by one that is riven by deep divisions
and disorder. His world is essentially one of flux where nothing
is fixed or final. Dostoevsky himself was deeply aware of living
in a time of crisis, where not only the content of the traditional
novel was insufficient, so too was its very form. The calmly nar-
rated novel simply could not express adequately the chaos he
saw around him.

Another crucial issue is that of topicality. For Dostoevsky,
good art *must* be highly topical, dealing with social issues of
immediate and direct concern to the artist and his public.
Dostoevsky's own writing is, indeed, intensely topical. As Fanger
shows,[33] *Crime and Punishment*, for example, even though it

may now be discussed primarily in terms of its psychological and philosophical investigations, deals directly with such contemporary problems as drunkenness, prostitution, crime and the radical question. He can, indeed, be seen as the chronographer of his times, and when he was abroad in the 1860s he became acutely aware of the need to keep in touch with Russia through the newspapers and his correspondents and blamed the relative failure of *The Idiot* on his own sojourn abroad during its creation — just as he had attacked Turgenev for looking at Russia through the wrong end of a telescope in *Smoke*. So, too, he defended his journalistic work because it kept him in touch with the very latest developments in Russian society.

Dostoevsky accounts for his concern with immediate reality in *Diary of a Writer* in 1876. 'What can be more fantastic, more unpredictable than reality?'[34] he asks. This emphasis on the fantastic within reality leads on to an answer to the question of why Dostoevsky was so intensely interested in topical issues. For Dostoevsky, only by looking at man as he *was becoming*, could one perceive the 'higher reality' about life. In a letter to Strakhov Dostoevsky sums up this approach to art. On 26 February 1869 he writes:[35]

> I have my own idea about art, and it is this: What most people regard as fantastic and lacking in universality, *I* hold to be the inmost essence of truth. Arid observation of everyday trivialities I have long ceased to regard as realism — it is quite the reverse. In any newspaper one takes up, one comes across reports of wholly authentic facts, which nevertheless strike one as extraordinary. Our writers [i.e. the 'landowners'] regard them as fantastic, and take no account of them; and yet they are the truth for they are facts.

In order to convey this deeper reality Dostoevsky allows himself many techniques which would not usually be considered admissible in 'normal' literary realism. Thus, intensification, distortion, the grotesque and fantastic are not mere adjuncts to Dostoevsky's realism, they are essential to it. And, as for Gogol, this peculiar realism undercuts the very basis of existence and our perception of it. *Everything*, then, in his art acts as polemic against the world of Tolstoy and, in particular, of Turgenev, whose harmony and tranquillity Dostoevsky viewed as a shallow falsification of the real truth about life.

This desire not to falsify life is particularly apparent in Dostoevsky's characterisation, wherein he does not try to 'play God', but rather to let his characters speak for themselves, even if this is in direct conflict with his own ideas.[36] Dostoevsky has no final approach to his characters, however tendentious he may appear to be at times, or even try to be. Their ideas are *theirs*, growing logically out of their characters and Dostoevsky accepts them as such.

Dostoevsky, that is, wrote, to use Bakhtin's term, *polyphonic* novels. Whereas, Bakhtin argues, most novels ultimately represent only one point of view (the author's), Dostoevsky refuses to do this. His characters represent opposing views — and ones which often oppose even him. As Bakhtin puts it: 'Dostoevsky . . . creates not voiceless slaves . . . but rather *free* people who are capable of standing *beside* their creator, of disagreeing with him, and even of rebelling against him.'[37] There is throughout a plurality of consciousness and no single character can be taken to be Dostoevsky's representative. The characteristic mode is questioning, a dialectic between a variety of conflicting points of view. Dostoevsky's own ideas are countered as soon as they are uttered. Father Zossima, for example, may seem to be the fullest embodiment of Dostoevsky's late ideas, but his ideological opponent Ivan Karamazov has all the best arguments. Many other instances could be adduced.

Dostoevsky depicts his ideological world as one of conflict because he saw the world around him as one of deep conflict and crisis, the crisis of nineteenth-century capitalist society, to which, Fanger argues,[38] the polyphonic novel is peculiar. None of his characters is fully Dostoevsky, because he was so deeply aware, through his own personality and place within society, of the contradictions of the social world he experienced and observed. Lunacharsky catches this aspect of Dostoevsky brilliantly:[39]

The disintegration of his personality, its cleavage, the fact that he wished to believe in ideas and feelings which inspired no real faith in him and wished to refute that which persistently troubled him and seemed to be the truth — this made him subjectively fitted to be the painful but necessary voice of the confusion of his times.

So then, the polyphony of Dostoevsky's world springs directly from the contradictions of the social world. He saw himself surrounded by opposing forces – the young nihilists and then populists, the Slavophils, the liberals, the reactionaries – and felt bound to convey the truth of each faction. Opposing viewpoints coexisted in the world around him, so too do they coexist in his imaginative depiction of it. It was Dostoevsky's great gift not only to represent the dialogues of his age, but also to see the age as one of great and intense dialogue.

As is frequently noted,[40] dialogue is a principal element of Dostoevsky's narrative mode. His novels are peculiarly dramatic. This is no accident for, in order to convey the conflicts of his time, Dostoevsky felt it necessary not only to change fundamentally the author's approach to character, but also to reshape the very genre of the novel. The calm social novel as it had emerged in England and France, and as was now developing in Russia, was insufficient too and, moreover, too orderly: so instead, and quite deliberately, Dostoevsky wrote 'loose, baggy monsters', to use Henry James' infamous phrase. His novels are not, of course, without precedent. They have close connections with the adventure and picaresque novels,[41] with carnivalesque literature,[42] with – significantly enough – the Socratic dialogue. In this sense Dostoevsky was profoundly eclectic as a writer.

Despite all that has been said about Dostoevsky's polyphony, doubts remain. As Mochulsky notes,[43] *Crime and Punishment* ends in a 'pious lie', and most readers of it find Raskolnikov's conversion highly unconvincing. Most of the novels, after all the drama and conflict, do have monologic endings, as if Dostoevsky, for all his awareness of surrounding chaos, still wished to impose some order on his world. Indeed, many other monologic, ideological and even didactic elements can easily be discerned in Dostoevsky. Even within his creative writing there are strong elements of a tendency: for all his polyphonic abilities, his preferences are not hard to discover. Dostoevsky may have felt strongly the need, as an artist, to convey the truth of life as he saw it, but he was also careful to make sure that it was, precisely as *he* saw it. *The Devils* is the prime example of this. While writing it, Dostoevsky wrote to Strakhov, on 5 April 1870:

I also set great hopes on the novel which I am now writing . . . I don't mean as a work of art, but because of its tendencies; I mean to utter certain thoughts, whether all the artistic side of it goes to the dogs or not. The thoughts that have gathered themselves together in my head and heart are pressing me on — even if it turns into a mere pamphlet, I shall say all that I have to say in my heart.[44]

Now, it may be true that Stavrogin, an essentially non-political character, moves to the centre of the work, but the political *judgement* of characters remains a very potent force in Dostoevsky's depiction of the nihilists. Pyotr Verkhovensky, in particular, stands as a mere caricature of Nechaev. He is characterised not psychologically, but ideologically, and becomes virtually a character out of a tragi-comic farce, or a melodrama.[45] Without question, even if the artist struggles hard against the polemicist in this work, *The Devils* remains an *attack* on the nihilists. The work, that is, had a specific *aim*, of developing the idea, latent in *Crime and Punishment* and *The Idiot*, that nihilism and crime are closely linked. In the end the book remains a terrible warning on Dostoevsky's part against the dangers of radicalism. Similar tendencies can be discerned in all Dostoevsky's major work. *Notes from the Underground* is quite clearly an attack on Chernyshevsky and his utilitarian politics and aesthetics. Indeed, this attack on an over-reliance on rationalism permeates all of Dostoevsky's post-Siberian writing.

While much of the above ideological critique of character may possibly be open to question, and is usually countered in most instances by an alternative viewpoint, it remains true that the ultimate intention of much of Dostoevsky's work remained didactic. Dostoevsky, in fact, denied the possibility of pure objectivity in art, and accepted quite freely that a certain tendency was inevitable — and he chose a specifically *moral* tendency. The 'pious lie' at the end of *Crime and Punishment* is a case in point. Whereas Raskolnikov might more logically have committed suicide, this would have weakened the efficacy of Sonya's exemplary humility, and so Dostoevsky, in what is a relatively arbitrary fashion, *brings* Raskolnikov to a reversal of his previous attitudes. Similarly, while Ivan Karamazov may argue more persuasively than Zossima it is *his* life which ends in grotesque visions and insanity, rather than that of Alyosha or Dmitry. Indeed, Ivan, Raskolnikov, Stavrogin and many others stand as a warning of the fate that awaits those who are separated from the soil and the people, who do not embrace the simple

peasant Russian faith. Conversely, Sonya, Myshkin and Alyosha
are introduced and depicted to *demonstrate* the true greatness
of the meek, even if occasionally, as in the case of Myshkin,
their efforts prove unsuccessful and unredemptive.

Just as much of Dostoevsky's writing had intimate links with
the Romanticism of the 1830s, so too his aesthetics were deeply
influenced by the Romantic (and specifically German) literary
theories of the same period. That is, art for Dostoevsky was a
form of philosophical inquiry, in which the poet (or the artist)
was a philosopher, or even a seer, and art itself was regarded as a
form of revelation — to the writer and his audience. Art was
quite simply the broadest avenue for the study of mankind's
deepest nature. As Steinberg notes,[46] Dostoevsky's art is essentially heuristic: it is 'destined to probe the mysteries of historical
existence beyond the reach of purely theoretical, conceptual
exploration'. Following on from Lermontov, Dostoevsky
attempted to unite art and philosophy and became perhaps the
most outstanding metaphysical novelist in the history of Western
literature.

Moreover, and again very much in line with the 'religion of
art' of the 1830s, Dostoevsky saw artistic creation as a quasi-
mystical experience. In 1846 he wrote to his brother Mikhail:[47]
'He [the artist] must consecrate all his toil to the holy spirit of
art — such toil is holy, chaste, and demands single-heartedness.'
Furthermore, Dostoevsky saw poetic inspiration as intuitive and
irrational, and the artistic instinct and insights are inexplicable.
Indeed, the artist in creation becomes an agent of some myster-
ious, quasi-divine force that works *through* him. To the poet
Maykov Dostoevsky wrote in May 1869:[48]

> The essence and even the metre [of poetry] depend on the
> soul of the poet, and they come suddenly completely ready
> in his soul, even independently of himself . . . I'll make a long
> digression: a poem, in my view, makes its appearance like a
> virgin precious stone, a diamond, completely ready in the
> poet's soul, in all its essence. . . . If you like, it is not even he
> who is the creator, but life, the mighty essence of life, the
> God living and real, concentrating his power in the diversity
> of creation.

Given this Olympian view Dostoevsky rejected any utilitarianism in art, even if he conceded that a certain tendency was inevitable. He consistently argued for the freedom and independence of art: it should have no tendency, apart from the purely artistic. It was in the early 1860s that Dostoevsky expressed this view of art most clearly: 'Since its [art's] interest and goals are one with the goal of man, whom it serves and with whom it is indissolubly united, then the freer its development is, the more good it will bring to humanity.'[49] Accordingly, any external pressure is bound to be harmful to art. Art *is* of some purpose within society, as the above quotation clearly reveals, but it can only be of value to society by being free.

It is significant that these arguments were most fully developed in the early 1860s, that is, when Dostoevsky, like Turgenev and Tolstoy a few years earlier, became acquainted with, and was horrified by the utilitarian aesthetics of Belinsky's immediate successors, Chernyshevsky and Dobrolyubov. If utilitarian ends were sought in art, then art as such would no longer exist, but would descend to the level of mere propaganda, and he was determined that 'holy' art should never become this. Paradoxically, indeed, Dostoevsky criticised Dobrolyubov and his ilk for demanding socially useful art, precisely because such demands lessen the chances of art serving society.

If art could serve society — yet remain free — how was it to do so? Like Turgenev, Dostoevsky answered the tough new generation by returning to his Romantic heritage of the 1830s and insisting on art's total autonomy. This would be sufficient in itself, because true, free art would serve mankind precisely because of its intimate connection with all that was noble, great and spiritual in human history. Art for Dostoevsky, particularly in his post-Siberian period, was important precisely because it was a *spiritual* activity, and, increasingly, a specifically Christian activity. He was especially appalled by Dobrolyubov's anti-aesthetic, extra-literary demands because of the deep schism he saw developing within Russian society of the 1860s. Now more than ever, the high moral responsibilities of true art had to be heeded to save mankind from imminent collapse: paradoxically, Dostoevsky echoed the words of his then ideological opponent Nekrasov in calling upon the artist to be not only a poet, but a *citizen*. Obviously, though, they understood this term rather differently. As his aesthetic views crystallised during the intense artistic controversies of the early 1860s,[50] Dostoevsky came to view the historic function of art as man's aesthetic (and therefore, spiritual) education, and no true artist should demean or betray his part in this elevated tradition. Instead, because true art more than any other human activity (except religion) came closest to the vision of an ideal life, and the true artist, in his role as a seer, revealed man most fully to himself, in the completeness of his religious destiny, then the artist should attempt to communicate this divine message — rather than depict trivial surface reality which might bring about petty, unimportant social reforms. Art, that is, could become the very embodiment of man's highest ideals, and give a whole moral system to the nation — and this it *must* do. Essentially, that is, art and religion are one, and art must attempt to call man to his religious destiny. As Jackson puts it,[51] what was central to Dostoevsky's views was 'his own aesthetic optimism, his belief in art as an awakener of human culture, his conception of Russian literature as the embodiment of Russia's ideal of moral truth and beauty'. And even if his own works were disfigured and disturbing, this was precisely because of the discrepancy implied in them between the religious potential of man and the fallen life he actually led. Art's task in the Russia of the second half of the nineteenth century was to emphasise this chasm.

In its increasingly intimate connection with religion, art for Dostoevsky had a purpose, even if at the same time it had to remain free. This is why, I think, Dostoevsky's art *is* ultimately didactic, because the purpose of tendency he envisaged was to convey his own ideas — or message — about man's historic and religious destinies. Art was too serious a business, the age he lived in too crisis-ridden, and what he had to say too important and deeply felt, for him, in the final analysis, to allow his message to go unheeded. Whatever his asseverations to the contrary in the early 1860s, Dostoevsky did believe, in the last twenty years of his life, that art should have a tendency, and that it should be a moral tendency. Certainly, according to his contemporaries, Dostoevsky had a very normative approach to art. V. V. Timofeeva, a young writer of the time, records him as remarking that the 'true artist must not praise traitors or liars',[52] while Strakhov notes that Dostoevsky went even further in his demands on art. 'The artist', Dostoevsky maintained, 'must follow the development of society and bring to people's consciousness the good and evil found within it; he should be therefore a teacher, an accuser, a guide.'[53] That is, art should be devoted to a faithful depiction of contemporary life but, at the same time, the depiction should make it absolutely clear what the author's view of this life was.

Perhaps the most important concept of the three that Strakhov refers to is that of 'guide'. Once more, in fact, Dostoevsky here follows the views of Belinsky, who in his last years advocated that 'the creation of artistic types indicates through both its positive and negative aspects the road which the development of society has taken and the road it should take in the future'.[54] Quite obviously Dostoevsky in the 1860s and 1870s interpreted 'positive and negative aspects' and the future road very differently from Belinsky, but the two were united in their basic approach to the role of art and artist in society. Increasingly, that is, the balance between freedom and purpose in art, in Dostoevsky's view of it, shifted from the former to the latter — just as it had in Belinsky. Few artists in nineteenth-century Russia were able to escape this pull. For Dostoevsky the purpose of art came to be moral guidance: indeed, more than that, he came to view art as the most potent force for the regeneration of Russian reality. The artist could change reality, that is, by his very depiction of it, and central to this was the importance of beauty in art. Not only was beauty essential to human survival for Dostoevsky, but for him beauty could save the world. But what sort of beauty?

Here the connection between art and religion, which had always been strong, became closest of all. Again Jackson makes the point well:[55] 'The craving for beauty is a craving for that highest moment of life which anticipates Olympian tranquillity and eternality of time: it is a craving for transfiguration.' Man's ultimate aspiration in Dostoevsky's novels is towards divine beauty, the beauty in repose of icons, for example. However, Dostoevsky was well aware that man's sinful nature inhibits this striving and he descends into the hell of ugliness, both physical and moral — though particularly the latter. For Dostoevsky, art was so important for this reason too. In its perfect form (which did not, incidentally, include his own work — Pushkin was his ideal in this respect), in its harmony, peace and repose, an artistic work approached the truly divine, the Christ-like. Indeed, the aesthetic dimension was extremely important in his conception of Christ, who almost came for Dostoevsky to equal perfect

beauty. And so art, which had always been of the utmost importance for Dostoevsky, in the end became identified with Christianity. Through art he hoped to transfigure reality, to make it
more Christ-like, and by holding up this image of perfect beauty
and of beautiful perfection, he, the artist, could help to regenerate
the fallen world he perceived so intensely and described so
vividly.

The lofty idealism of Dostoevsky's approach to art in theory
did not, however, carry over into his dealings with his fellow littérateurs. The first and most illuminating instance is his encounter
and breach with the *Contemporary* group. After the 'discovery'
of the young Dostoevsky, the writer of *Poor Folk*, he entered
this milieu in glory. Unfortunately, the ardour of their relationship was to be short-lived. Some of the group perhaps behaved
rather shabbily in the affair, but it seems certain that Dostoevsky's vanity played the major part in the rather rapid disin-
fatuation experienced by his new admirers: they soon found his
excessive, even grotesque self-advertisement ludicrously out of
proportion to his actual achievement. Reading Dostoevsky's
letters and contemporaries' accounts, one is not suprised: there
was even talk that Dostoevsky wanted *The Double* to be printed
in *The Contemporary* with a special border to distinguish it from
all other contributions.[56]

However, the causes of the split were various. Initially, perhaps the main reason was Dostoevsky's conceit and arrogance,
which repelled the group, and this personal animosity was
worsened by their changing opinions of Dostoevsky's work. The
enormous success of *Poor Folk* was not to be repeated. Dostoevsky's interest in the fantastic, in *The Double* and subsequent
works, left Belinsky at first ambivalent and then decidedly cool.
Partly for financial reasons, but also to spite them, Dostoevsky
submitted *Mr Prokharchin* in 1847 to the rival *Notes of the
Fatherland*, and the rift now became public. They in turn, especially Belinsky, were extremely critical of Dostoevsky's latest
work, and Dostoevsky 'replied' by starting work as a feuilletonist
for the *St Petersburg News*, a journal generally hostile to the
Gogolian tendency in Russian literature.[57]

Dostoevsky's reponse was true to character. After his rapturous
accounts to Mikhail of a few years before, there came a complete
turnabout in his opinion of them. Moreover, he whitewashed
the affair, putting it down to financial complications.[58] Nekrasov,

he claimed, had been angry that Dostoevsky had broken faith with the group by working for another journal. But, Dostoevsky argues, he *had* to, because he had already accepted the publisher's (Kraevsky) advances. Dostoevsky's tone, as it was to be so often on such occasions, verges on the hysterical: 'As soon as I roundly abused Nekrasov, he curtsied and whimpered like a Jew that's been robbed.'[59] The whole affair, in Dostoevsky's version of it, turns out to have been a great conspiracy on their part.

In the same letter, Dosteovsky said of Belinsky: 'But as to Belinsky, he is so pliable that even about literary matters he changes his views five times a week.' Part of the cause of the break was over different attitudes to art, it is true, but Dostoevsky's later accounts of Belinsky suggest that more than Dostoevsky's aesthetic sensibilities had been offended. What is particularly unpleasant is that there are two versions to the later story – the public and the private. When Dostoevsky later wrote for a wider audience about Belinsky, he was fulsome in his praise. In 1873 he published an account of Belinsky in the first issue of *Diary of a Writer*,[60] which although rather ambivalent and an attempt to depict Belinsky as a Christian socialist, is generally very warm. He remarks, amongst other things, on Belinsky's ardour, warmth, insight and passion for ideas. 'This most blessed human being' is how Dostoevsky refers to Belinsky here, for public consumption.

Yet only two years before, in letters to Strakhov and Maykov, Dostoevsky seemed to be of a rather different opinion. To the latter in October 1870, Dostoevsky wrote of his early liberalism and remarked:[61] 'I still retained a leaven of scabby Russian liberalism, preached by . . . the dung-beetle Belinsky and the rest' (*sic*). A year later, in May 1871, Dostoevsky wrote to Strakhov and continued this attack on Belinsky's Westernism, which one might expect, but proceeded to denounce him as a critic. He gives his correspondent a long (and very biased) list of Belinsky's 'ridiculous' mistakes, and concludes:[62] 'I could give you, on the spur of the moment, countless proofs that he had not an atom of critical sense, nor that "quivering sensibility" of which Grigorovich babbled.' Over twenty years after the rejection of his early works Dostoevsky had not meekly forgotten and certainly not forgiven his Christian brother, even if the Russian public, two years later, was led to think so.

Dostoevsky also quarrelled bitterly with Nekrasov in the mid-

1840s. In the end they at least seemed to be reconciled. After he broke with Nekrasov along with the rest of the *Contemporary* group, relations were severed for many years. In the early 1860s some contact was resumed, only for relations to be embittered again after a polemic between Dostoevsky's journal and *The Contemporary*. Only in 1872 did they become reconciled, although their real rapprochement took place in 1875, with the publication of *A Raw Youth* in *Notes of the Fatherland*, which was now in Nekrasov's hands. Indeed, Nekrasov came to Dostoevsky to buy the novel — perhaps a rather surprising gesture, given Dostoevsky's blistering attack on the left only a few years before in *The Devils*. None the less, Dostoevsky was generally pleased to accept the offer: he had always regarded Nekrasov's work highly, and after some misgivings about publishing in an apparently hostile journal, was glad to make a break from Meshchersky's journal, *The Citizen*. As Mochulsky notes,[63] he realised that his path did not lie with the official reactionaries, and moreover, his own views on the new radical generation, the populists, were rather different from those on the nihilists, as expressed in *The Devils*. Nekrasov, too, was delighted to renew an old literary alliance, and was equally pleased with Dostoevsky's new work, sitting up all night reading the first part[64] — an ironic echo of the reception of *Poor Folk*! Later he even dedicated some of his works to Dostoevsky, who reciprocated the tribute when Nekrasov died in 1877. Dostoevsky had spent some considerable time with Nekrasov during his last days and was very upset by his death and stayed up all night reading his work. Even though, as with Belinsky, Dostoevsky rather white-washed the original conflict,[65] this time there was no public insincerity, as the funeral oration and his similar article in *Diary of a Writer* concur with his private sorrow.[66]

After his split with the *Contemporary* group in the 1840s Dostoevsky moved to an even more radical circle, that of the *Petrashevtsy*, the first major 'conspiracy' (if it can be called that) against the regime since the Decembrists in 1825. The Petrashevsky group, although it achieved virtually nothing, was an important symbolic development. After two decades of de-pression and reaction, the late 1840s, with the development of the 'natural' school in literature, the increased awareness of the concrete needs of Russia, in particular the question of serfdom, as well as the revolutionary events in Western Europe, marked a regeneration of the Russian intelligentsia, a resurgence of hope and expectations, even if the period 1848–55 proved to be worse than the years which preceded them.[67] Petrashevsky, who was regarded by some as 'an extreme liberal, radical, atheist, republican and socialist'.[68] kept more or less open house where such crucial topics as the emancipation of the serfs and the abolition of censorship were discussed. The dominant influence was Christian and French Utopian Socialism and the talk was very radical. However, the Petrashevsky circle could not really be considered a revolutionary group; they were utopians, albeit passionate utopians, who desired escape from the oppression they saw all around them. They did not even have any concrete objectives or common policies.

Dostoevsky – who, typically enough, later claimed that he had never liked Petrashevsky[69] – was drawn to the group for a number of reasons. After his débâcle with the older generation of radicals linked to *The Contemporary*, he became aware of his true class interests, which clearly did not lie with the aristocracy, however enlightened, liberal, or even radical it might have been. More importantly, the discussions of the new group corresponded better to his own sense of justice and hatred of oppression which he had already manifested in *Poor Folk*. He first met Petrashevsky in the spring of 1846, and a year later was visiting the circle regularly.[70] He became an active participant, reading the Utopian Socialists, speaking with passion about serfdom and oppression, and publicly reading Belinsky's *Letter to Gogol* three times. He may have later accounted this 'mere liberalism' or 'mere literary interest', but this was clearly a pretext to minimise his guilt. It seems certain that he felt as passionately as anyone else about the issues discussed.

Indeed, Dostoevsky, along with a few others, including Mikhail, went rather further than undirected discussions of topics of mutual interest, becoming an active member of the Durov splinter-group which was both more extreme and more genuinely conspiratorial than the Petrashevsky circle as a whole. They may not have had any specifically revolutionary aims and no concrete plan of action, but they were much more serious about what they were doing. Their objective was the liberation of the serfs, even if this meant an uprising, and in order to prepare for such an eventuality they set up, in 1848, a secret printing press, with Dostoevsky's involvement. There was even a threat of death against anyone who broke the secrecy of the cell — which to most intents and purposes it was.

Although both at his trial (to which we return later) and later in *The Diary of a Writer*, Dostoevsky was at great pains to disclaim the extremity of his views in the late 1840s and his close connections with the most radical group of the time, up to his arrest Dostoevsky was very much on the far left of contemporary Russian society in his affiliations. And he was not to swing to the opposite extreme until the mid-1860s. For example, on the way to his exile he encountered the wives of the Decembrists and was deeply moved by their self-sacrifice, treasuring the Bible they gave him for the rest of his life. Even upon his return to European Russia he remained relatively moderate in his dealings with oppositional groups. *Time* was set up by Dostoevsky to capture the middle ground between the Westernisers and the new radicals, and the Slavophils, and at first he polemicised with both sides. For a time his journal even had relatively friendly relationships with *The Contemporary*. This was largely due to Dostoevsky's own conciliatory efforts — such colleagues as Strakhov were much more hostile, and it was all Dostoevsky could do to curb their extreme attacks on the young nihilists. Soon, though, Dostoevsky was drawn into open hostilities — indeed, in the early 1860s it was extremely difficult, even for someone as opportunistic as Dostoevsky, to appear uncommitted. The crucial issue which established Dostoevsky on a firm anti-nihilist footing was that of aesthetics. A bitter polemic between *Time* and all the St Petersburg journals ensued, primarily over this question. The student disturbances of 1862 shattered any hope of reconciliation and the ferocity of the campaigns only ended with Chernyshevsky's arrest.

By now Dostoevsky had realised where his real sympathies lay, as *Notes from the Underground* and the anti-nihilism of his first three major novels make abundantly clear. The polemic was also continued in a more open form, firstly in *Winter Notes on Summer Impressions* (1863) and then in Dostoevsky's second journal, *Epoch*. From the first issue Dostoevsky made no attempts at conciliation and his anti-nihilism in his second journal is both more open and more pronounced. He ridiculed the various splits within their ranks, attacked their utilitarianism and theoretical nature and conducted personal attacks on, amongst others, Chernyshevsky, who was, of course, in prison. (Dostoevsky was to deny this in his *Diary* in 1873.) He also allowed his journal to be used for other anti-nihilist material such as Aksharumov's *A Funny Business* (1864). The radicals, in turn, disliked *Epoch* intensely and *The Contemporary* published frequent attacks against it. Nekrasov and Shchedrin, in particular, satirised the journal and, as in the last months of *Time*, Dostoevsky was the object of abuse from all the St Petersburg journals, which, at least according to Strakhov, got the better of this particular duel.[71]

By about 1865, then, Dostoevsky had finished his dealings with the radicals: *The Idiot* and especially *The Devils* merely exacerbated the rift between Dostoevsky and this wing of society. One of the chief critics of Dostoevsky's excessive distortions in the latter work was Mikhailovsky, the Populist leader. This review helped bring about a rather unexpected change in Dostoevsky's attitudes and alliances. As we have already seen, in 1873 Dostoevsky resigned the post of editor on Meshchersky's *The Citizen*, partly for ideological reasons. In the same year, Dostoevsky referred to Mikhailovsky's critique of *The Devils* as a 'new revelation',[72] and by the following year, in his work on *A Raw Youth*, he seemed to have accepted Mikhailovsky's view that *The Devils* was *not* representative of the new generation of Russian radicals.

In these years (1874–5) Dostoevsky and Mikhailovsky established closer contact with each other. At the same time, Dostoevsky became reconciled with Nekrasov: indeed, the mid-1870s saw something of a general rapprochement between Dostoevsky and the Populists, based on his realisation that socialism need not be either revolutionary or atheistic — a realisation which was probably reached, at least partly, through Mikhailovsky's work. Dostoevsky in the 1870s, even though he was now a close associate of Pobedonostsev and was received at the Imperial court, also frequented the literary evenings of such as E. A. Stakenschneider, a feminist and friend of Lavrov.[73] He also had very close contacts with A. P. Filosofova, another radical feminist.[74] Clearly he again realised that there was much that closely corresponded to his own humanitarian sympathies in the radical wing of society.

Generally, the radicals distrusted him, for *The Devils* and his work on *The Citizen*. Many of his central concerns, such as Christianity, were no longer even of interest to them. To them

Dostoevsky often seemed something of a *yurodivy* (a holy fool).[75] His political views, as expressed in his *Diary*, enraged them – in particular, his rabid anti-Semitism and chauvinism during the Turkish war. Despite all this negative credit in Dostoevsky's account, he was not totally rejected. When he met the radicals at literary evenings his relationships with them were quite harmonious, with Dostoevsky playing the part of a teacher.[76] For all his 'mistakes' he was still considered, by some at least, as their own and, like Tolstoy in Lenin's famous phrase, he was regarded as a 'mirror' of their revolutionary activities because of his idealisation of the people, his call for a return to the people and the soil, which corresponded very well to some of the Populists' own aims.[77]

None the less, Dosteovsky was by now closest of all to official government circles – even though it had taken many long years to gain their trust after his rebellion of the 1840s. The discovery of the 'conspiracy' could not have occurred at a worse time. Nicholas I was profoundly shaken by the events in Europe of 1848 and decided that the intense oppression of the first twenty-two years of his reign was insufficient for the maintenance of order. The heads of the Third Section, Orlov and Dubel't, became even more energetic in pursuing their activities and for the next seven years until Nicholas' death there was a total clamp-down on all freedom of expression.[78] In fact, the Petrashevsky circle had been known to the authorities since 1845, but was thought to be innocuous: in February 1848, however, a truer picture emerged and Orlov instigated an investigation by planting the spy Antonelli, who in turn began submitting reports to the Ministry of Internal Affairs. A year later a memorandum on their activities was sent to Orlov, who passed it immediately to Nicholas. Both agreed that the 'conspirators', seen by Nicholas as descendants of the Decembrists, should be immediately arrested. The Tsar remarked: 'I have read everything; the matter is important for if it was but only foolish prattle, even then it is in the highest degree criminal and intolerable. Set about the arrest as indicated. Go with God! May His will be done!'[79] And so, on 22 April 1849, Dostoevsky found himself amongst those arrested and in imminent danger of receiving an 'exemplary' punishment. After interminable investigations, he was charged with having taken part in meetings which criticised government decrees and the institutions of censorship and serfdom, and above all, with reading Belinsky's *Letter*. In the end, guilt could not be proven but still, such dangerous conspirators had to be punished, for 'crimes against the security of the state'. Fifteen were to die (including Dostoevsky) and seven to be deported. As is well known, the executions never took place — nor were they intended to. Instead a vicious trick of a 'last minute' reprieve was played, and Dostoevsky was exiled to Siberia.[80]

Dostoevsky's attitude to his imprisonment varied. As usual, he later reinterpreted his experience and was indeed thankful for it, in that it had 'cured' him of his 'ideological illnesses'. None the less, he had no wish to remain in Siberia any longer than necessary, and once he had been released from the labour camp in 1854 he made every attempt to secure permission to return to European Russia. He wrote patriotic odes, petitions to Alexander, pleaded to General Totleben for his intercession, admitted his guilt and the error of his ways and begged forgiveness. Now he 'idolised' the 'kind and compassionate Tsar'[81] and expressed the most fervent nationalism, which was, at least in part, sincere. Gradually he was rehabilitated, becoming first an officer and allowed certain privileges. In 1859 he returned to European Russia, first to Tver' and then St Petersburg.

But his negative dealings with the Tsarist authorities were not over. The next major clash occurred during the incidents leading up to the closure of his journal, *Time*. As we have seen, Dostoevsky aimed the journal at the middle ground of contemporary Russian politics but it was not pro-government and was far from the chauvinism of Dostoevsky's later venture, *The Diary of a Writer*. In general *Time* was regarded as dangerous, even oppositional.[82] A renewed political crisis in Russia, this time centring on the student troubles of the early 1860s and the Polish insurrection of 1863, proved calamitous for Dostoevsky and his faltering journal. Strakhov's article, 'A Fatal Question', concerning these events, was published in April 1863 (having, of course, passed the censor). Mistakenly, the piece was then considered to be pro-Polish and rumours soon spread that the journal might be closed. Accordingly, Dostoevsky wrote a note, attempting to explain their true, patriotic position. But it came too late: the censor refused to pass it, as the matter had already gained the attention of the Tsar, who deemed the journal guilty of the 'charge' and suppressed it. Appeals to influential conservatives such as Katkov and Aksakov were unavailing and once more

Dostoevsky became the victim of arbitrary and summary justice.

Dostoevsky spent most of the rest of the 1860s abroad trying to work and avoiding his creditors. Despite this, and his own now very conservative views, he did not escape the attentions of the Tsarist authorities, twenty years after his 'crime'. From the time of his return from Siberia, and indeed, until one year before his death, he remained under police surveillance. Thus, for example, when he met Herzen abroad in 1862, the fact was noted by the police, even though nothing was done about it. Throughout the 1860s and 1870s, moreover, his letters were always intercepted and opened, despite his avowed monarchism and, in the 1870s, his friendship with Pobedonostsev. When Dostoevsky finally returned to Russia from Europe, he burned most of his papers in advance, for fear that he might be searched.

During the 1870s, however, Dostoevsky's relationship with official circles improved markedly, much to his own satisfaction, as he himself now fully supported the regime. After *The Devils* and Dostoevsky's acceptance of the editorship of *The Citizen*, in the eyes of most of society he had become fully identified with reaction, and he mixed mainly with leading reactionaries.[83] Yet even now, Dostoevsky's path was not entirely smooth: he spent a day or so in jail for a minor infringement of the censorship laws, and the journal was later watched closely for one and a half months, following what was, in fact, a very innocuous article.[84] At the same time he was developing very close links with the Procurator of the Holy Synod, Pobedonostsev, and through him, with the Imperial Court itself. The two men first met in 1871 or 1872, via Meshchersky, and in 1873 became friends. From the first Pobedonostsev had a warm regard for Dostoevsky, who was deeply affected by this, as well as being influenced by Pobedonostsev's views. Pobedonostsev followed *Diary of a Writer* with sympathetic interest, supplied Dostoevsky with material and congratulated him on his success — particularly at the time of the Pushkin speech. Now at last Dostoevsky had achieved fame to a degree beyond the wildest dreams of his youth — at the court of the Tsar of All the Russias! Equally, he was now looked on with favour by the highest authorities. As early as 1873, in fact, he had sent a copy of *The Devils* to the future Alexander III, who had expressed the wish to discover the author's own opinions of the work, and in the later years of the decade it was well known that the *Diary* (which, incidentally, experienced very few censorship problems) was read in the highest echelons of society. By the late 1870s, then, Dostoevsky was almost totally acceptable to the regime — in 1878 he became a corresponding member of the Academy, he was asked to visit the Tsar's children, surveillance was abandoned and in December 1880 he reached his final triumph when he personally presented a copy of *The Brothers Karamazov* to the future Alexander III. His death in 1881 brought fitting official tributes. Pobedonostsev wrote to Ivan Aksakov, expressing his great sorrow and commenting that 'he was the very man for our cause'.[85] To Alexander III he termed Dostoevsky 'a close friend', who alone wrote of the 'true' Russia, of religion, nationhood and patriotism.[86] There followed official tributes from the court, and his widow was granted a pension of 2,000R — a striking contrast to the official reception of the deaths of Pushkin, Lermontov, Belinsky and even Gogol. But then, in the end, Dostoevsky had proved himself a worthy patriot.

As for virtually all writers in nineteenth-century Russia, ideological factors were also very important in the critical assessment of Dostoevsky's work. We can now turn to this aspect of his career. Ideological factors are especially obvious in the work of Belinsky and his successors. By the time Dostoevsky's first work appeared in the mid-1840s, Belinsky tended to judge literature almost exclusively by the extent to which it was 'progressive' or fitted in with the 'natural' school. This approach underlies his opinions of all Dostoevsky's early work. Thus, he received *Poor Folk* in a state approaching ecstasy. His review of the work is without reserve or reservations. Everything in it is 'excellent' — the humanitarian pathos, the accessible plot, the living realism of all the characters. Above all, Dostoevsky has shown the plight of the 'little man', and has revealed that Devushkin and his kind are 'our brothers'. In brief, he regarded it as a perfect exemplar of the 'natural' school and Gogol had found a worthy successor. Belinsky's praise was doubly important, in that it stood as a counter-balance to the generally hostile reviews in the conservative press, especially in Bulgarin's *The Northern Bee*, which had been the principal vilifier of Pushkin, Lermontov and Gogol in their turn.

Unfortunately his next work, *The Double*, did not meet with the same kind of acclaim. Belinsky was at a loss to know what to make of it and wrote very ambivalently. He praised its originality, but criticised it for being rather prolix, and especially for the fantastic elements, which were definitely taboo for the 'natural' school. As yet, however, he was not too severe, putting down Dostoevsky's 'mistakes' to inexperience. Other critics were no more friendly, and Dostoevsky was particularly accused of excessive imitation of Gogol. Konstantin Aksakov wrote: 'Quite plainly we do not even understand how this tale could appear. Gogol is known to all of Russia, known almost by heart — and here, right under everyone's eyes, Dostoevesky paraphrases and literally reproduces Gogol's very expressions.' Shevyrev wrote much the same.[87]

The real collapse in his reputation was to come with his next two works, *Mr Prokharchin* and *The Landlady*. Belinsky was now unequivocal. The former he termed confused and pretentious, while the latter he regarded as a total flop, which would not even have deserved a mention in the press but for Dostoevsky's famous name. Throughout the review, Belinsky is sarcastic and venomous, and feigns total incomprehension of what Dostoevsky might be trying to achieve. But it is clear why Belinsky did not like the works: he was now well aware that Dostoevsky's apostasy to the 'natural' school was not a temporary aberration, and he was determined to expose the renegade. The recurrence of the fantastic, the use of melodrama and the apparent abandonment of the key virtues of realism and humanitarianism all evoked the critic's anger.

Now Dostoevsky was neither a promising beginner nor an established writer. However, he was not entirely without support, for in the 1840s it was still possible to write unideological criticism. Such a view came from the poet Maykov, who was later to become a close associate of Dostoevsky's[88]. He responded rather better to Dostoevsky's innovations, to his concern with man's inner world and with psychology in general. Indeed, he saw him not as an imitator of Gogol, but as one who attempted to deepen and rationalise the strange superficiality of Gogol's depiction of his fellow beings. Dostoevsky could also perhaps draw comfort from Maykov's lack of surprise that Dostoevsky was so brutally attacked for his originality — after all, Pushkin, Lermontov and Gogol had all recently received exactly the same treatment for their innovations.

When Dostoevsky returned from Siberia he had to struggle hard to re-establish his reputation. He was a forgotten man, a dimly remembered young writer of the past, whereas his close

contemporaries – and rivals – Turgenev and Nekrasov had
already established secure positions. In the late 1850s Nekrasov,
in fact, had rejected *The Inhabitants of the Village of Stepanchikovo* while *The Humilitated and Wronged*, which appeared in
1861, was harshly received by the critics. Dobrolyubov considered it 'below aesthetic criticism', while even Apollon Grigorev, who was later to work for *Epoch*, abusively dismissed
Dostoevsky's characters. The attacks indeed were unanimous.[89]
However, acclaim was soon to come, primarily with the publication of *Notes from the House of the Dead*. Even so, Dostoevsky
continued to struggle in the early 1860s. As we shall discuss in
more detail later, the radicals, sensing Dostoevsky's emergent
hostility, began to take up where Belinsky had left off, while
the collapse of *Time*, and especially *Epoch*, which had been of
a consistently lower standard, did nothing to enhance Dostoevsky's general standing. Much of what he wrote in the years
1860–65 was, indeed, journalistic hack-work, which did not even
maintain what reputation he had regained. *Crime and Punishment* went a long way to restoring what Dostoevsky had again
lost, except, of course, among the radicals, who were very displeased by the 'slander' of Raskolnikov. Dostoevsky's next
major novel, *The Idiot*, however, again represented something
of a reversal in his fortunes; it was coldly received and Dostoevsky
himself was dissatisfied with his attempt to depict a positively
beautiful individual. The critics, as twenty years before, simply
did not know what to make of Dostoevsky's strange new work
and saw it as a falling-off in his abilities.

*The Devils* fared even worse, though this time for more obviously ideological reasons. The left wing was in uproar, and even
liberal opinion came out against him, denouncing the 'retrograde'
Dostoevsky.[90] Some praise there was, particularly from Strakhov,
but generally speaking the novel was buried under an avalanche
of abuse. Dostoevsky's view of the left wing of Russian society
was much more sympathetic in his next major work, *A Raw
Youth*, and, accordingly, it was much better received, even by
those who had attacked *The Devils*. Nekrasov was impressed by
the new work and from this point onwards Dostoevsky was
almost universally recognised as a great writer. Only his more
conservative friends were rather guarded in their opinions of the
work, mainly because of Dostoevsky's renewed connections with
Nekrasov.

The last years, the years of *The Diary of a Writer* and *The*

*Brothers Karamazov*, generally reinforced this outstanding critical reputation. Above all else, Dostoevsky achieved immense acclaim with his Pushkin speech. Following the euphoria of the occasion, however, the press on all sides was not slow to attack. The liberal *Herald of Europe* regarded the speech as 'national self-glorification', while the radical writer Gleb Uspensky, in *The Notes of the Fatherland*, was even more severe. *The Word* regarded the speech as a kind of 'conjuring trick', and even the conservative Leont'ev, in a long article in *The Warsaw Diary*, remarked: 'Dostoevsky's speech is a fiery, inspired, red-hot speech but its foundations are utterly false.'[91] Not surprisingly, Dostoevsky was extremely angry about this apparent *volte-face* in critical opinion.

Throughout his career it was the radicals who were fiercest in their criticism of Dostoevsky. Dobrolyubov started where Belinsky had ended, in his article 'Downtrodden Folk'.[92] As a year earlier in his review of *On the Eve*, Dobrolyubov begins his article (on *The Humiliated and Wronged*) with disarming praise, calling the novel the best so far that year. In it there are many good sections, and the characters are well drawn. Now Dobrolyubov, in his familiar style, begins to turn to the negative aspects and builds up a totally damning critique. The plot, he claims, has certain inconsistencies; in fact, it is all rather contrived (i.e. unrealistic). What is worse, the characters are abnormal types, with no attempt on Dostoevsky's part to explain their abnormalities. That is, Dostoevsky has broken all the rules of the 'natural' school — the plot is not simple and accessible, the characters are not real and typical and in the end, Dobrolyubov decides that the novel is not really worthy of aesthetic consideration. Having dismissed most of Dostoevsky's originality as a writer, Dobrolyubov, again like Belinsky, attempts to 'encourage' him to return to the humanitarian school in which he had begun his career, and in the second half of the review Dobrolyubov says little of the novel in question but praises his earlier work, in particular *Poor Folk*, of course, for its sympathetic depiction of 'our brothers', the 'little men'. Dostoevsky was not yet, then, beyond recall and could still be considered within the revered Gogolian tradition (as Dobrolyubov rather mistakenly understood Gogol), despite his aberrations.

Pisarev, in two major reviews, adopts much the same line. His praise for *Notes from the House of the Dead* is, accordingly, of the highest. (Here, of course, the Belinskyan tendency to regard literature as social documentation is more in keeping with the work concerned, and so the review is less of a distortion of Dostoevsky's basic approach.) Pisarev applauds Dostoevsky's humanisation of the convicts: Dostoevsky has done great service to the humanitarian cause by showing the criminals not as 'lost souls' but as possessing some hope of regeneration. The work, indeed, stands as an implicit plea for improvement in penal conditions, and Dostoevsky, interestingly enough, is still considered a sympathetic fellow-traveller by the radical critics — even if they had slightly to reinterpret his intentions.

A major task of reinterpretation was needed in Pisarev's next review, 'The Struggle for Life' (1867), which, in considering *Crime and Punishment*, brilliantly stands Dostoevsky on his head. Pisarev, who almost alone of the radical critics had applauded Turgenev's *Fathers and Sons*, was profoundly moved by the novel, but still wrote an extremely polemical review, principally as a response to Strakhov's view that Raskolnikov's allegedly nihilist theories were responsible for his crime. In line with his own convictions, Pisarev sets out to disarm Dostoevsky's anti-nihilism by demonstrating that Raskolnikov's theories are virtually irrelevant to the murder. His material conditions in themselves provide sufficient explanation for his desparate behaviour. That is, his poverty, his class position, his family circumstances, are the cause, and his theories are mere rationalisations of the root problem. Pisarev's outstanding analysis of the plot is entirely directed to this end. Taking the point further, he argues that Dostoevsky has misrepresented the nihilists: Raskolnikov is in no way typical of radical youth, who shared none of his ideas, which are in essence a product of the *isolation* which produced the crime. As always, Pisarev is rather less tendentious than Dobrolyubov, and despite his ideological disagreements, still manages to acclaim the work as continuing the humanitarian tradition, primarily in his sympathetic treatment of the Marmeladov family. Obviously, Pisarev's review is partial, but it remains a convincing attempt to cut through Dostoevsky's metaphysical superstructure — indeed to dismiss it — and regard him still as a major author of the 'natural' school, retaining the old values of realism and sympathy for the downtrodden.

The next major radical critic, the Populist leader Mikhailovsky, continued this tradition of reinterpretation, of rescuing Dostoevsky from himself, as it were. His response to *The Devils* took something of the middle ground among the radicals, in that he did not consider that Dostoevsky had misrepresented the Nechaevists, but was wrong to present a pathological exception as a typical representative.[93] He too, however, distrusted Dostoevsky's fondness for the abnormal. Unlike Pisarev, however, Mikhailovsky is frankly polemical and considers Dostoevsky almost exclusively as a publicist, and hardly at all as an artist: it is a return, that is, to the ideological approach of Dobrolyubov. Although he could not deny the quality of Dostoevsky's work, he rejects almost all his ideas — their Slavophil coloration, the cult of suffering and advocacy of acquiescence in the face of oppression. Later Mikhailovsky, despite the relative closeness of the two men in the mid-1870s, was to become one of the most hostile of Dostoevsky's critics: the task or reinterpretation and rehabilitation of the renegade 'naturalist' was finally abandoned.

Mikhailovsky's most bitter attack on Dostoevsky was a general review of his work in an article written shortly after Dostoevsky's death, 'A Cruel Talent' (1882). From the beginning, claims Mikhailovsky, Dostoevsky had been interested in cruelty, especially of the sadistic variety. At first he had been more interested in the tormented, but later in the tormentors, with Dostoevsky as the *primus inter pares*! Now it is the abnormality of Dostoevsky himself that is stressed and Mikhailovsky, writing with an air of enstranged bewilderment, attacks above all the unnecessary and arbitrary acts of cruelty which fill Dostoevsky's pages. In the end, then, Dostoevsky had undermined all that was good and pure in mankind and the humanitarian thread in his work had long ceased to be the central current. It is Dostoevsky himself who had humiliated and wronged his creations. Seduro puts Mikhailovsky's view well: 'The world of Dostoevsky's heroes seemed to Mikhailovsky to be a menagerie of beasts of prey, in which the writer was assigned the role of cruel trainer.'[94] Mikhailovsky had clearly lost whatever sympathy he once had for Dostoevsky's work and later remarked of him: '[Dostoevsky was] an unfortunate man, and at the same time, a weak man, a man who is pitiable.'[95]

And so, by the time of Dostoevsky's death, he had completely alienated the radical critics: he was now recognised for what he had clearly been for the last fifteen years of his life — an enemy of democratic ideals. The final blow was dealt by Antonovich who, twenty years before, had attempted to butcher Turgenev's reputation in his hysterical review of *Fathers and Sons*. In a similar vein he tears his way through the pages of *The Brothers Karamazov* in his article, 'A Mystico-Ascetic Novel' (1882). Somewhat ironically, considering his own brand of criticism, Antonovich opens by accusing Dostoevsky of allowing tendency to intrude too much into the novel. He then goes on to attack this tendency — Dostoevsky's increasing subjectivism and conservatism — and deals him the worst insult of all by terming the novel a direct descendant of Gogol's *Selected Passages*. The humanist streak has vanished and once again Dostoevsky is belaboured for his apostasy. Antonovich proceeds to pour out his wrathful loathing on what he sees as the essence of Dostoevsky's work — his mystical religiosity, his reactionary views and his summoning of the Russian people to the monastery, away from a concern with real social problems. After a brief aside on the aesthetic weaknesses of the novel, he returns to his main task of demolishing Dostoevsky's views. The article is poor criticism, but is symptomatic of the final view of the radical critics who in a fury of revenge against a writer they had once espoused, attempted to leave no doubt as to the true nature of the dark and evil world of Dostoevskyan fiction.

For all the critics' efforts, Dostoevsky's wider popularity remained undiminished. His first success with the public was *Poor Folk*. Public readings were held and he was invited to all the leading literary salons. Dostoevsky's name 'was on everyone's lips'.[96] The subsequent works, at least according to Belinsky (who was not exactly impartial), were not such a success.[97] *The Double*, he claims, had no success among the public, *Mr Prokharchin* reduced all Dostoevsky's admirers to a state of unpleasant amazement, while *The Landlady* was a total failure.

On his return from exile, Dostoevsky regained public recognition fairly quickly with *The Humiliated and Wronged*, which was an enormous success. Even according to Dobrolyubov, it was the only novel being read that year. *Notes from the House of the Dead* strengthened his rapidly growing reputation. It was a literary sensation. Dostoevsky was hailed as a new Dante[98] and his position was now secure. Both these works were published in *Time*, thanks to which the journal quickly achieved great success. Dostoevsky had gone out of his way to make it popular, publishing not only his works, but those of his already popular rivals: Turgenev, Nekrasov, Shchedrin and Ostrovsky. His objective was assured: the number of subscribers doubled within the first year of publication, and by the end of its third year of existence it had become profitable. At least according to Strakhov, *Time* emerged as the closest rival to the principal journal of the day, *The Contemporary*.[99]

The débâcle of *Epoch* in 1865 did nothing to enhance the public's opinion of Dostoevsky's work, but this soon returned to its former high level with the appearance of *Crime and Punishment*. It received immediate acclaim and, like *Fathers and Sons*, became something of a *cause célèbre* with its intensely topical and political interest. The journal in which it appeared, Katkov's *The Russian Herald*, gained an extra five hundred subscribers within a year and the novel's success was enduring: by 1877 it had already entered its fourth edition. As with the critics, however, *The Idiot* had little success with the public. Dostoevsky had wanted to publish a second edition immediately to ease his desperate finances but he soon abandoned the idea.

None the less, when Dostoevsky returned to Russia in 1871, he was received as a major contemporary figure. Everyone, it seemed, wanted to meet him, hear him read his works, or correspond with him.[100] Dostoevsky was delighted by this reception and endeavoured to answer all the letters, unless they were purely abusive. The appearance later in that year of *The Devils* (again of great topical interest) finally established Dostoevsky as perhaps the most popular writer of his age. However abusive the critics may have been, the public rushed to buy it, and the first edition of 3,500 copies sold out very quickly. Even his open connection with the reactionary *Citizen* could not harm his popularity now, which rapidly grew throughout the 1870s. The major success of this period was the enormously popular and influential *Diary of a Writer*. Russian society was in a highly turbulent state at the time. Political violence was increasing while semi-feudal institutions were finally crumbling, to be replaced by democratic *zemstvo* committees, new courts and other aspects of a more liberal, westernised country. A war was being fought with the Ottoman Empire which was viewed by many, including Dostoevsky, as a Holy War in the defence of their enslaved Slav brethren. Dostoevsky responded to the deepest felt needs and seemed to answer the most difficult questions with

almost visionary intuition. E. A. Stakenschneider remarks on
the extraordinary success of Dostoevsky's new journal: '*The
Diary of a Writer* made his name known to all of Russia, made
him a teacher and the idol of the young, and not only of the
young, but of all who were tormented by the questions which
Heine termed "accursed".'[101] And in mere numbers the success
was enormous. Within the first year the readership grew from
four to six thousand, editions would be sold out within a few
days and some would be reprinted as many as five times. The
journal was a constant topic of conversation and every issue
was fiercely debated. Now, at last, the prophet had found honour in his own country, Much of his immense correspondence
was from complete strangers seeking his advice and guidance on
all aspects of life. People flocked to him, thirsting for truth, expecting magical, almost divine answers from him. *The Brothers
Karamazov* finally established him as the premier novelist of his
day, but now he was not valued so much as an artist, but as a
teacher of life.

This spectacular success reached its apogee in the years 1879–
80, culminating in the Pushkin celebrations. The celebrations had
to be temporarily postponed and Dostoevsky wrote to his wife,
with evident self-satisfaction, of the tumultuous reception accorded to him everywhere. Magnificent banquets, long speeches,
standing ovations, all are detailed to her with almost childish
delight, down to the dried sturgeon 'a yard long' and 'two hundred magnificent and expensive cigars'. As in 1845, Dostoevsky,
Khlestakov-like, revelled in his success among titled digni-
taries.[102] Elsewhere he remarks on his appearance in the Moscow Tavern, which 'is always crowded, and it is seldom that
people do not turn round and look at me: everyone knows,
everyone knows who I am'.[103]

But this was a mere warm-up for the amazing scenes when he
finally delivered his oracular interpretation of Pushkin. Dostoevsky described the scene in a letter to his wife (8 June 1880)
which conveys much of the atmosphere:

The hall was packed. No, Anya, no, you can never represent
to yourself nor imagine the effect it produced! What are my
Petersburg successes? Nothing, nothing at all compared to this!
When I *came* out, the hall thundered applause, and for a long,
a very long time, they would not let me speak. I bowed, made

gestures, asking them to let me read — nothing was of any avail: raptures, enthusiasm (all because of the *Karamazovs*). At last I began reading: I was interrupted positively at each page, and at moments at each phrase, by a thunder of applause. I read loudly, with fire. All that I wrote about Tat'yana was recieved with enthusiasm. . . . When at last I proclaimed the *universal union* of people, the hall was as though in hysterics, and when I finished, — I cannot tell you about the roar, about the wail of ecstasy: strangers among the public cried, wept, embraced one another.[104]

And so on — cries of 'prophet', kissing, embracing, fainting and shrieking. Eye-witnesses concur exactly, in fact, with Dostoevsky's version — even Uspensky noted that the reception was not so much an oration as an adoration.[105]

The six thousand copies of the printed text were sold out within three days. Everywhere Dostoevsky was asked to read — usually Pushkin's *The Prophet* — everywhere he was received with rapture as a great teacher and prophet. Soon he was dead, and the public tribute to him showed finally his position within Russian society. An estimated 30,000 people (four or five times as many as when Nekrasov died) accompanied the funeral procession, with seventy-two separate delegations, from students to the government, presenting wreaths. No writer's death since that of Pushkin had caused such national mourning.

It was, of course, Dostoevsky's 'teaching' that inspired the Russian public and we can now consider in what this teaching consisted. A number of problems immediately arise. The most central difficulty is a very basic one — that of establishing exactly what Dostoevsky thought of his country, the West and so on. Perhaps the main reason this problem arises at all lies in the very nature of his thinking. Again going back to his Romantic heritage of the 1830s (in this case to Hegel), Dostoevsky perceived the world dialectically. Religious belief, for example, did not exclude a profound understanding of atheism — as is most clearly illustrated in the *pro* and *contra* of *The Brothers Karamazov*. Indeed, for Dostoevsky, the dialectic was the very essence of the age. For him the only path to resolution was through the dialectic: good could not destroy evil, as each existed by virtue of the other, but could triumph only by assimilating evil. Given the age in which he lived, surrounded by the strident voices of conflict,

Dostoevsky sought some answer that might save him and the world from imminnent chaos. Some critics maintain that ultimately Dostoevsky could find no answer, that unbelief was always as attractive to him as belief.[106] Like Shatov in *The Devils*, that is, Dostoevsky can only proclaim: 'I will believe in God.' It has also been argued — as is frequently done for Tolstoy[107] — that it was the greatest tragedy for Dostoevsky never to find the single, final answer for which he so longed. In a famous letter, Dostoevsky put the matter thus: 'I want to say to you about myself, that I am a child of this age, a child of unfaith and scepticism, and probably (indeed I know it) shall remain so to the end of my life.'[108] However, this letter was written in 1854, and while it remained true that the deepest appeal of Dostoevsky's life and works lies in their dialectics, their polyphony and constant search for ultimate truths, it is equally true that in the last decade of his life, if one is to judge by his *Diary* and correspondence of the time, Dostoevsky had achieved some very definite beliefs.

But it was a long and arduous path which took him to this final position, and we must now consider this road. Once again, Dostoevsky's ideas have their origin in the 1830s. In much of what he believed he shows himself to be essentially a Romantic. In the 1840s, in his period of rebellion, Dostoevsky was Romantic in his espousal of the current aesthetic humanism. Dostoevsky's radical views of the mid-1840s were born of a general sense of injustice, and he obviously held his views very sincerely. However, it is difficult to be precise about his political views at this time. His letters have little political discussion, and his artistic works express only the most general sort of humanistic protest. His later accounts of the period shed little light on the matter. He claimed, for example, to have split with Belinsky on religious and political grounds, and elsewhere he maintained that in his youth, but for his arrest, he could well have become a Nechaevist. There is, however, some more concrete evidence, which has not been reinterpreted by the later, very unreliable Dostoevsky — that of an article of 1847, 'The St Petersburg Chronicle'.[109] Here Dostoevsky reveals himself as a thoroughgoing Westerniser. He rejects the Slavophil 'fetish' of the people and writes a fine eulogy to St Petersburg and, in particular, to its creator, Peter I, who was considered the very symbol of Westernism.

It is most likely, though, that Dostoevsky's early radicalism was of a rather vague and unsystematic variety. The traces of it were none the less to be long-lasting. Certainly, the 1840s humanitarian tradition *is* implicit in many of his later works, particularly in those immediately following his return from exile, such as *The Humiliated and Wronged* and *Notes from the House of the Dead*. However, alongside these vestiges were developing new views of man and society which were to form the corner-stone of Dostoevsky's later ideas and which were inspired by the central experience of his life — his imprisonment and exile. It was in the prison camp — or so he claimed — that he discovered himself, Christ, and most importantly of all, the *narod*, the common Russian people. In 1874, Dostoevsky commented on his experiences in Siberia to Vsevolod Solov'yov:

> Siberia and hard labour! . . . It was only there that I lived a healthy, happy life, I understood myself there, my friend . . . I understood Christ . . . I understood Russians and felt that I too was a Russian, that I was one of the Russian people. All my best thoughts occurred to me at that time, and only now are they returning to me, and then, not as clearly. Ah, if only you could be sent to hard labour![110]

Whenever he later thought or wrote of the common people, it was always with the convicts in mind.

Yet the camp had an even more profound impact on Dostoevsky. He had gone there still retaining much of his youthful idealism. Through his observation of the criminals, he discovered that many of his humanitarian convictions were totally inappropriate to the realities of life. On the one hand he met convicts who felt no remorse whatever, and on the other, 'criminals' who were more humane, sincere and religious than many respectable pillars of the community. No longer could he believe in the naive morality of the 'natural' school and its humanising depiction of the oppressed classes of society. The humanism of this approach was powerless before the evil Dostoevsky saw in the camp, the pleasure in inflicting and experiencing suffering, the terrible blow that the loss of freedom caused to all in the camp. Quite clearly, there was no such thing as the 'natural' morality that Dostoevsky had espoused. And so Dostoevsky had to begin afresh, to search for deeper truths about life — to seek

out, that is, his 'new word' — which would encompass his discoveries about the truth of mankind. How was he to reconcile
all the conflicting facets of mankind, as well as his own essential
idealism, with the amorality and absolute freedom he had observed in the camp?

The first work which presents these problems fully is Dostoevsky's fictionalised account of his experiences, *Notes from the
House of the Dead*. It is a transitional work, in that, alongside
the presentation of these new problems, there exist strong traces
of the old manner — the humanising approach. In the early
1860s Dostoevsky was, in general, at a watershed in his ideological development, retaining aspects of his pre-Siberian beliefs
while moving towards his later reactionary interpretation of
Russia's destiny. This vacillation was most apparent in the
editorial stance of *Time* as regards the student disturbances of
1861 to 1862 and the Polish question in 1863. After brief support for the students, Dostoevsky and his brother took fright
in the face of the worsening situation and gradually moved to
the government's position. In more general terms, and partly as
a result of the apparent ascendancy of the radical position during
these years, there was an upsurge of its antithesis, mystic
nationalism, which Dostoevsky came increasingly to support.[111]
Through his journal he developed an early version of his later
beliefs concerning his country. *Pochvennost'*, the creed of 'the
men of the soil', became the rallying-call of *Time* and its ad-
herents. It was to be a rallying-point between Slavophilism and
Westernism, though it is obviously much closer to the former.
Dostoevsky still recognised the validity of Peter's reforms, but
they had cost the country too dear, because they had separated
the cultured elite from the soil and the mass of the people. His
journal fought for a *reconciliation* between the two principal
sections of society, a union which would transform not only
Russia, but the whole of Europe. As yet, Dostoevsky did not
reject Europe but rather saw Russia as the potential summit of
its culture:

> We forsee, and forsee with reverence, that the character of
> our future activity must be to the highest degree *universal to
> mankind*; that the Russian idea perhaps will be the synthesis
> of all those ideas which Europe is with such obstinacy, with
> such courage, developing in its separate nationalities; that

perhaps all that is hostile in these ideas will find its reconciliation and furthest development in the Russian national
spirit.[112]

The essential difference between these ideas and those of ten
years later is their moderation; the intelligentsia, Peter and
Europe were still assessed positively, and Dostoevsky at this stage
was still critical of the Slavophils, in particular their iconographic
representation of pre-Petrine Russia. He argued quite specifically
that one could not return to this allegedly Golden Age of the
past, and the only path was onwards, to a reconciliation between
those who are still of 'the soil' and those who had been removed
from it by Peter's reforms.

However, as Dostoevsky thought through his camp experiences
and perceived more closely the discords of Russia in the 1860s,
he was to find that this moderation was insufficient in the face
both of the increasing violence and misery within society, and
his further 'discoveries' about man's nature. In particular, he
became increasingly aware that, *pace* Chernyshevsky, man was
not a rational being who could order his world according to
enlightened self-interest. The force of the irrational and perverse
was too great for such naive views to be appropriate to an understanding of man in society. *Notes from the Underground*, written
in part as a reply to Chernyshevsky's *What is to be Done?*, is
the first work which highlights the irrational aspects of man,
with its rejection of the utopian world of the Crystal Palace. The
Underground Man takes equal pleasure in his own humiliation
and in humiliating others: at least he proves he is alive and that
he is not a cog in the machine. It was a theme which Dostoevsky
never abandoned, even if it became subsumed by more metaphysical and religious aspects in his work, as in the characters
of Katerina Ivanovna in *Crime and Punishment*, Liza Khokhl-
akova in *The Devils*, and many others who possess or are oppressed by a 'cruel talent'.

What was even worse was that the whole world order appeared
to be unstable. He may have continued to cling to golden visions
of Russia's future, but the present resembled a grotesque asylum
populated by criminals, lunatics, epileptics, liars and social
'deviants' of every type. His characters are frequently ill, poor,
underfed and their perception of the world comes to us as if in
a bad dream — especially in Dostoevsky's first major depiction

of the modern metropolis, *Crime and Punishment*, much of which is mediated to us through Raskolnikov's distorted consciousness. Here, as in Gogol, the abnormal is the norm. To Gogol's irrational world of illness, madness and dreams, Dostoevsky added much of his own. One major difference was crime, which became central to his view of the world — and usually it is crime against the person rather than property. It is no accident that all his major fiction, and especially his *Diary*, is full of murder, rape, and other acts of violence. Nor was this a product merely of Dostoevsky's 'cruel talent': for him the crimes were painfully typical of a cruel and abnormal age. Yet, despite the basic similarities between Gogol's and Dostoevsky's world, the two strike one as very different. We find little explanation in Gogol's work for his irrational world, it just *is*. Dostoevsky was a much better diagnostician of the pathological phenomena he depicted: for him the main underlying causes are social and political. That is, Dostoevsky was depicting the materialisation of values and alienation of man which are so typical of an emergent capitalist country and bourgeois order.[113] Dostoevsky's whole work and thinking indeed stands, again in the Romantic tradition, against this materialisation and alienation. It is for this reason, as well as for the others already discussed, that Dostoevsky was so obsessed with topicality, with the 'plague' of radicalism, with drunkenness, the torturing of children, prostitution and so on, for only by depicting them and their causes could he cure his country of these diseases, could he protest on behalf of the crying children and other victims of this emergent order.

The new teeming urban metropolis was the most potent symbol of a new oppression which far outdid the old one in terms of savage brutality.[114] The theme of the city begins in Dostoevsky's work in the 1840s and it is the same phantasmal St Petersburg as in Gogol, where everyone is faceless, depersonalised, reduced to the level of his rank rather than his individual personality. In the stories of the 1840s, for example *White Nights*, there is still some latent glamour in the St Petersburg world, but by the time Dostoevsky returned at the beginning of the 1860s, such vestiges of the eighteenth-century odic tradition have vanished. The action is usually concentrated in the back streets, the Hay Market and the seedier, vice-ridden quarters, far from the fashionable and Imperial areas beloved of Lomonosov and

even Pushkin. Life for its inhabitants is a struggle for mere sub-
sistence in the face of grinding poverty, crime, prostitution and
drunkenness. Dostoevsky's fiction is dominated by this hell of
St Petersburg: even *The Devils* and *The Brothers Karamazov*,
which are set in provincial towns, are pervaded by this ethos of
dirt, decay, corruption and the incipient collapse of all traditional
values. 'Traditional' is precisely the term Dostoevsky envisaged.
The city was so evil, both in fact and symbolically, because it
was there above all that his diseased and pathetic individuals
were most cut off from the life of 'the people' and the soil, where
the old values of Russian life were dissolving, to be replaced by
immorality of every kind.

Nowhere is the nefarious impact of city life so apparent as in
his depiction of the family. The 'accidental family' was to become one of his principal themes in the 1870s (in reply to
Tolstoy's familial idyll of *War and Peace*), primarily in *The Raw
Youth* and *Diary of a Writer*, but it emerges at least as early as
the Marmeladov family in *Crime and Punishment*, with its drunk-
ard father, hysterically insane mother, prostitute daughter and
starving children.[115] They may, in principle, be termed a 'family',
but each of their destinies remains separate. In their chilling
tale of death and insanity (which was originally to be the main
theme of the novel) they provide a graphic microcosm of the
traditional world on the verge of extinction. Raskolnikov's links
with his family are, for most of the novel, even more tenuous —
and it is this theme of the isolated intellectual which has moved
to the centre in the final version. Dostoevsky had long been concerned with the isolated individual, alone in St Petersburg without family, roots or permanent home; indeed, it is the central
theme of most of his work of the 1840s. They — that is Devushkin, Prokharchin, Golyadkin (of *The Double*) — live in fear and
oppression, and escape into their dreams and fantasies. (The links
with Gogol's work are again obvious.) Each lives as if he were
the only person on earth, with no responsibilities for others,
which is, in Dostoevsky's terms, their greatest sin. The Underground Man and Raskolnikov take up the theme with renewed
intensity: both, to use Clive's phrase,[116] provide views of 'the
dissolving bourgeoise ethos . . . observed by a distraught indi-
vidualist in a total state of exile'.

However amenable to sociological analysis Dostoevsky's
work may be, he, of course, would have rejected this interpre-

tation as inadequate, indeed as dangerously spurious. For him the collapse of the old moral order was not simply reducible to the rise of capitalism, for example. The life of modern man in a more fundamental sense appeared to Dostoevsky to be profoundly tragic: and it is a tragedy of loss. Man stands alone in the dim streets of St Petersburg because he has abandoned the forces which for Dostoevsky could alone provide a defence against this darkness — the soil, the people, and most centrally, God himself. A world without God is, for Dostoevsky, one which has lost all meaning, even its basic reality. Both *The Idiot* and *The Devils* explore this theme most fully. Dostoevsky sees the plague of nihilism with which the young of Russia are possessed[117] as stemming directly from their lack of belief, which in turn has caused the disintegration of the Russian cultured classes as they descend into sensuality, violence and political terrorism. Even the saintly Prince Myshkin is powerless to resist this contagion and is driven back into the darkness of his own insanity by his confrontation with the Godless modern world.

In place of God, nineteenth-century intellectual man, in his sinful pride, has put his own rational self. Pride, reliance on rationalism, are for Dostoevsky the progenitors of all the other sins of the age. From *Notes from the Underground* through to the tragedy of Ivan Karamazov (the ultimate man of the rational *logos*), Dostoevsky argues persistently against the new ethics of Chernyshevsky and Dobrolyubov, and what he considered their logical extension, the 'ethics' of Nechaev. Raskolnikov is the first major study of the punishment which befalls those who attempt to live without God and who try to replace Him by their own proud intellect. He commits the main sin in Dostoevsky's scheme of things: the intellectual abrogation of the rights of God. And he is inevitably punished for his *hubris*.

Rational self-interest was no guide to morality, for it could only lead to the domination of individual by individual, to groups competing for power in a disintegrating social structure. Morality stemmed exclusively from God: if He did not exist, or if He were rejected, however 'respectfully', then anything was permitted, be it the rape of young girls or political assassinations. Murder was indeed, in Dostoevsky's view, the 'logical' consequence of a morality based on man alone. Each of the characters who abandons God in Dostoevsky's world — Raskolnikov, Stavrogin, Pyotr Verkhovensky, Ivan Karamazov — commits murder or sanctions it, or commits suicide. This is perhaps the most strikingly simple and obvious 'message' of Dostoevsky's artistic work. Man without God cannot survive.

Belief in God and acceptance of His law did not, however, imply loss of freedom. On the contrary, Dostoevsky did not seek mere subservience but placed unparalleled emphasis on man's potential for absolute freedom. 'Man's whole business is to prove that his is not a cog-wheel,' the Underground Man observes in what is the prologue to Dostoevsky's major fiction. Every individual in Dostoevsky's world, however humiliated or depraved, has this essential spark of humanity: no one is a mere louse, worm or 'trembling creature', as Raskolnikov at first believes. For Dostoevsky, every individual was an end not a means, and *everyone* had this right to absolute freedom. As long as a man was alive, the last word of his destiny could not be spoken. It was precisely because he recognised this dimension of man's destiny that Dostoevsky was so concerned with the problem of belief and morality. For, given man's freedom, how was he to use it without descending into mere self-will? Freedom was man's greatest gift, but it was extremely dangerous if it was not freedom in Christ, as Raskolnikov discovers.[118] This was the only possible creative form of freedom that Dostoevsky admitted. For freedom meant to him not licence to kill and torture, but implicit within it was absolute responsibility to and for others. Everyone in Dostoevsky's world, from the 1840s until the culmination in *The Brothers Karamazov*, is responsible for others, everyone is guilty, not only for his own sins, but for the sins of others.

Given the schism within the modern world, which Dostoevsky perceived more acutely than any other nineteenth-century writer, how was he to prevent total collapse? Many voices, many answers presented themselves, and Dostoevsky rejected almost all of them. Some looked to salvation from the West, as Dostoevsky himself had done in the 1840s, and even during the period of *Time* he had remained sympathetic to Western culture. In 1862, however, he visited Western Europe for the first time and, as with Herzen and Belinsky, his impressions were almost uniformly negative. Beginning with *Winter Notes* and continuing throughout the 1860s, he set out to demolish the value of European culture.[119] The West was decaying and had become a source of dangerous corruption for the pure, untainted Russians.

Paris had rotted in its bourgeois stagnation, while London had been transformed into a capitalistic inferno. Europe in general had been overwhelmed by the three poisons which now threatened Russia – positivism, atheism and socialism. European civilisation was dead: it had rejected the true Christ, had become spiritually bankrupt and could offer Russia nothing. In the 1870s, the attacks are ceaseless, culminating in his Pushkin speech, Dostoevsky's final assault on a declining civilisation, on Russian émigrés and, inevitably, on Turgenev.

Just as Dostoevsky now poured abuse on Western Europe, so too, he constantly exposed the dangers of Russian liberalism and radicalism. Neither could provide the answers to the 'accursed questions': on the contrary, they were the main contributors to Russia's ills. His work of the 1860s and 1870s is full of abuse at the expense of his own generation, the sentimental utopian liberals of the 1840s, who were cast in the role of the progenitors of the new and even more deadly 'devils'. Stepan Verkhovensky, even though he is treated fairly sympathetically, is seen as a vital link between the idealist fathers and the nihilist sons, between the *Petrashevtsy* and the Nechaevists. Indeed, this strand in Dostoevsky's thought is essentially autobiographical: Russia's tragedy was his own personal tragedy. In private Dostoevsky was his usual nasty self when describing the Russian liberals: 'When will these obsolete and retrograde dregs be washed away? . . . Recall the best liberals – recall Belinsky: isn't he a conscious enemy of his fatherland – isn't he a reactionary?' (Letter to Maykov, 1 March 1868.) It is somewhat ironic that *Dostoevsky* should term such people as Belinsky and Turgenev reactionary.

Such attacks were relatively mild, however, compared with his views on the deadliest enemy of Russian society – the demonic radicals. To Dostoevsky, they represented everything he loathed – rationalism, utilitarian aesthetics and ethics, atheism – all of which led, in Dostoevsky's view, to the end of culture and enlightenment as he understood them. Nihilism was politically motivated crime, but crime none the less. The revolutionaries denied or distorted all he stood for – man's spirituality, his noblest ideals, Christ and the Russian people – and he could scarcely find sufficient abuse to hurl at them, to eradicate them from the political arena in Russia. His most celebrated attack on them occurs in a letter to his niece from Geneva where, in 1867, he witnessed the International Peace Conference. He writes:

It was really incredible how these socialists and revolutionary gentlemen, whom hitherto I had known only from books, sat and flung down lies from the platform to their audience of five thousand! It's quite indescribable. One can hardly realise, even for oneself, the absurdity, feebleness, futility, disunion and the depth of essential·contradictoriness. And it is this rabble which is stirring up the whole unfortunate working-class! It's too deplorable.[120]

Elsewhere he describes them as 'wild beasts', they 'deserve the knout'. they are 'scum' and 'scoundrels', who will only bring darkness and obliteration to the whole world.

So Dostoevsky was unable to unravel this particular 'mystery' and remained uncomprehendingly hostile to the radicals and all the other genuinely progressive forces in nineteenth-century Europe. For him, hope lay in not crossing over the abyss to 'the other shore', but in clinging to the traditional and most conservative aspects of Russian society, to religion, the Church and the holy Russian people. Essential to this position was Dostoevsky's increasingly *anti-political* viewpoint. In fact, he had never really been interested in politics as such and after the grim recompense for his early enthusiasms, and the alarums of the early 1860s, he refused to interpret history in political terms, but rather within moral and then religious parameters. Even in the 1830s and 1840s in fact, Dostoevsky's views had been based on moral and emotional impulses and this remained the prime source of his intuitions. Feelings were more important than deeds and society could only be transformed by changes within the hearts of men. In line with his Romantic education, his guiding light was the religion of the heart. As early as 1838, Dostoevsky wrote to his brother: 'Nature, the soul, love, and God, one recognises through the heart, and not through the reason.'[121] And this Romantic view was to be life-long, underlying much of the later anti-rationalism and irrationalism.

Religious belief, as such, appears as essential in Dostoevsky's thinking relatively late, that is, sometime in the second half of the 1860s. (Even *The Idiot*, for example, is still more concerned with ethics than religion.) Dostoevsky's religious upbringing had not proved to be based on very strong foundations: his early understanding of Christianity was rather clouded and vague, and in his early works the pious tend to be hypocrites and tyrants.

In 1854 he wrote his famous letter to Madame Fonvizina, expressing doubts as to whether he would ever be able to find faith, and, while in Siberia, he was not a regular church-goer.[122] Only really around 1870, with his work on *The Life of a Great Sinner*, did religious belief move to the centre of his preoccupations, although even now Dostoevsky still admitted he was tormented by the very question of the existence of God. Even if Dostoevsky himself was not convinced, there is, throughout the 1870s, an increasing emphasis, culminating in the quasi-ecclesiastical world-view of *The Brothers Karamazov*, on the need for active belief to save mankind from the abyss. In this last period Dostoevsky finally arrived at the conclusion, which had been implicit in his work for the previous ten years, that a lack of clear belief leads directly to social sedition and anarchy. The Russian Christ became the only hope against positivism, atheism, socialism — and the Roman Catholic Church!

Central to Dostoevsky's religion was the notion of humility and acquiescence in suffering. It is in *Crime and Punishment* that the theme of salvation through suffering first emerges in a developed form. The problem embodied in the conflict between Raskolnikov and Sonya is the struggle between self-assertion and self-abasement and the 'pious lie' of the Epilogue reveals that only the latter course can bring about the process of renewal and regeneration. By the time of his next novel, *The Idiot*, the theme of positive acceptance of suffering has moved to the centre, embodied in the principal protagonist, Prince Myshkin. Both he, even if he is defeated, and Sonya represent the greatness of the truly meek, who, of course, shall inherit the earth. Alyosha Karamazov, even if he is a rather worldly version, still clearly counsels acquiescence in the social, political and economic status quo. Of the two paths —rebellion and acceptance — which were considered by Dostoevsky throughout his life, the latter has clearly triumphed. Protest destroys, while acceptance of suffering ennobles and becomes the only path to truth and salvation.

Dostoevsky's views on acquiescence in suffering are well within the mainstream of Christian teachings, even if he placed unusual emphasis and a slightly idiosyncratic interpretation upon it. Dostoevsky, however, extended the doctrine by moving into the historical sphere and by the 1870s regarded the craving for suffering (and oppression) as one of the basic instincts,

indeed needs, of the Russian people. That is, a central Christian
doctrine was taken to an absurd conclusion and acted as a
mystical justification of the repressive status quo: in his *Diary*
of 1873 Dostoevsky wrote:

> I believe that the main and most fundamental quest of the
> Russian people is their craving for suffering — perpetual and
> unquenchable suffering — everywhere and in everything. It
> seems that they have been affected by this thirst for martyr-
> dom from time immemorial. The suffering stream flows
> through their whole history — not merely because of external
> calamities and misfortunes: it gushes from the people's very
> heart.[123]

There could, of course, be no logical counter-argument to
such beliefs. In general, by the 1870s, Dostoevsky's view of the
Russian people had moved entirely into the realm of categorical
assertions about its unique spiritual nature. His attitude to his
homeland had become totally religious: his peculiar amalgam of
Slavophil theories and his Siberian experiences was divorced
from current realities, but then Dostoevsky made no attempt to
base his ideas on facts: he confuses his dream with the reality.
From Dostoevsky's own accounts it would seem that he 'discovered' the people and his own Russianness in the Siberian
prison-camp. By the time he began publishing *Time*, Dostoevsky
had already moved far from his Westernist leanings of the 1840s,
when the intelligentsia was regarded as the leading force in
Russian society, to a quasi-Slavophil position, in which he regarded the common people as the main hope for Russia's future.
This tendency deepened over the next decade, so that, by the
beginning of his *Diary* in 1873, he idealised the people. He was
aware, obviously, that they were not perfect (as witnessed by
his vivid depictions of peasant cruelty) but, in all respects, the
Russian peasantry, in Dostoevsky's view, was *special*. Russia
became a kind of New Israel, a Holy Land in which the Russian
people were the new God-bearing race.[124] The Russian soul was
a peculiarly *broad* one, capable of containing within itself all
extremes of human life because of Russia's unique history, which
had not placed the normal bourgeois restraints upon them. The
Russian was somehow a universal man, who loved all other men
and understood them. Russia became the light of the East whose

own rebirth would mark the regeneration of the whole world: it was Russia's mission to save the rest of mankind, who had abandoned the one true faith.

Dostoevsky's idealisation of his holy people is most marked in the prophetic publicistics of his *Diary of a Writer*. Here he gives frequent characterisations of the Russian people as a whole, their love of extremes, their 'special' form of drunkenness, their profound love of Christ, who is perhaps their only true love. Salvation for the country can only come from this divine source, from below. Elsewhere in the *Diary* he insists that the Russian people are incapable of sustaining hatred, that they alone are the repositories of truth, they are bestowed with unique 'candour, purity, gentleness, breadth of mind and benignancy'.[125] Pushkin is the sum of the people in his universality of spirit, but also, and more importantly, because he turned to the people and realised their truth and mission.

These views, of which Dostoevsky is 'somehow blindly convinced',[126] do not deviate essentially from those of the earlier Slavophils. Dostoevsky's particular contribution to the myth of the Russian people and its unique soul and mission is in the relationship he perceived between the intelligentsia and the people. For him, the intelligentsia must throw off its false Europeanisation and rediscover its links with its native land. All the problems of Russian society stemmed from this split. The intelligentsia had lost Christ and thereby had divorced itself from the holy people of Russia, and had been tempted and had fallen before the false European gods of atheism, positivism and socialism. All his heroes are judged by their alienation from the people and the soil. Raskolnikov symbolically kisses the earth to acknowledge his great sin of pride, while Dmitry, the eponymous man of the earth, is ultimately saved because of his close connections with the soil, and therefore with the people and Christ. Dostoevsky was quite explicit about the centrality of this conception to his overall view of Russian life. He viewed the Nechaev 'movement' for example as a 'monstrous phenomenon' which was 'a direct consequence of the great gulf between all educated Russians and the original native springs of Russian life'.[127]

This contrast between false intellectual learning and the true wisdom of the people is once more most fully expressed in *The Diary*. Near the beginning of the first entry Dostoevsky, in com-

menting on Herzen, notes that since the time of Peter I the educated elite had lost their roots among the people. He continues:

> Having detached themselves from the people, they *naturally*
> [my italics] also lost God. The restless ones among them
> became atheists; the apathetic and placid ones waxed indif-
> ferent. For the Russian people they felt nothing but contempt,
> believing, however, that they loved the people and wished
> them the best of everything.[128]

Dostoevsky sets the tone of his whole diary. It is, again, an autobiographical theme: Dostoevsky frequently returns to his own
experiences, in the belief that he had been saved from the
modern ills by his contact with the people of Siberia. All must
follow his example and return to the people, begging their
forgiveness, or else catastrophe will ensue.

Much of Dostoevsky's *Diary of a Writer* is written in the same
apocalyptic tone, and it makes depressing reading. Whereas
Gogol's similar defence of Tsarist oppression can be regarded as
naive and rather harmless, Dostoevsky's aggressive chauvinism,
racism and hostility to social progress is much more chilling.
Even given the mood of the country in the late 1870s, the pan-
Slavic hysteria, the militarism of Europe in general and the very
different attitudes to war, race and crime in the Victorian period,
Dostoevsky's arguments can only be described as deeply reactionary. Society, he argues, is in a state of collapse because of
Russia's internal enemies – the Westernising liberals and radicals.
Suicide, the torture of children, drunkenness, the love of money,
are all symptoms of the diseases Dostoevsky saw emanating from
the rotten cesspool of the West and the corrupt and corrupting
educated elite. Another internal and external enemy was the
Jews. 'Yiddishers', Dostoevsky notes, 'will be soaking up the
blood of the people and subsisting on their debauch and humiliation.'[129] The Turks, in turn, are described as 'a savage, dis-
gusting Mohammedan horde, the sworn enemy of civilisation',
and as 'sadistic beasts'. They, the Jews, the Catholics, the Poles,
the English, are all conspiring to thwart Russia in its Holy War,
to liberate the oppressed Slav peoples and regain Constantinople
as the true capital of the Orthodox world. 'Constantinople must
be ours,' he cries. The Russians, of course, do not fight for greed
or self-interest: they have entered the war as a disinterested

party for the sake of others, but also to carry their true Christian message to save the rest of the world. War itself is beneficial, it is glorious activity which unites and refreshes the nation. Men, in fact, need war, as they need suffering, and too long a peace merely weakens the nation. And so he constantly supports the war effort, calling on his readers to enlist and to fight for the Russian Tsar, the Russian Church and the Russian Christ.

So Dostoevsky continues, invoking the all-loving, universal Russian man to crush the Turks and the rest: Dostoevsky the preacher of universal love, forgiveness and harmony, advocates Russian imperialism. Quite apart from the frenzied chauvinism, his arguments are full of the most bizarre paradoxes. This is hardly surprising. Dostoevsky's vision of universal harmony, of a Golden Age before the Fall, could hardly be achieved in the sinful, criminal and dislocated world of the nineteenth century. Perhaps the greatest irony and tragedy of Dostoevsky's life and work was the discrepancy between his startling insights and explorations into the divided world of nineteenth-century man and his society, and his remarkably banal and unoriginal remedies for this crisis. Again, the parallel with Gogol is most striking. Both saw beneath the surface of everyday life and achieved a 'higher realism'. Equally, both seemed to have been terrified or appalled by what they saw and sought refuge in tradition, the rule of established authority and an end to conflict through reconciliation between the opposing parties. Even in 1840, when Gogol was writing, and certainly by 1880, this was clearly impossible, and the utopian hopes of both now strike us as naive in the extreme. Dostoevsky may have found success for his ideas, which Gogol never did, but in many ways his tragedy remains the same, and even though his illumination of the 'accursed questions' is unparalleled in its depth and intensity, his answers to them stood little chance of solving them. At the end of his life, Dostoevsky, the radical of the 1840s, the voice of the oppressed and the spiritual revolutionary, chose to identify himself with an order far more corrupt than the West and one which was to disappear forty years later.

# Dostoevsky: Important Biographical Dates

| | |
|---|---|
| 1821 | Born in Moscow. |
| 1833–7 | Attends boarding schools in Moscow. |
| 1837 | Dostoevsky's mother dies. |
| | Pushkin killed in a duel. |
| | Dostoevsky moves with Mikhail to St Petersburg. |
| 1838 | Enters Engineering College. |
| 1839 | Dostoevsky's father murdered by serfs. |
| 1841 | Receives commission. |
| 1843 | Transferred to Corps of Military Engineers. |
| 1844 | Retires and takes up writing full-time. |
| 1846 | Publication of *Poor Folk* and *The Double*. |
| 1847–9 | Publication of *The Landlady*, *Mr Prokharchin*, *Netochka Nezvanova* and *White Nights*. |
| 1849 | Arrest, trial and 'mock' execution. |
| | Sentenced to four years' penal servitude, and subsequent service in the ranks in Siberia. |
| 1850–4 | Penal servitude in Omsk. |
| 1854–9 | Military service in Semipalatinsk. |
| 1855 | Nicholas I succeeded by Alexander II. |
| 1856 | Dostoevsky restored to officer's rank. |
| 1857 | First marriage to Mariya Isayeva. |
| 1859 | Finally allowed to return to St Petersburg. |
| | Publishes *The Uncle's Dream* and *The Village of Stepanchikovo*. |
| 1861–3 | The journal *Time* with Mikhail. |
| 1864 | *Notes from the Underground*. |
| 1864 | Death of Mariya Isayeva. |
| 1866 | *Crime and Punishment*. |
| 1866 | *The Gambler*. |
| 1867 | Marries Anna Snitkina. |
| 1867–71 | Lives abroad, mainly in Geneva, Dresden and Florence. |

| 1868 | *The Idiot.* |
| 1870 | *The Eternal Husband.* |
| 1871 | *The Devils.* |
| 1873 | Takes job as editor of Meshchersky's *The Citizen.* Begins publication of *Diary of a Writer.* |
| 1874 | *A Raw Youth.* |
| 1879–80 | *The Brothers Karamazov.* |
| 1880 | The Pushkin speech. |
| 1881 | Dostoevsky dies in St Petersburg. |

# 3 Lev Tolstoy

The dominant theme of Tolstoy's relationship with the world around him was the opposite of Dostoevsky's. Whereas the latter attempted to resolve the conflicts of Russia in the second half of the nineteenth century on their own terms, and was accordingly intensely topical in his work, Tolstoy's art and thought represent a rejection of the modern world. His answers are usually antihistorical, absolute. Tolstoy's background and education provide the starting-point for this struggle. His early upbringing was set in a close family circle on the Yasnaya Polyana estate, where his tradition-bound, conservative father and doting mother provided a rich, comfortable and easy life. The deaths of his mother in 1830, and his father in 1837, when Tolstoy was still only nine, were the principal shocks to disturb this tranquil gentry existence, but it was not until the year of the death of Tolstoy's father that he left the estate and realised for the first time that he and his family were not the centre of the universe.[1]

After the typical aristocratic home education from mainly foreign tutors, under whose guidance Tolstoy made little progress, he entered Kazan University in 1844 to study Oriental languages, with the intention of becoming a diplomat. Although he worked quite hard he failed the first-year examinations and switched to law, rather than have to repeat his first year. This time he managed to pass his examinations, but both at Kazan and later when he transferred to St Petersburg, he continued to do rather badly. What was taught within the conventional university system simply did not interest him: indeed, he felt it obstructed rather than advanced his pursuit of knowledge. For the first time he questioned the accepted wisdom on educational methods: this rejection was the first in a life-long struggle against traditional pedagogical practice.

Instead, his own omnivorous reading acted as his main education. Among his main complaints during his brief university career was that he did not have enough time for his own reading, and, in turn, the hours devoted to his favourite authors, Pushkin, Gogol, Dickens, Schiller, Dumas, Goethe and Hegel, occasioned his poor academic performance. These authors were the standard material for the educated young of the period, but Tolstoy already revealed his somewhat 'archaistic'[2] tendencies in the choice of his principal masters — Rousseau and Montesquieu. Already Tolstoy had begun to look to a former era with conceptions very different from those of Russia in the 1840s.

That Tolstoy was able to indulge his own interests derives almost entirely from one single fact: he was a wealthy aristocrat. His class origins were to affect him for the rest of his life. Indeed, even in terms of his education Tolstoy can be viewed as representative of the landowing aristocracy, and he remained cut off from the contemporary intellectual and literary world centred in St Petersburg, and to a lesser extent, Moscow. From the 1840s Tolstoy built his own private world on Yasnaya Polyana and established it on the moral principles deriving from the apogee of progressive Russian aristocratic culture, the end of the eighteenth century. It was to the world of Novikov, Karamzin and especially Radishchev, that Tolstoy looked, bolstered by foreign illuminati of the period, Rousseau, Sterne and Stendhal.[3] Tolstoy's view of the world was in many ways that of the eighteenth century — he viewed man morally rather than sociologically.

Tolstoy led a life typical of his class. In his early years he treated the servants and tutors with the contempt which, in his eyes, they deserved, while at Kazan he displayed the sort of snobbery that had made Lermontov unpopular at Moscow University. Significantly, when he returned to his ancestral estates Tolstoy felt comforted by the atmosphere. Yasnaya Polyana held a central, even sacred significance for Tolstoy. (He was to spend almost his whole life there.) As Troyat puts it:[4] 'Russia for Tolstoy was neither St Petersburg nor Moscow, but Yasnaya Polyana.' Tolstoy viewed himself not simply as an aristocrat, but as a *landowner*, and his estate continually acted as a support, spiritually as well as materially. (For example, when in the 1860s he found himself in conflict with both the government and all political factions, he retreated to his estate with his new bride, almost like a feudal baron.)[5]

Before settling down to a writing career in the early 1850s Tolstoy followed a pattern of life which was typical of a young aristocrat. He drank, played cards, amused himself with women, writing and his estates. Tolstoy distinguished himself from the normal pattern only by taking all this seriously. Tolstoy also considered the army as a suitable career and made full advantage of his social position. He was well received for his high birth, he enjoyed the benefits of the 'nice evil' of slavery, and even had himself moved from the front line through his family connections. Tolstoy continued this pattern during his foreign travels of the late 1850s. He criticised the idle rich, but mixed freely with them, stayed in the best hotels and shared their pleasures, which, of course, as Tolstoy was later to point out so vociferously, derived from their exploitation of the poor.

Tolstoy became involved with this latter section of society on his return from abroad, setting up a peasant school. Paradoxically, it was his very exploitation of the poor which allowed him to indulge this particular interest. (Again, Tolstoy was to realise this paradox all too painfully, especially in *What Then Must We Do?* (1886).) It can be argued that all his social work and flouting of accepted practices derive from his class position. So too, his clashes with established authority stem in no small part from Tolstoy's aristocratic *hauteur*. The first of these occurred in July 1862 when Yasnaya Polyana was searched in his absence. With the offended dignity of a grand seigneur whose privacy has been invaded, Tolstoy demanded a public apology — or else he would leave the country.

It was in the 1860s, isolated on his estate and in conflict with the rest of society, that Tolstoy became increasingly conscious of his own class position. This rise in class consciousness can be seen in a number of ways. For example, his major work of the period, *War and Peace* (1865–9), has as one of its main themes the role of the aristocracy in Russian history. Tolstoy saw his own class as the most important in the development of his country. (More specifically the first plans of the work reveal great interest in the Decembrists, the members of which had been, in the eyes of many, the last representatives of the enlightened aristocracy as a political force.)[6] In more social terms Tolstoy's turning to the peasantry in the early 1860s was very typical of his own class in his attempt to achieve some measure of harmony between the two classes. In both these respects Levin in *Anna Karenina* (1875–7) stands as the representative of Tolstoy's thinking. Again one of the main themes is

Tolstoy's concern with the fate of the landed gentry, which Tolstoy still considered central to Russia's future. Levin is the true conservative aristocrat. He is anti-liberal in his politics, rejecting any public service, but prefers to work on his own estate, proud of his economic self-sufficiency. He, like Tolstoy, may be democratic in sympathies, but hates to see the old order in general, and the old estates in particular, breaking up.

Both Levin and Tolstoy, then, reject modern civilisation and stand on the defensive against rising capitalism which was threatening their whole class. Tolstoy all his life belonged in spirit to the pre-capitalist world, and it is this he reflects in his art. Certainly up to 1880, and even afterwards in his major fiction such as *Resurrection* (1899), he is chiefly interested in his own class. His main protagonists are rich and can indulge themselves in their private lives and introspection. He may not idealise them, but he does give a very positive view of his class — with the later work *Resurrection* being a notable exception in this respect. Apart from the aristocracy the only class of any real interest to him was the other side of the feudal society he inhabited — the peasantry. The middle classes and lower aristocracy are almost entirely absent from Tolstoy's fiction.

However, he frequently found his class position onerous and oppressive. As early as 1859 he talked of becoming a peasant, of giving away all his money and property,[7] and the guilt which occasioned these aspirations intensified in the last period of his life. None the less, even when writing savage exposés of the moral hypocrisy of the landowning class, he continued to own land himself and remained aristocratic in his approach to the world. Levin's pride in his economic self-sufficiency underlies Tolstoy's Christian anarchism, and the contempt he felt for all those who were not aristocrats or peasants remained long after 1880.

Considerable wealth, though, was the most obvious benefit Tolstoy derived from his class position. When the estates were divided up he received his beloved Yasnaya Polyana, which comprised 4,000 acres, as well as 330 serfs.[8] Tolstoy set about spending his considerable income. In the mid-1840s, in St Petersburg, he had built up gambling losses of 3,500R and was spending more or less everything he received from his estates. In the Caucasus, while in the army, he lost even more, and for a time in the early 1850s his circumstances became slightly difficult, and briefly his debts threatened to cause him to sell Yasnaya Polyana. (In the end he only had to part with one small section of it.) His relative lack of money kept him quite busy in his new literary career and caused some minor difficulties with his first literary 'agent' Nekrasov, to whose *Contemporary* Tolstoy was contributing. Tolstoy was rather annoyed that he received nothing for his first published work, *Childhood* (1852), and Nekrasov was obliged to inform him that beginners were not remunerated.

Tolstoy helped pay off his losses by setting up his *Military Gazette* while in the Crimea, but his gambling continued. In 1854 he lost 5,000R in two days. Like Dostoevsky, Tolstoy for a time became an obsessive gambler, practising by himself to improve his chances, but he always had his estates to rely on and never found himself in the appalling circumstances that Dostoevsky did. Tolstoy continued to throw his money away, and in 1862 lost 1,000R at billiards in Moscow. *The Cossacks* (1863) covered this particular debt, and now Tolstoy's already comfortable financial situation was being even further improved by his now considerable literary income. Tolstoy received 300R per sheet for the first part of *War and Peace*, and when he decided to print it in book form he sold 4,500 copies of the six-volume edition at eight roubles per copy. In total contrast to the normal practice of the nineteenth-century literary market in Russia, Tolstoy *himself* advanced money to cover the printing costs.

When, in 1871, Tolstoy temporarily abandoned literature to devote himself to his pedagogical activities, he was offered 500R a sheet for anything that he might publish in the future. This is what he later received for *Anna Karenina* and he then sold the rights to the novel for 20,000R. In 1880 he received 25,000R for the fourth edition of his works.[9] During this period he not only lived comfortably off his literary income and estates, but was able to buy more land, and in 1882 bought a house in Moscow for 27,000R. By the time Tolstoy decided in 1891 to divide up his estate, it was worth 580,000R, and during the last years when his wife Sonya was publishing his works, as the main source of the family income (Tolstoy had relinquished all rights to his literary royalties), she received 20,000R per annum.

Tolstoy, then, never *had* to work as a writer for his living, so too, interestingly, he never fully regarded himself as a writer, and even in those (relatively infrequent) periods when he did devote himself exclusively to writing, it was never to literature *as such*, but to literature as part of a wider moral activity. Unlike most writers of nineteenth-century Russia, Tolstoy had no early literary ambition. As late as 1848, when he was twenty, he had given little thought to becoming a writer and only drifted into a literary career because this was one of the 'done' things for a man of his age and position. In 1845 he had begun writing, but commentaries on philosophical and jurisprudential textbooks, and not fiction. During the 1840s and early 1850s, he occupied himself with a variety of activities – his estate, music, the army and his earlier interests of law and philosophy. Even when he did begin to think more seriously of literature towards the end of the 1840s his other commitments precluded any fulltime concentration on it. None the less, Tolstoy was growing bored and dissatisfied with himself and looked around for something worthwhile: literature seemed to be the answer.

By the early 1850s Tolstoy had begun to take literature seriously and whenever he could he worked hard, both at his own writing and in the analysis of literature. He derived great pleasure from his new pastime (which it still was) and liked the direction literature now lent to a previously rather aimless existence. In 1852, while working on *Childhood*, he wrote: 'I am writing not out of ambition, but because I like to; work gives me pleasure and a sense of purpose, and I am working.'[10] He did not abandon his other pursuits, but gradually, and particularly after the success of his first works, he became bored with everything else and longed to retire to devote himself exclusively to it. Literature was seen by him as a means of self-fulfilment, but also, and already, as a *moral* activity. He would never, he maintained, write for mere pleasure, but always with some idea or purpose, and considered himself, with typical self-assurance, to be the most moral writer in Russia.[11]

However, almost immediately Tolstoy began to have serious doubts about the worthiness of his new career. From 1855, in fact, he found himself in something of a complex position. His first contacts with the St Petersburg literary world singularly failed to impress him. He found the controversies emerging in the *Contemporary* group very petty,[12] and defiantly declared he was not a littérateur.[13] He was no longer a solider, did not wish to be a *professional* writer, certainly had no desire to be a civil servant and the only remaining possibility was the life of a landowner, to which he was drawn, but which was considered to be rather a lowly occupation by his new literary acquaintances. Not only was he torn between being a writer and doing something more practical: he also felt that to be a worthy, that is, a *moral* writer, he had to escape what he saw as the petty, professional literary world.

As the 1850s wore on (and literature in Russia became more social and engagé), the basic conflict between life and literature came to haunt him more and more. He was pursued by the feeling that 'life' was more important and that it was here that he should make his mark. The years 1858–9 marked a crisis in his literary activity: he was very dissatisfied with *Family Happiness* (1859), work on *The Cossacks* was going badly, and he thought literature a waste of time with so many other important things to be done. He almost abandoned literature and made a final break with *The Contemporary*. Tolstoy was not alone: Fet also left the increasingly radical journal (as Turgenev shortly was to). The idea of the writer as a free artist was disappearing in Russia and on these terms Tolstoy no longer wished to be a writer.

1859–62 marked a cross-roads in Tolstoy's career.[14] He forsook literature, travelled abroad, mainly to study education, and in 1861 opened his first peasant school. (He was also working as the local Arbiter of the Peace. Another important event which turned him away from the 'beautiful lie' of art was the shattering blow of the death of his brother Nikolai.) Education also served as a kind of escape for Tolstoy from the literary career in which he felt he had failed, but his interest in popular education was also symptomatic of the role writing already played in his life. That is, literature was *always* for him a form of education, not an end in itself but a means to self-fulfilment, self-betterment and ultimately, and most importantly, the betterment of others.

His confusion persisted. Between 1859 and 1865 much of his work remained either unfinished or unpublished, and his feelings of dissatisfaction were exacerbated by the hostile criticisms of the works that did appear.[15] Gradually, however, literature began to reclaim him. He still viewed himself as an amateur in the literary world but under the influence of the more ambitious and worldly Sonya he plunged into his new project, *War and Peace*. His work on it took a very serious form, with detailed research into the historical background (even if he only looked at what he needed to prove his polemical points).[16] The first parts, after some initial doubts, met with great success, and Tolstoy felt confident enough in his resumed career to work on the later parts almost without a break.

Tolstoy was never again to devote himself quite so whole-heartedly to 'pure' literature. In the early 1870s he again felt isolated from the literary scene. In 1872 he reopened his school, and popular education again became the corner-stone of his existence. For a while he abandoned fiction, wrote another peasant reader, bought a stud farm in Samara, and spend as much time as possible away from literature. The same process as ten years before — peasant schools and peasant stories — eventually led him back to literature, first to plans for an historical novel, and then to *Anna Karenina*. Once he had begun he worked rapidly and with some enthusiasm, but he could not still the doubts for long. His work was much more erratic, and he spent as much time directing the seventy schools he helped organise in his province as he did on *Anna Karenina*. The novel was a great success, but so utterly disenchanted with his artistic career was Tolstoy that he could only comment: 'What's so difficult about describing how an officer gets entangled with a woman? There's nothing difficult in that, and above all, nothing worthwhile. It's bad and *it serves no useful purpose*' [my italics].[17]

From then on Tolstoy never again regarded himself as a writer. Now he was a teacher and religion, its practice and propagation, became Tolstoy's main concern. Even when he did occasionally revert to works akin to those he had written before 1878, he created them as propaganda, as in *Resurrection*, or concentrated on his later religious and social themes, as in *The Death of Ivan Il'ych* (1886) and *Hadji Murat* (1904). Art *per se* seemed to him immoral at such a time of deep crisis in society and literature became one of the self-indulgent 'pleasures' (along with tobacco, meat and sex), which he felt must be renounced in order to live a more Christian life. One dominant trend in nineteenth-century Russian literature leads to a negation of aesthetic art. In Tolstoy's life after 1878 this tendency reached its ultimate conclusion.

Just as Tolstoy was to reject 'art', so too his own work often stands as a rejection of accepted artistic approaches. At first, he made no major formal innovations, but his *treatment* of accepted subjects (the autobiographical sketches and army life) marked a

considerable intensification of existing tendencies. A de-roman-
ticised approach to the Caucasus, and nature in general, for
example, may have already become accepted practice in Russian
literature,[18] but almost immediately he pushed this basic tendency much further. In all his works of the 1850s, that is (and,
of course, later), Tolstoy attempted to reveal the deeper truth
submerged beneath the accepted approaches. He was deliberately
unconventional and innovatory towards what was standard
practice in the existing literature of the time — just as he was in
the field of education, and as he was to be in his religious beliefs.

The most obvious example of this approach is, perhaps, the
polemical 'demythologising' of history in general, and Napoleon
in particular, in *War and Peace*, where Tolstoy attempts to turn
accepted views on their head. But the same applies to his earlier
work. Here he stands as the enemy of Romantic art. *Family
Happiness*, for example, breaks with convention in having marriage as the starting-point rather than the culmination. while *A
Landowner's Morning* (1856) again goes against the established
tradition of having love as the centre of interest.[19] This effort
to overcome literary clichés continued: he looked to older, in
particular eighteenth-century genres, to rejuvenate the newer
ones and later turned to folk art in polemical protest against
the dominant upper-class literature of his period. Never would
he take anything as given because the given, for Tolstoy, almost
always obscured the real truth.

In a sense, like Dostoevsky, Tolstoy attempted to put an end
to 'landowners' literature' — even if Dostoevsky would certainly
have considered Tolstoy as a pre-eminent 'landowner'. It was
for this reason that, beginning with the *Prisoner in the Caucasus*
(1872), he turned to folk language and literature, which stood
in sharp contrast to the 'long-winded rubbish' of *War and Peace*
(as Tolstoy later referred to it), and most nineteenth-century
bourgeois realism. A new kind of literature was needed, a literature that would not portray and flatter the upper classes, but
one that would be comprehensible and accessible to the 'dark
mass' of the peasantry, who provided the wealth that allowed
such 'self-indulgent' works to be written. And even if Tolstoy
could never quite resist the temptation to return to the old
forms, he increasingly eschewed the very art which had made
him famous. Instead, he resolved to write for the people, and in
their own language.

The same tendencies are even more apparent in Tolstoy's actual representation of reality. That is, from the very beginning he never attempted to record the 'body and pressure' of his changing times objectively as Turgenev did, but rather he depicted what he saw from a definite point of view. Tolstoy, long before 1878, was one of the least objective of Russian realists. Perhaps the keynote to Tolstoy's art is the term *ostraneniye*, the making strange of the familiar. The most famous example, from a study of which the Formalist critic Victor Shklovsky first systematically used the term,[20] is *Kholstomer* (1886), a story in which the world is viewed through the eyes of the eponymous horse. Another famous instance is Natasha Rostova's naive perception of the opera, through which Tolstoy reveals his abhorrence of the most extreme expression of upper-class (and, therefore, decadent) art. Through his frequent use of this device and, of course, in many other ways, Tolstoy depicts the world with a pitilessly severe candour, because of his constant desire to break .down conventional views and perceptions. Implicit in this desire and the resultant depiction of reality is a profoundly moralistic view of the world, which intrudes into Tolstoy's art from the 1850s onwards.[21] *Truth* and a purpose in art, from the first, were Tolstoy's major concerns. When *Sebastopol in May* was severely mangled by the Imperial censor, Tolstoy noted in his diary: 'I wish, however, that Russia will always have such moral writers as myself; but I can never be a sugary one, nor can I ever write from the empty into the void, without ideas, and above all without aim. . . . My aim is literary fame, the good that I can accomplish by my writings.'[22]

And this normative approach is evident in almost all of Tolstoy's early writings.[23] The Sebastopol sketches, for example, do not attempt merely to record Tolstoy's impressions of the Crimean War. Rather they can be best viewed (as the censor realised) as attacks on militarism and war in general. Already the *idea* was becoming the focal point of Tolstoy's art. This tendency was pushed even further in later works of the 1850s. *The Two Hussars* (1856), with its direct attack on the new generation, is perhaps the first work to make the underlying point so explicit, while *Three Deaths* (1859) is written almost as a parable in which the central idea stands not merely as a conviction, but as an absolute law with which it is impossible to argue.

However, while it would be a mistake to overlook the strong

polemical, even didactic intention of Tolstoy's early work, we should not exaggerate it. *War and Peace* is an interesting example of the tension in Tolstoy's artistic works between the idea and the realistic principle. Here, more than in any work before it, Tolstoy is concerned with maintaining the psychological truth of life. He conveys life as a process in which his characters appear to be allowed absolute freedom to seek out and to fulfil their destinies. Except perhaps in the Epilogue where Natasha, in particular, is suddenly reduced to a static ideal of family life,[24] Tolstoy's characters *do* seem quite stunningly liberated from authorial intrusion or even invention: the autonomy which Tolstoy allows his characters and the whole of the flow of life is perhaps the corner-stone of his creative genius. None the less, the whole work can, indeed must, also be read as an extended polemic. His aproach to historiography is essentially iconoclastic, while the basic contrast between the aristocracy and the people, with the moral advantage already given to the latter, shows Tolstoy's realism as having an underlying *point*. His treatment of history, though, is not merely iconoclastic. He falsifies the evidence, makes a ridiculous caricature of Napoleon and other leaders he disapproves of, and often descends to the level of publicistics.

*Anna Karenina* reveals the same ambivalence to the depiction of life in his writing. In some ways, indeed, Tolstoy attempts to be more impartial here than in *War and Peace*, and his aloofness from the narrative and the cold objectivity are reminiscent of Pushkin, one of whose short stories had initially given Tolstoy the tone for the whole novel. Certainly, his treatment of Anna, and to a lesser extent Vronsky, is immeasurably more sympathetic than he had originally planned.[25] Nevertheless, one can hardly mistake Tolstoy's intentions — Anna is condemmed to the 'false' St Petersburg world, while Levin and Dolly Oblonsky are more at home in the 'Russian' world of Moscow. Dolly, who stands as the moral centre of the novel, in particular expresses Tolstoy's own horror at Anna's fate, when she is reduced to the evils of drugs, and worst of all, contraception. Moreover, he constantly intervenes in the course of the novel and has no intention of letting his opinions be known. For all its 'fairness', *Anna Karenina* remains a tendentious work, a *roman à thèse*.

By the time he finished this novel Tolstoy was no longer satisfied with such ambiguous approaches to moralism in his work.

The times in which he lived were too extreme for there to be any ambivalence on the part of the writer and after 1880 any pretence of objectivity is, with rare exceptions, abandoned. His tales of the last period, with their parabolic simplicity, are excellent examples of this. The simple naturalism does not disguise the underlying moral messages. His dramas of the period, such as *The Power of Darkness* (1888), are vehemently satirical in their social content and stand, really, as dramatic counterparts to his tracts of the period.[26] Significantly enough, Tolstoy felt more interest in the dogmatic works and it is clear that his aprioristic approach to reality in his publicistics carries over into his *apparently* artistic works of the period. *Resurrection* provides the clearest illustration of this tendency. In some ways, the subject-matter and social background are reminiscent of the two major earlier novels. But such similarities merely emphasise the enormous leap Tolstoy had taken in his representation of reality. The novel is written with intense conviction, not to depict a world, but to denounce it in all its corrupt and corrupting rottenness. All of high society, the Church and governmental authorities are exposed with all the ruthlessness of the propagandist: *ostraneniye* dominates the whole narrative. Obviously, this leads on many occasions to crude irony and oversimplification,[27] but for Tolstoy this was now of no importance, provided he could convey his deep moral beliefs to the rest of society.

Underlying this approach was an exceptionally lofty view of the responsibilities of the artist. This was, of course, the prevailing approach in nineteenth-century Russian society, but in Tolstoy's case it took an extreme and somewhat idiosyncratic form. His views first began to crystallise in the mid-1850s and were provoked by his conflict with the *Contemporary* group. He rejected in the end both the 'aesthetic' and 'utilitarian' wings of *The Contemporary*. The principal spokesman of the former group was the writer Druzhinin, who in response to the demands from Chernyshevsky and Dobrolyubov for more socially committed art, was pushed into a polemical defence of 'art for art's sake'. In the mid-1850s Tolstoy took what might be termed a neutral position, in that his asocial yet morally committed art found favour with neither group. However, as the debate intensified towards the end of the 1850s, Tolstoy too was drawn into the conflict, on the side of the old guard. What he found particularly appalling was the increasingly utilitarian demands of the 'nihilists', which demeaned the very high value which he gave art at this time. In a speech in 1859 (at the time of his break with *The Contemporary*) he specifically rejected the socio-political bias that literature was acquiring, in favour of a more eternal form of art:

> However important a political literature may be, a literature that reflects the passing problems of society, and however necessary to national progress, there is still another type of literature that reflects the eternal necessities of all mankind . . . a literature that is accessible to all and to every age.[28]

As usual in his struggle with the world. Tolstoy takes an anti-historical, absolutist line, and, incidentally, in the last phrase anticipates *exactly* his view of art of the 1880s. Tolstoy turned to former views of art to bolster his position. Whereas the new wisdom of the artist was that he should be a *citizen*, to Tolstoy he remained what he had been to previous generations – a high-priest of a sacred calling.[29]

Tolstoy also looked to the past by taking a fundamentally classical view: literature should be written simply and with extreme clarity. Moreover, he resolved that upper-class art was essentially artificial and corrupt. Not only should the artist write simply and clearly, but he should do so for a specific reason – so that the common people, the *narod*, could understand and appreciate it. The true artist would serve them rather than exploit them by writing for a tiny proportion of the population. He wrote at the time:

> I became convinced that a poem such as 'I Remember the Marvellous Moment' [by Pushkin] or a piece of music such as Beethoven's Ninth Symphony, is less worthy of admiration than Vanka's song or the lament of the Volga boatmen, and that we do not like Pushkin and Beethoven because they are expressions of absolute beauty but because they flatter our hideously overstimulated sensitivities and our weakness.[30]

It was twenty years before Tolstoy finally resolved the con-flicts of the 1850s. In the meantime he continued to write upper-class art, occasionally abandoned literature altogether and sought a new style which would be genuinely accessible to the mass of the people. By the time he had finished *Anna Karenina* and entered the period of his 'conversion',[31] he had worked out his aesthetics of good and bad art which he reiterated in private and public for the next thirty years, principally in *What is Art?* (1898). We can now consider these aesthetics, which even though they only apply explicitly to Tolstoy's last period are implicit in his view of the preceding thirty years.

What, then, for Tolstoy was good art?[32] Firstly, one should have something important to say, otherwise literature becomes mere idle amusement and entertainment[33] — which art, Tolstoy had always condemned as worse than useless. But what was this 'something'? The only permissible themes were the eternal ones, those that elevated man to a higher awareness of life and taught him the underlying moral truths of human existence.[34] Shakespeare was condemned by Tolstoy, for example, because, amongst many other faults, he failed to give an answer to the meaning of life.[35] By this time eternal themes were specifically *Christian* themes: all good art must be permeated by a deep Christian feeling, and the best artists were those that wrote with Christ in their hearts.[36]

Tolstoy again and again returns to this point: there can be no true art without a religious basis. In *What is Art?* he writes: 'In every age and in every human society there exists a religious sense of what is good and what is bad common to that whole society, and it is this religious conception that decides the value of the feelings transmitted by art.'[37] In historical terms, Tolstoy explains the decline of upper-class art by the decline of religion among this section of society. Once the aristocracy had lost its faith, its art became what Tolstoy termed bad art. In a quite staggering manner, Tolstoy asserts that bad art began in the West with the Renaissance, whereas the same process began in Russia with the advent of Europeanisation, *circa* 1700. Conversely, of course, popular art is by definition good art because the people have not yet lost their faith, and their art, however secular in appearance, remains religious. And, of course, if traditional upper-class art was bad enough, then modern, decadent art was almost beyond description for Tolstoy.

It was not sufficient, obviously, for art simply *to be* religious and universal: the underlying truths had to be conveyed and one of the central tenets of Tolstoy's aesthetics was the usefulness of art, in terms of the artist's ability to communicate his feelings to his audience, or in Tolstoy's terms, to *infect* it. Art, therefore, was a kind of moral education for society. Tolstoy remarked to V. I. Alekseyev, tutor to his children: 'The task of art ought to be to bring to life the light of truth, to illuminate the darkness of life and to indicate its true meaning.'[38] Increasingly, he judged art by its usefulness to society: *Anna Karenina* was of no use, while his *ABC* for the peasants was. *What is Art?* again illuminates these ideas most clearly. Here Tolstoy argues: 'If only the spectators or auditors are infected by the feelings which the author has felt, it is art,'[39] and, more centrally: 'Art is a human activity having for its purpose the transmission to others of the highest and best feelings to which men have risen.'[40] The important word to emphasise is *transmission*, because elsewhere Tolstoy does reject *explicitly* didactic art: for example, he criticised Zola, whom he generally admired, for excessive didacticism. Art does not teach, but communicates.

But *how* was the artist to 'infect' his audience? One of the central requirements was sincerity: he considered sincerity of thought as the highest criterion of good art, followed by sincerity of expression.[41] Frankness and openness were also highly regarded, while clarity and simplicity were considered the main requirements of good style. Constantly, too, Tolstoy insists, somewhat naively, on *literal* verisimilitude and realism. Art was to be simple, plain, logically consistent and rationally lucid. (Tolstoy, in fact, had little to say about artistic technique, apart from these very general demands, because it did not particularly interest him. Indeed, he considered the modern preoccupation with formal aspects of art to be deeply pernicious, given that it was the content that took pre-eminence.) Next came the love of the author for his subject (however that was to be assessed!) and only then technique.

Such then were Tolstoy's main conditions for good art. Bad art, generally speaking, is the antithesis of good art in Tolstoy's somewhat simplistic scheme of things, but a couple of points should be high-lighted. A lack of moral centre he considered especially reprehensible. In an article of 1899 on Maupassant, for example, he reproaches the otherwise admirable writer for falling into the prevailing modern tendency of ignoring moral questions in his work. Shakespeare, in particular, received all Tolstoy's fury for his seeming lack of convictions or interest in eternal moral and religious issues. 'Drama', according to Tolstoy, 'should serve the elucidation of religious consciousness', and it was precisely this that Shakespeare had failed to do.[42]

In the same article, 'Shakespeare and the Drama' (1906), Tolstoy reveals his abhorrence for Shakespeare's style as well as his content. His art was the antithesis of everything Tolstoy now advocated and he launches into a savage attack on *King Lear*, incidentally revealing all the inherent naïveté of his over-simplistic view of literary realism.[43] In the play, he argues, there are too many elements which are incredible and fantastic, and so an audience could not possible be 'infected' by large sections of it. He dislikes Shakespeare's fondness, as he sees it, for exaggeration, maintains that the characters do not speak in a language which is peculiar to them (which is unrealistic) and that, in general, the language is too 'poetic'. Here Tolstoy makes it all too obvious that he found great difficulty in accepting any literary conventions which were not those of nineteenth-century realism, and that he had a very conventional view of drama, which consisted in the belief that a good play simply presents an illusion of reality so that the audience could share the feelings of the characters and, therefore, the author. Any imaginative boldness, metaphor, free expression of emotions were equally taboo.[44]

Although Tolstoy tended to dismiss most accepted art as 'long-winded rubbish', he did find some past examples of literature worthy of being considered good art, and it is quite revealing to glance at Tolstoy's literary preferences. Medieval art is admired for its religious basis, its simplicity and universality, as well as for the modest anonymity of its authors. Classical art stands even higher. Quite apart from its pre-eminent stylistic virtues of simplicity, restraint and rational clarity, it also, in Tolstoy's view, had the noble effect of elevating its audience and inspiring in it the higher feelings of life.[45] Somewhat surprisingly, Tolstoy also found good qualities in Romanticism, in that, despite its lack of restraint and irreligious basis, it did at least have certain high aspirations and qualities. Similarly Tolstoy always spoke well of Lermontov, primarily for the elements of *seeking* which are implicit in all his work: indeed, Tolstoy considered that Lermontov had the greatest influence on him of all Russian writers.[46] Other ninteenth-century authors escaped Tolstoy's condemnation of upper-class art — Grigorovich and Turgenev for being the first to give realistic portraits of the peas-

antry, Tyutchev for taking a serious attitude to his art and Zola
for showing the common people in a true light.

His particular 'dislikes' in art are also highly significant.
Very often in reading Tolstoy's conversations one has the feeling
that he regarded the very medium of poetry to be largely bad
art. Why write in verse, he would ask, when prose was so much
more comprehensible? Even Pushkin's best work, Tolstoy argued,
was his prose.[47] Modern art, that is the art of the last two decades of the nineteenth century, the Symbolists, Decadents and,
in painting, the Impressionists, were dismissed totally by Tolstoy
as bad art. The Symbolist Bryusov, for example, earned the description of a 'decadent, a spiritual degenerate' and the whole
movement he saw as a symptom of the general decline of Western
civilisation. In the Impressionists, in the manner of a Tula
peasant which he reserved for such occasions, Tolstoy could see
nothing but 'naked women'.[48] Modern music was no better — it
was artificial and fashionable, and that was all. As we have already
seen, he preferred peasant songs to Beethoven, and, obviously,
*a fortiori*, Wagner.

Tolstoy did not dismiss all post-realist art so obdurately
simply because he was aesthetically conservative, dogmatic and
puritanical — although he certainly was all these. No, his deliberate lack of comprehension of new movements in art was based
on the aesthetic theories already discussed. More important,
however, were the *social* factors which Tolstoy saw implicit in
such art and which occasioned his great disgust. We can now
return to Tolstoy's basic understandings and consider them
from this point of view.

Tolstoy rejected upper-class art not simply because it was not
religious, simple and natural, but also, and perhaps most importantly of all, because it was not universal, in that it appealed to a
very small privileged section of society. Its greatest crime was
that it was based precisely on the exploitation of those who
produced the only true art, and the very wealth that allowed
upper-class art to be created — the people. *What is Art?* begins
with a powerful and vivid account of the time, energy and money
Tolstoy saw as being wasted in the service of this kind of art
and it is a theme to which he constantly returns.

This type of art, then, is the very essence of bad art. Instead
of uniting all mankind by its appeal to all that is highest and
most universal it appeals to the basest instincts of the effete,

wealthy few, and obviously divides man from man. No, the only possibility for good art for Tolstoy was that produced either by or for the mass of the people. The central ideas of his later aesthetics is precisely that uttered in his speech of 1859. Good art must be accessible to all. All Tolstoy's later rejections of the Decadents and others are based on these principles. A Russian peasant would not understand such art, so it is, by definition, bad art. At one point he comments: 'Literature must attain such simplicity that laundresses and door-keepers could understand it.'[49] And, of course, such art will unite people, heal the divisions in society, and this too is a central aim of art.

Much of what Tolstoy says about art in these last years seems to be a rejection of art — certainly of the art that most readers of literature consider to be the finest products of Western civilisation. Few would agree that Shakespeare, Dante and Beethoven are not true artists, or that *Anna Karenina* is a worthless novel. Often it seems that his laudable desire that art should be accessible to all does lead him to gross absurdities. Yet this bizarre result was not the product of a grim puritan who in reality denied the value of art as such. On the contrary: Tolstoy dismisses so much of contemporary and earlier art precisely because of his intensely moral approach to this activity. Despite all his equivocations and ambivalence, Tolstoy belongs to the central line of nineteenth-century Russian thinking on art, whereby it was viewed not in isolation from society but as intimately and ineluctably interwoven with the social fabric. In other words, Tolstoy rejected upper-class art because he concluded that such art betrayed the immense responsibilities he and others placed upon it. Instead of improving society, ameliorating the lot of the oppressed peasantry, it pandered to the tastes of the luxuriating few. The art of the *fin de siècle* was the ultimate and fullest flower of this parasitic growth.

His conversations and publications on art of the last thirty years should not be viewed, than, as a rejection of art, but as a mighty, if vain, attempt to return art to its roots, to make it a vital part of the progress and future of mankind. In *What Then Must We Do?* Tolstoy sums up precisely what is the basic function of art in human society in his view: 'Since man existed, true art which was highly esteemed had no other purpose than to express man's vocation and welfare. Always till recent times, art has served the teaching of life.'[50] The 'recent times' have seen a

decline in this moral function of art and it is against this that
Tolstoy had struggled almost all his creative life. Towards the
end of *What is Art?* Tolstoy gives in brief both his whole
aesthetic and what he considers the role of art to be in the
future:

> Art is not a pleasure, a solace, or an amusement; art is a great
> matter. Art is an organ of human life transmitting man's
> reasonable perception into feeling. In our age the common
> religious perception of men is the consciousness of the
> brotherhood of man — we know that the well-being of man
> lies in union with his fellow-men. True science should indicate
> the various methods of applying this consciousness to life.
> Art should transform this perception into feeling.
>
> The task of art is enormous. Through the influence of real
> art, aided by science, guided by religion, that peaceful co-
> operation of man which is now maintained by external means
> . . . should be obtained by man's free and joyous activity. Art
> should cause violence to be set aside.[51]

Tolstoy could not have accorded art a higher destiny, for the
setting aside of violence had become the key to his view of life,
which we may now consider.

Certain basic tendencies should be highlighted. The central
idea is the quest for truth: in a sense, it could be argued, as
Lampert has,[52] that truth is the hero of Tolstoy's novels — certainly Pierre and Levin strive after this more consistently than
anything else. And, of course, in the treatises and parabolic tales
of the last thirty years of his life, Tolstoy is ultimately concerned
with this single quality which, for him, always remained dis-
coverable. Tolstoy was almost obsessed by the need to uncover
the truth beneath the conventions and illusions of society.
Similarly, from his earliest years he was obsessed with the need
for sincerity, both in his own life (as in the instance where he
showed his wife-to-be his shockingly private diaries) and in the
lives of his characters. Anna Karenina, for example, suffers precisely because she is so sincere about her motives and emotions,
whereas her brother Stiva escapes unharmed because he is prepared to lie and deceive. Levin, too, cherishes his sincerity above
all. Tolstoy, like his autobiographical hero, has been most aptly
characterised as a latter-day Alceste.[53]

Insincerity was unfortunately deeply characteristic of the modern world, especially in the bourgeois and upper-class worlds which he flayed so mercilessly in his last years. Against their easy self-deceptions and hypocritical immorality he placed an absolute, eternal morality. Tolstoy tried to ignore the modern world, and dealt instead with what he regarded as more fundamental human issues — the family, love, religion and death. He was, in this sense, the least 'social' and topical of nineteenth-century Russian writers. He dealt with man not so much as he was in the modern world, but as he ought to be: the basic opposition of all Tolstoy's arguments is between man's law, which he rejects, and God's Law.

Tolstoy approached the world in this anti-historical manner because he did not really believe in progress. Human life seemed unchanging and so the problems that faced him and his contemporaries were not 'topical' — the women's question, crime, nihilism and so on — but those that had confronted man throughout his history. He stood outside his own time and condemned it from the distance of Yasnaya Polyana, and from the starting-point of the values of other times. If one were, however, to place Tolstoy more exactly in historical terms, then he appears more a product of the eighteenth century than of the nineteenth — as in his deism, love of the country and opposition to the nineteenth-century metropolis, his utopian, even arcadian hopes. His attitude to the propagation of knowledge must also be seen as intrinsically that of the Enlightenment. Like the *philosophes* he attempted to popularise knowledge, to lead it back from the over-specialisation of the modern era to its popular roots. So too, his own approach to knowledge is essentially that of the eighteenth century in his ultimate reliance on rationalism. There is almost no Romanticism in Tolstoy's work (with the exception of his view of the peasantry). Instead he approached Romantic beliefs with the power of his reason, and attempted to destroy them. Even in his discovery of God there is no élan or mysticism. Rather he insisted that his God was one that was amenable to reason: indeed, he rejected precisely those aspects of established religion which offended his intellect.

Tolstoy stood apart from his own times in other ways. He was a sectarian, not a builder but a dissenter. Although Tolstoy did offer some positive alternatives, more often it is easier to establish what Tolstoy did not wish for. He preferred, that is, to condemn and could offer only the most generalised answers to the problems he discerned so clearly. In particular, he rejected all those who, in his view, sought to alienate the people from their own labour — the doctors, scientists, lawyers, teachers and intellectuals in general. Tolstoy believed, quite sincerely, that the peasants knew more that was worth knowing than the intelligentsia, and while the notion of the superior wisdom of the people was popular throughout nineteenth-century Russia, Tolstoy again took it much further than his predecessors.

While dissent, even subversion, may be considered healthy and desirable, certain serious reservations must be made. So intense was Tolstoy's rejection of the world that a frightening minimalism (as in his views of art) emerges. Tolstoy ultimately taught that this life is worthless — however much he may celebrate it in his artistic writings. And even in his advocacy of Christian love one senses that he was not moved by charity but by a cold rationalism and logical quest for truth. Gorky was especially aware of this side of Tolstoy. In a brilliantly acute memoir he wrote: 'Leo Tolstoy does not love men; no, he does not love them. The truth is that he judges them, cruelly and too severely,' and later: '. . . He is not a sincere person, he is exaggeratedly self-preoccupied, he sees nothing and knows nothing outside himself. His humility is hypocritical and his desire to suffer repellent.'[54] Tolstoy wished to save *himself* above all else, and for all his anguished analyses of contemporary evil, he remained concerned principally with his own soul and its salvation. Moreover, he set such impossibly high standards for his fellow-men (to which even he did not measure up) that he was bound to lacerate their weaknesses rather than have compassion for them. Ultimately one is forced to agree with Gorky, and other critics, that Tolstoy was not a loving, and certainly not a forgiving man: his morality is that of the Old rather than of the New Testament.

Significantly, as Tolstoy notes in his *Confession* (1882),[55] his only early belief was *self*-perfection — in a period of intense altruism and desires for the amelioration of the peasants' lot. While others looked to the improvement of society Tolstoy, fired primarily by self-disgust, wrote his 'Rules of Life' and resolved to work harder, to make something of *himself*. Throughout the 1840s he would draw up regulations for himself, concerning mainly his moral and religious behaviour. Usually he broke them fairly promptly.[56] Equally frequently, he would

castigate himself for *achieving* nothing. Self-reproach mingled
with self-aggrandisement — as it was to throughout his long
struggle towards the self-perfection he desired but could not
achieve: the life within him proved stronger than his will to
asceticism.[57]

At the same time Tolstoy was studying law and philosphy
and beginning to write, and other wider concerns came to interest
him. Already he began to show a deeply anarchistic strain in his
ideas which, in part at least, derived from his profound egotism.
Through his reading of Rousseau (which he declared he might
have written himself, so closely did it correspond to his own
ideas) he began to attribute all human evils to a corrupting
society. In his natural state man was good. By the mid-1850s he
was able to declare: 'All governments are alike in their extent of
good and evil: the best ideal is anarchy.'[58]

Tolstoy had always felt a close kinship with nature, which was
dramatically reinforced by his sojourn in the Caucasus at the
end of the 1840s. His belief in the 'natural man' was intensified
by the same majestic grandeur that had impressed the previous
generation of Russian writers, in particular Lermontov. The
Caucasus to him represented *real* life, far from tainted civilisation
which he had already come to despise. This contrast between a
more 'real' natural life and an 'artificial' civilisation was to remain
life-long. Again his belief in the eternal, natural law ties him very
closely to his eighteenth-century heritage.[59]

Wherever he travelled in Russia and Europe in the 1850s
Tolstoy constantly remarked upon the evils of civilisation. He
disliked Moscow, and St Petersburg all the more: he never stayed
in either place longer than necessary. France, in particular, and
Europe in general merely reinforced these earlier impressions of
the artificiality and unnaturalness of modern city life.[60] All of
modern life, indeed, seemed intolerable in the 1850s. Tolstoy's
more specific social views of the 1840s and 1850s were rather
more ambivalent. A case in point is his view of serfdom. By the
1840s most members of the Russian intelligentsia were united
in the view that emancipation of the serfs was the first priority
for social improvement, whatever their different motives were.
Even the government was forced to admit that emancipation in
some form was now inevitable.[61] At first Tolstoy was not
entirely persuaded: he was appalled by the wretched state of
the peasantry, but did not attack serfdom as such. Later, in his

*Reminiscences*, he noted: 'The idea that the serfs should be liberated was quite unheard of in our circle in the forties. The hereditary ownership of serfs seemed an indispensable fact of life.'[62] And at the time he commented: 'It is true that slavery is an evil, but an extremely *nice* evil.'[63] None the less, even in the 1840s Tolstoy endeavoured to improve the material lot of his own serfs. His efforts though were met with inertia and suspicion, so Tolstoy abandoned his efforts in disgust and looked for other channels for his youthful idealism.

One such avenue was army service, and here too we see contradictions and vacillations in Tolstoy's opinions. He first decided to join the army in 1848, to help put down the Hungarian rebellion, and quickly involved himself in army life. For almost the first time he felt fully satisfied with the action and *purpose* his military career gave to his existence. His enthusiasm continued for a number of years: at the onset of the Crimean War, seeking greater involvement, he asked for a transfer to the centre of action. But it was there that he first realised and exposed the grim futility of both the heroism and slaughter he encountered. All his work of this period met with serious censorship problems because of Tolstoy's explicit anti-militarism. He calls for more humane and efficient methods in the army, the abolition of slavery and corporal punishment.

But, of course, the Imperial government would hardly have agreed with Tolstoy's view that war was the greatest crime of all and so once more in frustration, Tolstoy turned elsewhere for a central belief. The family became one of the central concerns of his thinking. To Tolstoy it appeared at this stage one of the surest ways of achieving what was becoming one of his principal aims – the overcoming of the purely *self-ish*. His advocacy of the traditional family was also, though, a response to the social mores of the intellectual world he encountered for the first time in the mid-1850s. There the 'women's question', as developed primarily in the work of George Sand, was gaining favour. Tolstoy rejected the view that love was the centre of sexual relationships, but once more turned to the past and argued, especially in *Family Happiness*, for an extremely traditional, even archaic, family life.[64]

For the twin ends of escaping the contemporary Russian world which he already loathed and of rendering his own existence more meaningful, Tolstoy travelled through Europe in the late

1850s. Unlike Dostoevsky Tolstoy approached the countries he visited with an open mind, always endeavouring to learn whatever and whenever he could. In particular, he sought support for his own position in the Russian world, which was already outside the normal categories of Left and Right, or of Westerniser and Slavophil.

On his return to Russia, after the relative prosperity of Europe, he was even more appalled by the backwardness of his own country – the hypocrisy, the inefficiency, the dull inertia of the peasantry. Emancipation was now inevitable and Tolstoy resolved to work hard on his own estates to give his serfs an equitable settlement. At first he opposed freeing the serfs with land, but none the less, inspired by moral guilt, his plans were relatively liberal for the landowning class.[65] Problems immediately developed and Tolstoy, as always in his anger and frustration, cursed both the peasantry and the Slavophils as well for what he considered to be a naive idealisation of the peasantry. But Tolstoy already was realising his own brand of Slavophilism and began to work with the peasants on the land, and even though he still failed to communicate fully with them he persevered. Eventually he signed a petition in Tula advocating Emancipation *with* land – which made him extremely unpopular with the local gentry who were almost unanimously opposed to such far-reaching reforms.[66]

However, the real breakthrough for Tolstoy in his discovery of the moral treasure of the common folk was when he set up his peasant school in 1859. Popular education, on the eve of Emancipation, had become a central topic of debate in Russian intellectual and academic circles and, as always, Tolstoy went his own way. For his times, Tolstoy's views were progressive to the point of subversion. 'Nature', in the eighteenth-century understanding of the term, again acted as Tolstoy's starting-point. Coercion and compulsion were the last things that would develop the thirst for knowledge in his peasants. Instead, the emphasis was on free spontaneity and creativity: they learned what they wanted and Tolstoy offered no rewards nor threatened punishment. As in other areas, Tolstoy sought support in foreign theories for his views which were unacceptable to both wings of the Russian intelligentsia, to say nothing of the official view.[67] While he was not working with his own peasants, Tolstoy continued his travels abroad, meeting the progressive educationalist

Froebel and visiting schools in France, Germany, England and
Belgium. Everywhere he reacted with indignation to the coercion
and conformism of the educational institutions he visited. He,
instead, opened more and more schools in his area, always
attempting to reveal the peasants to themselves, to purge them
of the corrupting forces of civilisation. He tried to show them
that education was not the painful grind it so often was in
traditional schooling, but a precious, even joyous, heritage. Contemporary memoirs certainly attest to the success of his methods.
The teachers Tolstoy hired had never seen such freedom, nor
such enthusiasm for education. One commented on the central
aim of Tolstoy's schools:

> In introducing literacy among the people we were to facili-
> tate, to help the people express their inner essence, to say
> *their own word*, and we were to listen to this word, and not
> inculcate anything of our own. *Civilisation* seemed to Lev
> Nikolaevich a perversion of the healthy life of the people.[68]

All of Tolstoy's early pedagogical experiments were, of course,
directly related to the Emancipation and were inspired by the
spirit of the epoch. The year 1861 was a crucial turning-point,
and Tolstoy, as an active and class-conscious member of the
landowning aristocracy, felt the break with the old order more
intensely than most. It could, indeed, be argued that much of
the rest of his life was an attempt to understand and come to
terms with this change. Levin, in particular, reflects all the confusion and consternation that Tolstoy himself must have felt,
faced with the new social organisations, the rising policital
tensions, and the breakdown of the old order.[69]

His initial reaction was to turn to the peasants, whom he already regarded as the 'source of truth'. When he returned to
Russia in 1861 he summoned his peasants to explain to them
his terms of the Emancipation, which he determined to make
as generous as possible. Now the peasantry became his touch-
stone in all he did: he envied their simplicity, above all, their
apparent ability to live without struggling over the enigma of
their existence. All questions of culture and civilisation were
now to be decided from the viewpoint of the peasants.[70]

Despite all this Tolstoy took little interest in politics as
such.[71] In the early 1860s he married and settled even more

resolutely into the life on his estate. From a distance he viewed the rise in left-wing views and actions (the first attempt on the life of Alexander II was in 1866) with growing alarm and fury. He became ever more traditionalist in his views, and while still disdaining to enter the political debates publicly and openly, he did so covertly and implicitly. The initial forum was his debate over education with *The Contemporary*. Tolstoy's article in the first issue of his journal *Yasnaya Polyana* in February 1862 opened the argument.[72] He, in response to the left-wing theories, argued that not only was it impossible to teach the people, it was unnecessary: instead, popular education should simply try to respond to its needs. To all but Tolstoy this article seemed to be not so much *on* popular education as *against* it. Chernyshevsky replied with a derisive dismissal of almost all Tolstoy's ideas; Tolstoy responded in turn and gradually the basic contradictory conservatism of his ideas emerged. However laudable his insistence on freedom and spontaneity may have been, he was at the same time refusing to raise the people above their existing level – which was precisely the objective of popular education in the eyes of the intelligentsia. Tolstoy criticised universities just as much as popular education, but he reserved the most venomous attack for the student circles: his account of their activities, as Eykhenbaum notes, reads like a government denunciation.

But Tolstoy's fight against the radicals took him much further. As the 1860s wore on and Russian society became even more deeply divided, Tolstoy came to reject even more forcefully the modern world, and the notion of progress as such. For him human life was basically unchanging and the radicals' 'issues' and 'questions' simply hid the real, underlying problems of human existence. Tolstoy discovered Schopenhauer about this period, and once again took from him what he needed – a fatalistic view of human history which reinforced the ideas of predestination implicit in *War and Peace*. *Anna Karenina* takes up and develops the fatalism of *War and Peace*. Life now seems to go on *outside* the course of history. But Tolstoy could no longer ignore modern 'questions'. The emancipation of women, materialist philosophy, the *zemstvo* committees and other modern issues all play a prominent part but are all cast aside by Tolstoy. In any case, he deliberately makes them of less importance than the novel's central issues – private morality and the working out of God's eternal law. It is before *this* that Anna and Vronsky are guilty, and not in the eyes of society whose hypocritical judgements Tolstoy vehemently scorns.

After the relative happiness and optimism of the 1860s Tolstoy's old doubts returned with renewed force. What concerned him now was the question which had perplexed him from the 1840s and which had been submerged by his writing, his educational interests, his marriage and his devotion to his estates and family. Why did he do all this if death awaited him? What was the purpose and meaning to his existence? None of his activities now sufficed and as the 1870s progressed, Tolstoy withdrew more and more into his spiritual life as he sought an answer to the only important question. He read widely, particularly the Idealists – Plato, Spinoza, Kant, Schelling, Hegel and Schopenhauer – but none of them seemed to persuade him that suicide was not the only reasonable answer.[73]

So, having rejected the 'experts' once more, Tolstoy turned whither he had sought hope so often before, to the peasantry, who in the eyes of this latter-day Rousseau were not tormented by the same problem as intellectuals. And so, like many 'repentant noblemen' before him, Tolstoy, through the people, discovered a faith – a belief in God which seemingly stilled all his doubts. The essential theme of all Tolstoy's later works was that the only life worth living was one devoted to God, or as Tolstoy puts it in his *Confession*, 'Live seeking God and then you will not live without God.'

At first Tolstoy turned to the Orthodox faith of his youth and read mainly religious works. He was now convinced that a society without God was inconceivable. But soon he declared war on the 'tissue of lies' of the official Church. Again rationality was his basis for judgement – he found the dogmas and rituals an insult to his intelligence, but, more importantly, he saw the Church's active support for the repressive policies of the state – persecutions, executions and war – as a direct contradiction of what he considered to be the essence of Christ's teachings.[74] Thereafter he reserved some of his most bitter invective for the Church, which instead of bringing the truth of Christ into the world had first perverted and then destroyed it.

Tolstoy sought, therefore, to go beneath the encrustations of the established Church, to discover the true essence of the Gospels, and from his reading of the Bible and the Church Fathers he developed his own basic, ethical system, around which he resolved to lead his life, and to encourage others to follow him. As usual, he resolved to go his own way. What is also characteristic is Tolstoy's minimalism, which we also find in his aesthetics of the same period, in that he reduces all religious teaching to a set of *ethical* principles, abandoning all mysticism, revelations or even the other-worldliness so typical of religion. There is little religious élan in Tolstoy's 'conversion': rather, it is a protracted logical travail. Indeed, Tolstoy managed to reduce all of Christ's teaching to five basic commandments, which are not so much a guide to a spiritual life but *practical* guide-lines for daily behaviour.[75] None the less, Tolstoy had great hopes for them, provided all people would follow them. If so, the whole of the old order would be destroyed, the kingdom of God would be created on earth, and peace would reign between man and man.

So, Tolstoy attempted both to practise and preach the fundamental Christian beliefs which he alone had rediscovered (or so he seemed to think) after two millenia of distortions, falsifications and lies. He sought love and forgiveness, beseeching Alexander III to show clemency to his father's assassins.[76] He visited prisons and lived the life of a practical Christian. Above all he denounced, and to a large extent, renounced a life of pleasure based on the exploitation of others' labour. Tolstoy's striving to asceticism knew no bounds — his views on sexual abstinence became notorious, particularly after his frighteningly passionate vehemence in *The Kreutzer Sonata* (1890). Poverty, peace and accord between men became the greatest virtues. He aimed also at self-sufficiency, making his own boots, consuming as little as possible and constantly dreaming of, and attempting, the abandoning of all his property, despite the justifiable protestations of his wife and some of his children who did not share his ascetic tendencies.

The central tenet was 'Resist not him that is evil'. If this were fully applied in practice, Tolstoy believed, all evils would disappear from the world, and man could begin to live in peace. All the lies of the Church and all the crimes perpetrated by and in the name of the State, stemmed from the refusal on the part of Christian institutions to follow this most subversive and important of Christ's teachings. Yet if non-resistance to evil was the very core of Christianity for Tolstoy, and if it was the belief that was to have the most far-reaching implications in the work of his followers then it was also the most contentious, and the most difficult for Tolstoy to practise. The first major test was in 1891 when famine ravaged the district of Samara. Tolstoy at first advocated that no charity should be collected or distributed as this would be resisting evil. The general public was outraged and Tolstoy, against all his principles, went off to organise the relief-work.[77] For the rest of his life he continued to take part in campaigns on behalf of the persecuted and suffering, the most notable instance being his work for the Dukhobors,[78] but he maintained his *belief* in non-resistance. During the 1905 Revolution, for example, he refused to take sides and condemned the violence of all parties, and a year earlier, during the Russo-Japanese War, he declared that even had Moscow and St Petersburg been taken along with Port Arthur, then no resistance should have been made.[79]

By any criteria the political implications of this doctrine are exceedingly naive. However, many other political applications of Tolstoy's practical Christianity in the last thirty years of his life are extremely cogent. For the first time in his life Tolstoy became interested in the wider ramifications of the politics of his own society. The central doctrine of Tolstoy's political views of the last period was a development of his earlier views — his anarchism. Now, more than ever, he regarded all governments, and indeed government as such, as immoral. All of them, of whatever political stance, oppressed the poor for the sake of the rich and his non-resistance to evil was directed principally against this institution. If all men, he argued, realised the kingdom of God within themselves, government would be at an end. The only way to peace was by the withdrawal of support for all governments, which he brilliantly and tersely characterises in *What Then Must We Do?*: 'The government, that is armed men using force.' Throughout this work he destroys all the illusions that had been used to justify the existence of organised society, whether they were theological, philosophical or sociological. A revolution to overthrow the present government is no answer for that would merely replace one system of oppression by another, one legitimisation of power by one possibly even worse.

The anti-militarism of the 1850s was also taken up by Tolstoy with renewed intensity and one of his main targets in these years was war, one of the greatest crimes of so-called civilised society. Again, Tolstoy is absolute in his condemnation. *Bethink*

*Yourselves!* (1904) sums up Tolstoy's approach. War appears before him as an insane nightmare. He begins his essay with an exposé of all its evils, made all the more devastating by the air of estranged non-comprehension:

> Again there is war! Again there is needless and quite unnecessary suffering, together with fraud and a general stupefaction and brutalisation of men.
>   Men who are separated from each other by thousands of miles — Buddhists whose law forbids the killing not only of men but even of animals, and Christians professing a law of brotherhood and love — hundreds and thousands of such men seek one another out on land and sea like wild beasts, to kill, torture, and mutilate one another in the cruellest possible way. Can this really be happening, or is it merely a dream?[80]

Yet Tolstoy does not simply attack and reject the more obviously negative aspects of modern society. Again, in an intensification of his earlier views, he denounces modern society *in its entirety*. Everything connected with existing social forms, whether it be science, education or art, was inevitably based on servitude and exploitation, so had to be rejected. Exploitation of man by man, in all its multifarious forms, was the chief social evil in Tolstoy's eyes. In all his conversations and publicistics of the last years, this was the overriding theme. Exploitation is an evil, but not merely because of the horrifying poverty it occasions. All land belonged to God, and so the people were the lawful owners of the land.[81] Moreover, philanthropic efforts on the part of the rich — that is, the exploiters — was a hypocritical self-indulgence, for it did not substantially improve the lot of the poor. Tolstoy explained his doubts about his own relief work. How can we feed those who produce the very goods we are collecting to feed them, who have always fed us with their labour, he asked, and continued: 'The only sure means of helping the starving is for us to get off their necks.'[82]

*What Then Must We Do?* has as its main theme the exploitation of the urban poor by the rich. Their luxury is a hideous social crime. Tolstoy, in his work on the Moscow census, had attempted to improve the lot of the wretches he encountered, but he soon realised the futility of such actions. It was merely the rich flaunting their wealth in the face of the poor and expecting the latter to be grateful. Tolstoy describes his feeling of shame with typically startling exactitude: 'And I was so greatly deluded that I called "doing good" this chucking away farthings with one hand to those whom it pleased one to select, while gathering thousands from the poor with the other! It is not surprising that I felt ashamed.'[83] The whole capitalist society is evil with the private ownership of property as the corner-stone.[84] All wordly possessions must be renounced by all and only then will the fundamental change which society so desperately needs be possible. Science, medicine and technology, while possibly good in themselves, are at present merely worsening the situation by serving the rich almost exclusively — and art *a fortiori*. Tolstoy appeals to the rich to help the poor, but only in *his* way. That is, they should share the shame which their position in society inevitably entails and help the poor in the only way possible — by ceasing to exploit them, by abandoning their goods and living as true Christians and peasants.

Tolstoy's view of his society is as revolutionary and radical as any of his contemporaries: his sympathies are with the oppressed and he denounces his own class utterly. Most of all he sympathises, indeed identifies with the peasantry to whom Tolstoy, throughout his life, had turned for inspiration. In this last period this basic tendency, like so many others, is intensified and Tolstoy invests all his hopes for the future in the people. *They*, the upper classes and the intelligentsia, have much to learn from the people, and not vice versa. Indeed, he envied them their apparent happiness and inner quiet, and loved the masquerade of dressing up as a peasant, pretending he could become a peasant. In the true Slavophil tradition he believed that the peasants were invested with a superior wisdom. Berlin puts it well:[85] 'Tolstoy believed that the child is closer to ideal harmony than the man, and the simple peasant closer than the torn, "alienated", morally and spiritually unanchored, self-destructive parasites who form the civilised elite.' Accordingly Tolstoy supported neither the government nor the radicals, but he was 'for the people, for the peasant, for the worker',[86] and criticised the intelligentsia for being cut off from its native roots.

Tolstoy, of course, was not so naive as to consider the Russian peasantry spotless. The grim view of their life in *The Power of Darkness* is sufficient evidence of that. Yet in most of his later works, in the *Tales*, in *Resurrection* and in his publicistic writings, the peasantry is always presented as the repository of the true Christian virtues, while the upper classes are effete, exploitative spongers. The peasants, that is, are closer to Nature, to God, and it is their lives which are worthy of imitation.

Tolstoy was, then, close to the Slavophils in his view of the peasantry. He thought that Russia could, and should, avoid the capitalist stage of development, and rejected Western capitalist society. Yet, unlike some of his radical contemporaries, he did not propose socialism, on the basis of the peasant commune, as a future alternative,[87] but a return to primitive Christianity of some rather vague, anarchistic variety. And this is the central weakness of Tolstoy's critique of society. That is, however acute his understanding of exploitation under capitalism may have been, he assessed it, as always, on a *moral* basis and failed, or rather refused to take account of the social, economic and political factors that his left-wing contemporaries advanced. Tolstoy did not fully understand capitalism: indeed, for a long time he tried to pretend that it did not exist, that in some way it was not real.[88] Even in his later work he continued to see Russian society largely as he had always done, as consisting of two classes — the aristocracy and the peasantry — and his point of view remained that of the country-dweller, a peculiar mixture of the aristocrat and the peasant. He reflects the profound dissatisfaction, but also the political naïveté of the peasantry — he reflects their protest and anger about what was being done to them, but signally failed to see the causes, or to propose adequate alternatives. The social disruption of Russia after 1861 may have been his main concern, but he did not fully understand what was happening.

Yet one should equally remember that, at least until 1905, many members of the left wing considered Tolstoy a fellow-traveller, and he deserved such a response because of his unrelenting attacks on the Church and government. Equally, he expressed considerable admiration for the radicals and revolutionaries. He strongly denounced the violence of some factions of the left, yet was forced to acknowledge their high ideals, their sympathy for the workers and peasantry, and their striving for a more humane society. He even at one stage argued that the only way to overthrow the government was with bombs and terrorism, as all peaceful, humane methods had failed.[89] None the less, to the last Tolstoy maintained his own attempts to change society,

hurling a stream of polemics and publicistics against the government in the hope that peaceful means would eventually triumph.
Even if, seven years after his death, other methods were employed
to sweep away Tsarist society, Tolstoy had played his part in
undermining the corrupt edifice he had so vividly portrayed and
condemned.

Indeed, throughout his life this had been Tolstoy's forte:
his is essentially a destructive genius. One thought dominated his
whole existence — death — and it was this agonisingly inevitable
final end which drove Tolstoy to shore up his life, in 1878, with
beliefs and hopes in a purpose and meaning to what had become
a futile existence.[90] But even after this, he was not entirely convinced and remained a very pessimistic thinker. There is little
joy or peace in his later works: instead he remained curiously
ill-at-ease in the world, and perhaps tried so hard to convince
others of the truths he had 'discovered' because he needed to
convince himself. Tolstoy's whole life had been devoted to find-
ing the meaning and purpose of it, but perhaps, as Berlin argues,
his vision was too complex to take in a single, comforting belief.
Berlin sums up brilliantly Tolstoy's predicament:

> Tolstoy's sense of reality was until the end too devastating to
> be compatible with any moral idea which he was able to con-
> struct out of the fragments into which his intellect shivered
> the world, and he dedicated all of his vast strength of mind
> and will to a life-long denial of this fact.[91]

Tolstoy's alienation from the official world was also true of
his dealings with the literary world: he never really liked writers,
and critics still less, and only in the 1850s had any close involvement with fellow littérateurs when he joined the most prominent
and most radical journal, *The Contemporary*. At the time the
group surrounding the journal was on the point of breaking up,
during the period of polemics concerning the social function of
art. For a brief period relations between Tolstoy and the journal
were mutually warm. Tolstoy had sent his first work, *Childhood*,
to the journal and Nekrasov, the chief editor, was very happy to
publish it, as well as material from the banned *Military Gazette*.
All of Tolstoy's early works were published in *The Contemporary*.
Tolstoy eventually arrived in St Petersburg in 1855, where he,
the new rising star of literature, was greeted with enthusiasm by

the circle. Everyone was enchanted, especially by his naive candour and striking 'freshness'.[92] In particular, the liberals regarded
him as a potential ally, in the hope that he would restore the
upper-class bias to the journal which was under threat from
Chernyshevsky and Dobrolyubov and the radical, more plebeian
elements they represented.

However, Tolstoy very rapidly became disenchanted with
both wings, as we have seen. For a while he turned to the Slavophils, in the hope that they might prove to be more serious in
their attitudes to literature and life, and began to associate with
Aksakov, Kireevsky and others of the group.[93] Equally quickly,
however, he discovered that they suited his old-fashioned approach to literary practice no better, and their allegiance to
Orthodoxy particularly alienated him. For the rest of the 1850s
Tolstoy sided most closely with the aristocratic liberals still
connected with *The Contemporary*. He became closest to Druzhinin, Botkin and Annenkov, the chief proponents of artistic
disinterestedness and Tolstoy decided to side with them against
Chernyshevsky, whom he detested.[94] Even among this aristocratic group Tolstoy felt the oppressiveness of mere 'convictions',
but he still did not withdraw, despite his weariness of all the
factions of contemporary opinion and, however reluctantly,
continued to argue on behalf of the Druzhinin group, ending
his involvement with his speech of 1859. This speech pleased
no one, and it should, of course, be noted that everyone was as
disenchanted with Tolstoy as he was with them. They all disliked his moralistic approach to literature and were angry that
he spent so much time on activities not connected with literature.

By this time the conflicts within *The Contemporary* had
reached breaking-point and once the old guard had been removed,
the new radicals were free to push for an even more openly
committed brand of literature. Tolstoy was now totally isolated
from the professional world of literature, in which no one shared
his specifically *moral* concerns. Tolstoy turned his back on this
world and devoted himself to education, on which front too he
entered a prolonged polemic with the radicals. Any return to
literature would have been regarded as a challenge – and the
open opposition between Tolstoy and *The Contemporary* was
reinforced by its very scathing review of *The Cossacks*, which
was viewed by them as an implicit rejection of the contemporary
world (which it was). Tolstoy found himself in the early 1860s

without a literary group, without a journal and with almost no support for his views. *An Infected Family* was his reply to the claims that his career was over, and to the radicals in general, but he was not to give a full answer to them until *War and Peace*, with its covert topicality.[95]

Tolstoy, then, joined the anti-nihilist trend of the 1860s, which had been initiated, however inadvertently, by *Fathers and Sons* and continued by Pisemsky, Dostoevsky and others.[96] He reinforced this position by his new choice of publisher, the conservative Katkov who published *Family Happiness*, *The Cossacks*, *War and Peace* and who was to handle *Anna Karenina*. He also became friendly with another conservative, Strakhov, but more significant was his renewed alliance with the Slavophils in the 1860s, which greatly influenced his work on *War and Peace*. Whenever he travelled to Moscow to continue research for his novel, he sought out the conservative Slavophils, Samarin, Yur'ev, and in particular, the historian Pogodin.[97] He welcomed especially the support their views gave him in his continuing battle with *The Contemporary*, the intellectuals and the modern world in general.

The 1870s saw a continuation of the same ambivalence in Tolstoy's relationship with the literary world. During the debate over popular education Tolstoy even published an article in the Populist *Notes of the Fatherland*, which the editor Nekrasov accepted because of Tolstoy's quasi-populist views, but the underlying tendency of the period, in particular in *Anna Karenina*, is Tolstoy's sustained hostility for the intellectuals and, in particular, the radicals.[98] So too, his quest for a new, more popular style marked what was soon to be finally achieved — a total and complete break with the literary world with which, after the brief honeymoon of the mid-1850s, Tolstoy had been more or less openly at war.[99]

Thereafter Tolstoy had as little as possible to do with the literary world which he had never liked and had now officially abandoned. Younger contemporaries visited him on his estate, including Chekhov, Gorky, Korolenko, Veresaev and Gleb Uspensky, but these encounters were very much pilgrimages to the sage of Yasnaya Polyana. Tolstoy's real associates were not writers, but his followers, the pilgrims and the peasants. And it must be noted that he felt much happier teaching them, and learning from them, than he ever had in the 'artificial' and 'false' literary salons which traditionally formed the centre of Russian literature throughout the nineteenth century.

The critical reaction to Tolstoy followed a similar pattern. Initially, *The Contemporary*, which was publishing Tolstoy's work, needless to say responded extremely favourably: he was viewed as their great hope for the future, particularly as there was little interesting new literature published in the depressed years of the early 1850s.[100] *Childhood* was immediately praised, as were all his other works of this period, and his rise to fame by 1855 was unparalleled in its rapidity. The *Sebastopol Sketches*, in particular, received great acclaim for their truthfulness, which in Nekrasov's view was precisely what Russian literature needed at this time.[101] Even Chernyshevsky, in a review of 1856, praised Tolstoy for precisely the qualities which had so impressed Nekrasov, Turgenev and the other critics of the group. He is almost without reserve in acclaiming all Tolstoy's literary merits, in particular, the power of the psychological analysis and the purity of his moral feeling. He too, at this time, had great hopes for Tolstoy's future efforts.[102] As late as 1859 Pisarev, in a review of *Three Deaths*, spoke highly of Tolstoy, again emphasising the profundity of his psychological insights. However, he was also rather critical of the type of hero Tolstoy chose to depict — the lazy, self-indulgent, aristocratic wastrels — and he reproached Tolstoy for not being sufficiently critical of his characters.[103]

What was remarkable about the first critical response to Tolstoy's work, given the almost universally polemical nature of Russian literary criticism after Pushkin, was that he was acclaimed by all shades of opinion. *Childhood* was almost unanimously hailed as a work of genius,[104] while *Sebastopol in December* impressed even Alexander II and his wife, and again received universal praise.[105] Annenkov, Apollon Grigorev, Druzhinin, Aksakov, all enthused about the Army Tales: liberals and Slavophils vied with *The Contemporary* to applaud the striking new writer.[106]

But soon the latter journal began to realise that Tolstoy's unaligned approach to society was not entirely to its liking. After his early success they thought that Tolstoy should make his social commitment much more apparent, but this was the last direction in which Tolstoy wanted to move. *Youth* (1857) was well received, but criticism began to mount, directed both at his content and his style.[107] *Albert* (1858) was a complete flop, while *Lucerne* (1857) perplexed everyone.[108] Almost before it had begun, Tolstoy's literary career seemed to be over: Nekrasov declared in 1856 that much of his thinking was worthy of the conservative *Northern Bee*.[109] Over the next year Nekrasov tried to heal the rift, but increasingly found Tolstoy's stubbornness and vanity impossible, and became more and more critical of his new work.

Tolstoy realised that he had reached a cross-roads in his career and turned to education. When he began to publish articles on pedagogy, the *Contemporary* group continued its campaign to discredit him. In an article of 1862 Chernyshevsky adopts the method, beloved of Dobrolyubov in his reviews of Turgenev and Dostoevsky, of beginning with disarming praise. Tolstoy's liberal methods are very welcome but, unfortunately, most of his more theoretical premises strike Chernyshevsky as ridiculously utopian: indeed, Tolstoy attributes to his peasants qualities which are scarcely human, so perfect do they seem to be. Primarily, Tolstoy, from his absolutist, moralising position, has failed to take account of the factors which seem most significant to the materialist Chernyshevsky: that is, Tolstoy deliberately omits the 'scientific' aspects, the socio-economic roots of the particular situation. In other words, Tolstoy's early anarchism was quickly detected by the more positivist radicals and in his usual polemical style Chernyshevsky was determined to make clear to the wider public the dangerous potential of Tolstoy's ideas.[110]

The next year, Tolstoy re-entered the literary scene with *The Cossacks* and met a very varied reception. In Dostoevsky's *Time*, Polonsky wrote a rather mixed review, while *Notes of the Fatherland* had much to criticise. Annenkov in *The St Petersburg News* was the most enthusiastic of the reviewers. He wrote that the work was 'a capital achievement in Russian literature, able to sustain comparison with the greatest novels of the last decade', and proceeded to praise the brilliant handling of local colour. In private Turgenev and Fet were equally enraptured.[111]

*The Contemporary* thought rather differently and perceptively noticed that the novel was a polemical refusal to accept contemporary European civilisation. It noted that the novel 'is not a protest, but a profound act of non-recognition of everything that has been achieved and is being achieved in literature and in life'. Moreover, the review argues against Tolstoy's view of the artist implicit in the novel. That is, as before, Tolstoy and his ilk should not stand aloof from society but should involve themselves as *citizens*, the same as anyone else.[112] Like Dobrolyubov's *What is Oblomovism?*, *The Contemporary's* review is a rejection of the entire old guard and its 'outmoded' literary attitudes.

Tolstoy had planned *The Cossacks* as the first part of a trilogy, but reacted rather painfully to the implicit view that it was time he wrote something modern or else gave up the literary profession. After the venomous *An Infected Family* he turned to an even greater rejection of the contemporary in *War and Peace*. In the usual fashion of the time he began publishing it in 1865 in serial form. The initial reactions were almost universally negative and it failed to please even those whose opinion Tolstoy still respected. Turgenev remarked:

> The thing is bad, positively bad, boring and a failure.... All those little details so cleverly noted and presented in baroque style, those psychological remarks which the author digs out of his heroes' armpits and other dark places in the name of verisimilitude — all that is paltry and trivial, against the broad historical background of a novel.[113]

The second part, published the next year, fared no better — only Fet gave it support — and Tolstoy, realising that his grand historical edifice was misunderstood, stopped serial publication.

When *War and Peace* finally appeared in its entirety, initial reactions were more favourable. Fet, Goncharov and even Turgenev wrote in private about the novel with great enthusiasm.[114] Annenkov, in *The Herald of Europe*, wrote most favourably. He praises the work's vividness and simplicity, regarding the whole as a brilliant panorama of life. There are some criticisms: like most of Tolstoy's contemporaries, he objects to the intrusion of his theory of history and, in more aesthetic terms, argues that the novel is perhaps too scenic and lacks movement. None the less, the tone of the whole review verges on the eulogistic and he rhetorically asks his readers: 'Is this not really a splendid spectacle from beginning to end?'[115]

Strakhov in *Dawn* also praised the work, and Pisarev, writing for *Notes of the Fatherland*, spoke of its 'truth, unadorned and unadulterated'.[116] However, the considered critical reaction was generally negative. Dostoevsky thought that Tolstoy had done nothing that Pushkin had not already achieved,[117] while Pushkin's old associate, Prince Vyazemsky, was even more abusive, in particular about Tolstoy's deliberate debunking of respected national heroes. In general, military veterans accused Tolstoy of lacking patriotism. Liberals, too, attacked Tolstoy for flaunting the people and accused him of being an aristocrat playing at populism. But the radicals were the most enraged group. Saltykov-Shchedrin declared: 'The military scenes are all falsehood and chaos. Generals Bagration and Kutuzov are made to look like puppets.'[118] Once again, their chief point of attack was Tolstoy's eschewance of topical problems. Even Pisarev accused Tolstoy of this, while also reproaching him again for insufficient criticism of the aristocratic 'wastrels'.[119] In general, they hated his historical philosophy and not just because it offended their aesthetic sensibilities. To them, Tolstoy's determinism seemed 'a philosophy of inertia' and they viciously took him to task for this. Thus War and Peace was called an 'apologia for the satiated aristocracy, for bigotry, hypocrisy and debauchery'; Tolstoy's sympathy for his characters depended 'on a feeling of a certain regret about lost rents', while he viewed war 'as drunken marauders viewed it'.[120]

Tolstoy took these attacks seriously and retreated to his pedagogical concerns. When he began to publish again on this subject he was to fare no better. Between 1870 and 1872 he published his readers as well as writing theoretically on educational methods. As he might have expected, his libertarian and anarchistic ideas were abused on all sides.[121] In particular, Tolstoy was accused of being a reactionary, of rejecting all the advances of contemporary pedagogical theory and practice. Whereas Tolstoy had publicly ignored the abuse of the literary critics, he now took up the challenge and after an initial setback with the local zemstvo committee, attended a meeting of the Moscow Society for the Education of the People. This confrontation proved inconclusive, so Tolstoy continued his battle in the press, publishing an article in Notes of the Fatherland. This in turn was attacked and, as ten years before, a furious polemic ensued, during which Tolstoy was, in fact, defended by the Populist Notes.[122]

Tolstoy's next major encounter with the critics was with the appearance of Anna Karenina. The response was a little warmer than it had been for *War and Peace*. His close associate, Strakhov, praised him eulogistically, while Suvorin and Stasov were almost as enthusiastic, and even Dostoevsky, who disagreed with Tolstoy's hostile approach to the Turkish war, wrote in *Diary of a Writer*: 'Anna Karenina is a perfect work of art, appearing at exactly the right moment, utterly unlike anything published in Europe; its theme is totally Russian.' Turgenev, who was not so enamoured of things which seemed to Dostoevsky quintessentially Russian, was rather less pleased. In 1875 he wrote to Polonsky: 'I don't like *Anna Karenina*, although there are some splendid pages (the race, the mowing, the hunt). But it is all sour, smells of Moscow, incense, of old maids, the Slavophils and the aristocracy.'[123]

But, as usual, the radicals were the most critical: even though the novel was more concerned with topical issues it was, of course, a profound rejection once again of contemporary solutions. The radicals were not slow to sense this, and abusively dismissed the whole ethos of the novel. Skabichevsky remarked that it was 'permeated with an idyllic aroma of nappies'. Anna's suicide seemed to him 'a melodramatic piece of nonsense in the manner of the old French novels, and a fit conclusion to a vulgar love affair between a snob and a lady of Petersburg society with a weakness for frock coats'. Tkachev, in turn, saw the novel as 'devoid of meaning' and thought that Tolstoy had sought to 'degrade public morality'.[124] Ironically enough, as we have seen, Tolstoy would now have agreed with such unsympathetic views of his account of 'how an officer gets entangled with a woman'.

Thereafter, Tolstoy had no time for the critics but they had not finished with him. Most reviews of his newer work in the last thirty years of his life tended to be more or less hostile. Turgenev was among the first to notice the ironic contrast between the gloominess of Tolstoy's work, indeed its potential deleterious impact on the public, and his great stature. Of Tolstoy's *Confession* he wrote in private:

> I read it with great interest; it is a remarkable work in its sincerity, truthfulness and power of conviction. But all of it is based on false premises — and in the end leads to the gloomiest negation of all living human life. . . . It is also nihilism of its own sort. . . . And all the same Tolstoy is about the most remarkable man in contemporary Russia![125]

*What is Art?*, for its equally depressing nihilism, was greeted with
a storm of abuse both in Russia and abroad where Tolstoy was
called a renegade and the enemy of free thought. A few, such as
George Bernard Shaw and the artist Repin, welcomed the work,[126]
but most critics and artists were deeply shocked by Tolstoy's
minimalist aesthetics.

The most sustained attack on Tolstoy in the last period came,
however, from left-wing critics within Russia. Just as they tried
to counter Dostoevsky's enormous popularity of his last few
years with a series of articles exposing the profoundly reactionary nature of his ideas, so too with Tolstoy. This time the matter
was even more urgent, for Tolstoy was not only the most
remarkable man in Russia, many of his ideas *seemed* to coincide
with those of the Populists and Marxists. Mikhailovsky initiated
the new campaign in 1880 with an article devoted to Tolstoy's
recent Popular Tales.[127] Mikhailovsky begins with a relatively
mild critique of some aesthetic points, although even these are
motivated by a desire to refute the ethos of Tolstoy's new world.
Thus, Mikhailovsky comments that the fantastic elements are
rather surprising after Tolstoy's former realism, while he finds
the overt moralism distasteful. Tolstoy's advocacy of passive
acceptance of one's fate, however unjust (as in *God Sees the
Truth but Waits*), is particularly obnoxious. Tolstoy's avowed
aim may be to enlighten the people, to communicate to them
the truth of life, but in reality he keeps them in darkness and
slavery. Mikhailovsky then goes on to reject utterly Tolstoy's
reactionary views on women, according to which they should
stay at home to produce children and feed their families; they
should not attend courses, but will receive all the learning they
need from reading the Gospels.

According to Mikhailovsky, Tolstoy has withdrawn from
life 'to an uninhabited island of his own self-satisfaction'. His
non-resistance to evil and rejection of charity are particularly
reprehensible: he has descended to the worst sort of nihilism in
which he refuses to help the people to improve their lot rather
than 'corrupt' them by introducing 'false civilisation' into their
midst. Tolstoy may claim to love the people, to support their
cause against exploitation, but this brand of conservative Populism is totally at odds with itself: 'But what an amazing muddle!'
Mikhailovsky writes: 'What revolting contempt for life, for the
most elementary and necessary aspirations of the human soul.'

That is, in taking his abstract love of the people to such extreme conclusions, Tolstoy ends up by preaching a continuation of the slavery and oppression the people are consigned to live in.

In the name of progress, then, Mikhailovsky rejects Tolstoy's later ideas as dangerous nonsense. First Korolenko followed this line, and then Plekhanov, in a series of articles in the 1910s. Tolstoy, he argues, is a magnificent writer, a brilliant critic of contemporary evils, but a confused and inconsistent thinker. Above all, and this is the implicit message of all three, his views are socially retrograde, and whatever the *apparent* similarities with left-wing opinions, Tolstoy should on no account be listened to. In the first article,[128] Plekhanov states this basic position. Tolstoy is essentially *outside* the liberation movement, because he has failed to take his views on exploitation to their logical conclusion. He is none the less to be valued as a great writer who exposed social evils, but should be seen as one who never really understood what was necessary to remove them. The second piece, also of 1910, restates this thesis, centring on the 'pernicious' doctrine of non-resistance. Plekhanov's main aim here is to weaken the potential of Tolstoy's influence by showing that his views are logically untenable because he is self-contradictory and inconsistent. Clearly, however, Plekhanov felt that Tolstoy's influence still needed to be fought, for he returned to the subject with even greater polemical direction the next year in his article *Karl Marx and Lev Tolstoy*. Now he rejects the increasing tendency among left-wingers of 'supplementing' Marx with Tolstoy. The two simply cannot be put together, because *philosophically* they are diametrically opposed. He then proceeds to give his fullest dismissal of all Tolstoy stood for. To the end, Plekhanov argues, Tolstoy had remained an aristocrat, always showing the brighter side of his class, even if he did not realise this. Even when he had depicted the peasants' suffering, it was always *moral* torment he was concerned with and not their actual physical hardship. Tolstoy was, and remained, a subjective idealist who had ultimately been unable to transcend the limitations of his class outlook. Plekhanov, of course, was no hack dogmatist and fittingly concludes with a tribute to Tolstoy's great art. This, he argues, has been of immense service to mankind because of Tolstoy's unsurpassed exposure of exploitation: may others, he argues, be inspired by this exposé to remove exploitation forever!

This partial acceptance of Tolstoy by oppositional forces was matched by total hostility from established forces of power. The first important clash was when Tolstoy was attempting to publish his *Military Gazette*. In the end it was not permitted — the army clearly did not favour officers who were too intelligent. A similarly enlightened and humanitarian approach to war imbued the *Army Tales* which Tolstoy based on his own experiences of the Crimean War, and severe cuts were made because of Tolstoy's alleged anti-patriotic sentiments.[129] The truth, as Nekrasov observed, was too much for the Tsarist censorship at such a sensitive time.[130]

Because of his sympathetic treatment of the peasantry in the period of Emancipation Tolstoy earned himself the reputation of a dangerous liberal, even a class-traitor, and within a year he resigned as Arbiter of the Peace. Shortly afterwards, while Tolstoy was away in Samara, his estate was searched, which ultimately led Tolstoy demanding and receiving an apology from Alexander II. Ironically enough, given Tolstoy's deepening conservatism of the 1860s, he had been suspected of dangerous liberalism, mainly because of his advanced educational theories. He had, in fact, been under surveillance for some time, and the Ministry of the Interior later tried to ban his educational articles, considering them a perversion of the fundamental values of religion and morality. In the end, the Minister of Education refused to do this,[131] but it is clear that the authorities were already suspicious of the rebellious Count.

Tolstoy's educational theories were to bring him into conflict with public authority again a decade later during the renewed controversy over public education. As he took his ideas from one committee to another, he felt he was waging war against the entire educational hierarchy. However, this was as nothing to him compared with the threat of a trivial charge which was almost brought against him the same year (1872) concerning a minor infringement on his estate.[132] Again Tolstoy threatened to leave the country, but Russia became habitable when the charge was dropped. Increasingly, however, as the 1870s progressed and Tolstoy's later ideas came more to the forefront of his thinking, he became more and more hostile to established authority. His 'anti-patriotic' attitude to the Turkish War caused the conservative Katkov to refuse to publish the last part of *Anna Karenina*, which appeared separately. And then, after his 'conversion', Tolstoy declared open war against the twin temporal powers of Church and State — a courageous act in such a country in such a turbulent period.

Shortly afterwards the 'Tsar-Liberator' Alexander II was assassinated and Tolstoy entered the public arena as a defender of the basic rights of all Russians. Although Tolstoy was disturbed by the revolutionary violence, in his new spirit of Christian love he sent the new Tsar a letter in which he pleaded with him to love his enemies and show clemency to the assassins.[133] Tolstoy could not send such a letter direct to the Tsar, so he sent it to his conservative friend, Strakhov, asking him to forward it to Pobedonostsev, the Procurator of the Holy Synod. At first Pobedonostsev refused to show the letter to the Tsar. Eventually, however, he received it, and was not particularly impressed. Pobedonostsev replied to Tolstoy pointing out that their respective interpretations of Christ's teaching had little in common. 'My Christ', he wrote, 'is a man of strength and truth who heals the weak, and yours seemed to me to be a weak man himself in need of healing.'[134] Tolstoy was furious, but made no reply.

The next few years saw a continuation of hostilities between the government and the outraged prophet. Tolstoy was already under surveillance as a serious threat to internal security, and the authorities took dim views of his plans to speak publicly at Turgenev's funeral. (The celebrations were eventually postponed.) The same year, 1883, Tolstoy was called to jury service and refused on religious grounds. He was fined 200R and the Minister of the Interior reported that measures should be taken against a writer whose views and actions were 'Undermining the people's confidence in justice and arousing the indignation of all true believers'.[135] Certain measures were already being taken against him, in the form of severe censorship and confiscation of almost all his new works, which continued for the rest of his life. *A Confession* was published in *Russian Thought*, but was immediately confiscated by the police, and only appeared freely abroad — as did most of Tolstoy's later works. In 1885 his wife Sonya attempted to publish Tolstoy's complete works, including those that had been banned, but permission was refused. *The Kingdom of God* was prohibited, and only appeared abroad, while *What is Art?* was so mutilated by the censor that Tolstoy disowned authorship. *Resurrection*, much to Tolstoy's surprise, was published in Russia, but with 497 deletions or alterations.[136] And so it continued. *Hadji Murat*, with its attack on Russian imperialism, was never published in Russia during Tolstoy's life-time, while most of his later articles concerning non-resistance to evil and attacks on the Church and State only received clandestine circulation.

Two artistic works attracted the particular attention of the authorities. Tolstoy had been trying to have *The Power of Darkness* performed. Alexander III, apparently, was quite impressed, but Pobedonostsev, who was outraged by the play's naturalism, considered it a 'negation of the ideal', 'degradation of the moral sense' and an 'offence to good taste'.[137] Under the influence of his chief adviser and arbiter of public morality, the Tsar concurred: the play was prohibited on the eve of the first performance and all copies were withdrawn from circulation. Only eight years later, in 1895, under a new Tsar, Nicholas II, was the play performed. *The Kreutzer Sonata* had a somewhat similar fate. Written in 1889, the work was circulated in manuscript form and caused a storm of controversy. The following year, the censor still could not reach a decision. This time both Alexander and Pobedonostsev agreed that it was a fine work — but the empress was shocked! In the end, under pressure from ecclesiastical authorities, the work was banned, although Alexander finally allowed the work to be published when Tolstoy's wife managed to persuade him that it was a highly moral work which deserved publication.[138]

By the 1890s Tolstoy was maintaining his campaign against established authority on two fronts — the printed word and his practical charity, the most striking example of which was the relief work he organised during the Samara famine of 1891. This caused considerable embarrassment to the government, because of the international appeals Tolstoy made on behalf of the starving peasants, which showed the government's efforts in a poor light. Pobedonostsev once more grossly misrepresented Tolstoy's activities and denounced him to the Tsar in the following fantastic terms: 'Count Tolstoy's appeal is based on the most rabid, wild-eyed form of socialism in comparison to which the pamphlets of the clandestine agitators are milk and honey. . . . He openly preaches social revolution.'[139] The government, while determined not to make a martyr of Tolstoy, began to respond. Articles were published against him in *The Moscow Gazette* (probably on the direct intervention of Pobedonostsev) and sermons were preached that he was the Anti-Christ![140] There was a real threat that Tolstoy might be arrested or exiled. Yet his devastating attacks on Church and State, in the form of articles and books published abroad and circulated in Russia, continued unabated, constantly undermining and subverting all legal authority. He even wrote to the new Tsar, Nicholas II, suggesting that the only sensible thing he could do would be to abdicate!

Tolstoy was not physically touched: the government was clearly afraid of the effect any drastic step would have on both internal and international opinion. Yet they maintained a steady campaign against him, in the vain hope that they might combat his enormous influence. He was constantly watched, spies were planted at Yasnaya Polyana, and official organs of Church and State ceaselessly attacked him. In all, Pobedonostsev was the chief activist, deliberately exaggerating Tolstoy's influence in the hope of getting some positive action against him. In 1890 he had written to Alexander:

> It is impossible to conceal from oneself that in the last few. years the intellectual stimulation under the influence of the works of Count Tolstoy has greatly strengthened and threatens to spread strange, perverted notions about faith, the Church, government, and society. The direction is entirely negative, alien not only to the Church, but to nationality. A kind of insanity that is epidemic has taken possession of people's minds.[141]

Meanwhile, Tolstoy courted martyrdom at every step. Not satisfied with his own activities, he took up the cause of sectarians who appealed to him for help. The Dukhobors, who, Tolstoy helped leave Russia and escape persecution, were the most famous case, but there were many others.[142] The government was furious: Tolstoy had transformed a fairly commonplace local event into an international incident. Then, as over the previous two decades, they acted against Tolstoy, through the campaign of words, but also by recourse to what had now become a familiar tactic — the persecution of Tolstoy's disciples, whom they could arrest and exile with far less anxiety about international repercussions. Throughout the last thirty years of his life he had to suffer this martyrdom by proxy, particularly when, in 1897, at the height of the Dukhobors' campaign, his two chief disciples, Chertkov and Biryukov, were arrested and exiled.

Tolstoy, of course, attempted to intercede on behalf of his followers, arguing that it was *he* they should persecute, and eventually achieved what, in a sense, he had been seeking – a form of martyrdom. By 1900 the Church, long the object of some of Tolstoy's fiercest attacks, which culminated in *Resurrection*, ran out of patience and excommunicated him. A storm of protest followed, but Tolstoy was quite pleased about what was, after all, a fairly painless punishment. For the last ten years the same processes continued. Tolstoy attacked Church and State, they responded, spied on Tolstoy and vilified him in sermons and in the press, and persecuted his followers. But, ultimately, he was now beyond their reach and they could only hope to diminish his appeal. Tolstoy had become an alternative tsar: Suvorin (the editor of *New Times*), shortly after Tolstoy's excommunication, noted in his diary:

> We have two tsars, Nicholas II and Leo Tolstoy. Which is the stronger? Nicholas II is powerless against Tolstoy and cannot make him tremble on his throne, whereas Tolstoy is incontestably shaking the throne of Nicholas II and his whole dynasty. . . . Let anyone lift a finger against Tolstoy and the whole world will be up in arms and our administration will turn tail and run![143]

And so, in the last decade of his life, Tolstoy's influence both within and beyond Russia was feared and attacked by both government and opposition. Through his immense popularity, first as a writer and then as an outraged publicist, he had become a majestic third voice bringing down curses on both houses.

Tolstoy had always been popular as a writer, but it was only after his 'conversion' that he became the world-famous celebrity who so threatened the government. Indeed, his 'conversion' had provoked a moral crisis in his devoted readers: they wrote to ask his advice, to congratulate him, or to insult him. Within a few years his new ideas were already having an enormous impact on the Russian public: as early as 1885 his views had a perceptible influence on society with young men writing to ask whether or not they should serve in the army.[144] Tolstoy spread his ideas partly by publishing cheap editions of his *Tales* and parables, which within six years had sold more than six million copies, while his regular enlightening journal *The Intermediary* flourished despite the governmental suspicion which surrounded it. His more purely artistic works of the period were also enormously popular. The reaction to *The Death of Ivan Il'ych* was extremely enthusiastic,[145] while in the 1890s *Master and Man* sold 15,000 copies in four days, plus 10,000 in another edition.

By the mid-1880s the first pilgrims were arriving to sit at the feet of the sage of Yasnaya Polyana, and the first Tolstoyan communities were set up. Foreign writers too came to Yasnaya Polyana. The publication of *The Kreutzer Sonata* gave an enormous impetus to the spread of what was now known as Tolstoyanism. His mail tripled and correspondents anxiously inquired whether he really desired the extinction of the human race. In a period of intense search for new faiths and hopes, Tolstoy's work became the forum for public discussion. His work grew more and more popular. *The Kingdom of God* was banned in Russia, but by now his 'new word' was so important that it was immediately published abroad. Every summer more and more visitors arrived, including Chekhov and later Merezhkovsky and Gippius, while Gorky also sought Tolstoy out. Everyone, it seemed, wished to listen to his wisdom: he had become the conscience of his times, a prophet who received ample honour in his own country, the arbiter of morals and literary values.

Whenever Tolstoy travelled away from Yasnaya Polyana in the 1890s and 1900s he was mobbed by huge crowds: such scenes had never been seen before in Russia.[146] And his new work merely added to the near hysteria that surrounded his every move. *Resurrection* had a reception which surpassed even that of *Anna Karenina*, and translations were simultaneously published in Germany, France, America and England. His excommunication was met with a storm of protest: he was acclaimed in public for his courageous stance and received hundreds of telegrams and letters from well-wishers.

By this time, his correspondence had reached enormous proportions: in the 1900s he would receive between thirty and forty letters a day from all over the world,[147] and each major publicistic work of the last decade increased the volume of letters addressed to Yasnaya Polyana. Indeed, in the last years of his life, Tolstoy probably had the largest personal correspondence of any man in the world: Tolstoy had become the conscience not only of Russia but of the whole civilised world.

Although his stubbornly moralistic stance on the events of 1905 caused him to lose some support among the radicals and even the liberals, his impact on Russian society and the wider world continued more or less unabated. In 1908 Tolstoy celebrated his eightieth birthday. The government attempted to keep the fuss to a minimum but, despite their efforts, it was the occasion for international celebrations. Tolstoy received 1500 messages of congratulation, including one signed by the English writers Hardy, Meredith, Wells and Shaw. Two years later Tolstoy died, having fled finally from his family and wealth, at the small station of Astapovo. Every heart-beat, it seemed, was broadcast to the world, and huge crowds of mourners arrived to bear witness to perhaps the greatest man of his age, while others marked his death in their countless telegrams.

Tolstoy's immense popularity derived not only from his greatness as a writer and his unflinching moral honesty. It must also, of course, be seen as a product of the disturbed times in which he lived. The last two decades of the Romanov dynasty witnessed in Russia an amazing number of new faiths, cults and movements, each with its own leaders and prophets. It also, of course, saw the rise to power of the Russian Marxist movement. Yet although Tolstoy had his followers and disciples, he seems not to epitomise his age, but to stand above and beyond it, following his own concerns and fulminating against all falsehoods and hypocrisies, the suppression and hardship which surrounded him. By the end he had become part of the past, and Russia perhaps no longer looked to *him* with expectant eyes, even if it had followed his every word and action for the previous two and a half decades. Tolstoy chose to die alone and it was fitting that he did. Despite this, one should never forget the immense stature and influence of one who all his life had struggled against the modern world in the name of permanent moral values and who, at last, was able to be entirely true to his own beliefs.

# Tolstoy: Important Biographical Dates

| | |
|---|---|
| 1828 | Born at Yasnaya Polyana. |
| 1830 | Mother dies. |
| 1837 | Father dies. |
| 1844 | Enters Kazan University. |
| 1847 | Leaves Kazan without taking a degree. |
| 1852 | Joins Army. |
| | *Childhood.* |
| 1854 | Receives commission. |
| | *Boyhood.* |
| 1855 | Serves at Sebastopol. |
| | *Sebastopol in December.* |
| | *Sebastopol in May.* |
| 1856 | *Sebastopol in August.* |
| | *Two Hussars.* |
| | *A Landowner's Morning.* |
| | Leaves Army. |
| 1857 | *Youth.* |
| | *Lucerne.* |
| | Travels in France, Switzerland, Germany. |
| 1859 | *Three Deaths.* |
| | *Family Happiness.* |
| | Organises peasant school at Yasnaya Polyana. |
| 1860–61 | Visits Germany, France, Italy, England and Belgium. |
| 1861 | Quarrel with Turgenev. |
| | Appointed as Arbiter of the Peace. |
| | Resumes school work. |
| 1862 | *Yasnaya Polyana* journal. |
| | Resigns from office of Arbiter of the Peace. |
| | Marries Sofya Andreyevna Behrs. |
| 1863 | *The Cossacks.* |
| | Begins *War and Peace.* |

| | |
|---|---|
| 1865–9 | Publishes *War and Peace*. |
| 1872 | Re-opens school. |
| | *A Prisoner in the Caucasus*. |
| | *God Sees the Truth but Waits*. |
| | *ABC*. |
| 1873 | Begins *Anna Karenina*. |
| | Samara famine. |
| 1874 | *On Popular Education*. |
| 1875–7 | Publishes *Anna Karenina*. |
| 1878 | Great moral crisis and 'conversion'. |
| 1879–83 | Intensive theological study. |
| 1881 | Assassination of Alexander II. Tolstoy appeals to Alexander III to exercise clemency. |
| | *What Men Live By*. |
| 1882 | Buys house in Moscow. |
| | *A Confession*. |
| 1884 | *What I Believe*. |
| 1885 | Founds *The Intermediary*. |
| 1886 | *The Death of Ivan Il'ych*. |
| 1887 | Tolstoyan colonies founded. |
| 1888 | *On Life*. |
| | *The Power of Darkness*. |
| 1890 | *The Kreutzer Sonata*. |
| 1891 | *A Critique of Dogmatic Theology*. |
| | Renounces copyrights and divides property among family. |
| 1891–2 | Famine relief in Samara. |
| 1892 | *A Union and Translation of the Four Gospels*. |
| 1893 | *The Kingdom of God is Within You*. |
| | *Master and Man*. |
| 1898 | *What is Art?* |
| 1899 | Dukhobor migration. |
| | *Resurrection*. |
| 1901 | Excommunication. |
| | Serious illness. Visits Crimea. |
| 1902 | *What Then Must We Do?* |
| | *What is Religion?* |
| 1903 | Protests about pogroms. |
| 1904 | Russo-Japanese war. |
| | *Bethink Yourselves!* |
| 1905 | First Russian Revolution. |

| 1906 | *Shakespeare and the Drama.* |
| 1908 | *I Cannot be Silent!* |
| 1910 | Dies at Astapovo. |

*Works published posthumously*

| 1884 | *Memoirs of a Madman* |
| 1889 | *The Devil* |
| 1898 | *Father Sergius* |
| 1904 | *Hadji Murat* |
| 1908 | *Recollections* |

# 4 Anton Chekhov

In creating his 'new word' Dostoevsky attempted to put an end to 'landowners' literature'. Chekhov's life and work can be read as the final conclusion to this tradition. He had no connection with *The Contemporary* or the 'natural' school; he had little concern with the metaphysical 'accursed questions'; he revitalised the neglected genres of the previous forty years – the short story and the drama – and wrote no novels. Coincidentally his writing career began as those of the 'giants' ended. Dostoevsky died in 1881, Turgenev in 1883 and Tolstoy attempted to abandon his own version of 'landowners' literature' after 1880.

Even Chekhov's background differed from that of other major writers of the period. His grandfather had been a serf, while his father was the owner of a small grocery shop in the provincial town of Taganrog.[1] Chekhov's childhood was gloomy. Later he remarked: 'In my childhood, I had no childhood.'[2] He was obliged to work long hours in the shop and was regularly whipped. His father's religiosity added to the gloom and Chekhov particularly loathed his obligatory duties as a chorister. Yet Chekhov managed to preserve his basic humanity. Indeed, like Belinsky he was to learn from his experiences the same compassion for suffering in the broader Russian life he was later to describe. In 1875 the family's troubles worsened when the business virtually collapsed. Yet this also acted as Chekhov's emancipation. His father moved with most of the family to Moscow and Chekhov was left in charge. His life, despite the increased responsibilities, was now his own and he relished the increased freedom.

Chekhov's education did little to relieve his hardship and for many years he remained one of the least well-educated of Russian writers, never having the advantage of the extensive private education of most of his predecessors. The Chekhov parents, despite their stern regime did at least have ambition for their children's advancement. But the choice of schools available in Taganrog hardly stimulated Chekhov's intellectual curiosity. He first entered the local Greek school (there was a large Greek community in the town). All subjects were taught in Greek and the stern discipline reinforced the general horror he experienced in the year he spent there. Taganrog gymnasium, with its reactionary atmosphere, was little better and against this harsh background Checkhov made little impression.

His later life proved to be his education and Chekhov became a conscientious autodidact. By the age of sixteen he was reading widely, mainly Russian classics and weighty intellectual matter.[3] Eventually he made his way to medical school in Moscow, and medicine acted as the next stage in his liberation from his oppressive background. He saw in it a means of satisfying his humanitarian feelings, while it also offered him a sense of self-respect and personal dignity. Determined not to waste this chance of emancipation, Chekhov became a conscientious and hard-working student.

Meanwhile his wider intellectual horizons were expanding. While in Moscow he spent summer evenings with friends in Voskresensk, and later in Babkino where he met the enlightened Kiselev family. The 'fat' journals were read and discussed, as was Russian literature, while the political and social world also played an important part in their conversations.[4] As the 1880s progressed, Chekhov's own reading reinforced these enlightening influences: scientific journals and books occupied him as much as literature. At the same time he encountered his main literary mentors, Tolstoy and the French naturalists – Zola, Flaubert and Maupassant were particularly important influences, from whom he variously learned the primacy of the moral dimension, a hatred of the philistine world, the colourlessness of everyday life as well as an almost all-pervading pessimism although Chekhov, in his last years at least, was rather more hopeful than his chief mentor, Maupassant.[5]

Chekhov's background was no more advantageous in financial terms. Quite apart from his own needs as a young doctor he had to provide for a large and impecunious family. From his early days as a doctor his professional income was insufficient and he was obliged to publish, at first short humorous sketches, to supplement his income. His main occupation and concern was now making money, accruing enough for himself and his family to survive. He was badly paid in these early years, receiving only five kopecks per line, and only eight a line from 1882 when he began working for the publisher Leykin. He frequently complained about his working conditions, the lack of privacy his crowded family flat afforded, the lack of free time, the sacrifices his low income forced on him. In 1883 he wrote, for example, to Leykin:

> I have a better topic and would gladly have written and earned more, but fate is against me this time. I'm writing under abominable conditions. Before me sits my non-literary work pummelling mercilessly away at my conscience, the fledgling of a visting kinsman is screaming in the room next door and in another room my father is reading *The Sealed Angel* aloud to my mother. . . . Someone has wound up the music box, and I can hear *La Belle Hélène*. . . . It makes me want to slip off to the country, but it's already one in the morning. It would be hard to think of a more abominable setting for a writer.[6]

None the less, with his usual self-discipline Chekhov persevered and sought additional income wherever possible. He augmented his sketches with a gossip column and worked as a part-time teacher.[7] Unfortunately, his medical career was not providing sufficient income for him to work under less 'abominable' conditions. He qualified in 1884, but little regular income ensued. Indeed it was hard even to collect the money due from his patients, although he made efforts that he should not be exploited. By 1885 his medical practice had become relatively successful, but already, and this was to become more and more typical of Chekhov's practice, he frequently treated peasants *gratis*. Constantly, in the first half of the 1880s, he had to borrow money and his literary earnings did not greatly improve the situation. For example, his first collection of stories of 1884, *Tales of Melpomene,* sold for six kopecks per copy.[8]

Slowly, through a combination of hard work, careful management and growing literary fame, Chekhov's situation improved. In 1884 the family was able to rent its first summer dacha, and in 1886 Chekhov began to work for the influential publisher Suvorin, and immediately received twelve kopecks a line! The same year he published his first important collection of stories, *Motley Tales,* and followed its sales with great excitement, even urging Suvorin to advertise it more prominently.[9] The second half of the 1880s shows a similar pattern. Through prodigious hard work Chekhov gradually ameliorated his position, but his working conditions remained difficult, and he frequently cursed his lot as a struggling writer. His family were able to move into a new flat but their living conditions were still far from luxurious. In 1887 Suvorin gave him an advance of 300R, which delighted Chekhov. His stories were now selling quite well but money remained scarce and his family flat as crowded and noisy as ever. *Ivanov* (1887) brought him 600R, while *The Bear* (1888) was already bringing in a regular income, but imminent financial ruin faced him and, in turn, Chekhov was forced to turn out stories, one-act vaudevilles and other work at a furious pace. As the decade drew to a close, however, his literary work and fame was gradually easing his burdens. *The Steppe* (1887) alone brought him 1000R, the Pushkin Prize in 1888 another 500R, the second version of *Ivanov* in 1888 another 900R, and by this year he could count on about 3–4000R per annum. Debts there still were but Chekhov, entirely through his own efforts, was able to write less and still survive.

The early 1890s marked a considerable improvement, and in 1892 he was able to fulfil a long-cherished dream when he bought his estate at Melikhovo for 5000R. By this time Chekhov, though still far from wealthy, earned considerably more than most contemporary writers.[10] Even so, he still had to work hard and the bitter complaints about his lot as a 'literary proletarian' continued throughout these years. A typical letter was one to Suvorin in June 1892:[11]

> My soul longs for space and height, but perforce I must spend a narrow life over scoundrelly roubles and kopecks. There is nothing more banal than bourgeois life with its pennies, its victuals, its absurd talks, and its useless conventional virtue. My soul has wilted from the consciousness that I am working for money and that money is the centre of my activity.

It was only by the end of the decade (only four years before his death in 1904) that Chekhov was comfortably provided for. He was not rich, nor did he particularly desire to be, but at least he could allow himself the luxury of writing little, and writing well. His royalties now were large: *The Seagull*, for example, brought 1300R, and he was able to buy a house in Yalta, even though he still had to borrow some money to do so. In 1899 he signed a contract with the prominent publisher Marx which, although not particularly to Chekhov's advantage, was sufficient for his needs. Even so, he still had to write for his living and in 1903 had to renegotiate his contract with Marx. By now Chekhov was the most popular living writer (with the exception of Tolstoy) and in the last year of his life he was at last handsomely rewarded for his efforts, receiving 1000R for the reprint rights of *The Betrothed* (1903) and 2500R for *The Cherry Orchard* (1904).

Given the difficult conditions under which Chekhov laboured, writing played a rather different role in his life than it did for many of his predecessors. Unlike most writers before him he had no early ambition to be a writer and when he became a serious artist in the late 1880s it was as the result of a number of accidents. He had begun writing as early as 1877, but had an extremely casual attitude to his 'art': he wrote for a specific, very middle-brow audience and merely responded to what his public wanted. Writing, as he later remarked to Korolenko,[12] was part amusement, part a means of completing his education, and nothing more. Gradually, however, Chekhov was drawn to the life of Grub Street: medicine remained his vocation, but he began to create his own artistic standards and demands. By about 1883 Chekhov reached something of a turning-point. The prime cause was the frustration he felt at the rigidity of Leykin's terms — never more than one hundred lines.[13] Chekhov, moreover, was beginning to add serious touches to his basically light-hearted sketches and Leykin did not approve of this. Yet he still had not thought of making literature his profession: he simply wanted a little more freedom. Moreover, apart from chance encounters with Leskov he knew no serious writers and received no encouragement to develop his talent. And, in any case, money remained his first priority.

This situation was to change dramatically in the mid-1880s. In 1885 he went to St Petersburg and met a number of famous writers[14] who all praised the great talent they saw submerged beneath the hack-work. Chekhov recognised that he had developed far beyond the requirements of Leykin's sort of publication and resolved to make himself more his own literary master. The following year he began to publish in Suvorin's

*New Times*, a much more serious journal and, freed of the restrictions on length and subject-matter as well as the necessity of meeting deadlines, Chekhov glimpsed the possibility of literature as a serious career. For the first time his real name appeared under a story, *The Requiem* (1886), his first story to appear in *New Times*.

Of course, Chekhov did not change his approach to writing immediately. That same year he was to publish 116 pieces! Much of what he wrote was still hack-work and literature was still a useful way of adding to his earnings. A letter from Grigorovich which acclaimed Chekhov as the most promising of the emerging writers, provided he worked more conscientiously, made a profound impact. He had been walking around in a daze since he had received it, Chekhov wrote, and proceeded to describe the extremely lowly nature of his attitude to literature:[15] 'If I do have a gift that warrants respect, I must confess before the purity of your heart that I have as yet failed to respect it.' All his associates had no respect, he continued, either for their work, or his. Moreover, as a doctor he could not possibly devote himself to literature. He then went on to describe his working methods:

> The only reason I am writing all this is to justify my grievous sin in your eyes to some small degree. Until now I treated my literary work extremely frivolously, casually, nonchalantly, I can't remember working on a *single* story for more than a day, and *The Huntsman,* which you so enjoyed, I wrote whilst I was out swimming. I wrote my stories the way reporters write up fires: mechanically, only half-consciously, without the least concern for the reader or myself.

In the future, he humbly suggests, perhaps he will find time to write something more serious.

Now at last Chekhov began to change his approach. Given the eulogy of the famous Grigorovich, who had been an associate of Belinsky, Nekrasov, Turgenev and all the other stars of past decades of serious Russian literature, he determined that he would no longer waste himself. Serious doubts remained – but he would at least try to make something of himself. The next couple of years saw a great increase in this seriousness, which brought its own problems. As his fame increased, Chekhov felt a growing sense of responsibility. He tried, that is, to become the serious writer that everyone seemed to expect him to be, to deal with social problems, to write less (he wrote 'only' 69 stories in 1887) and, most important of all, to produce a 'large' work.

Various attempts were made: *Ivanov* appeared – although Chekhov wote it in ten days – *The Steppe* was his attempt at a major prose work, and in 1888 he wrote only nine tales, all of which were longer pieces. Yet Chekhov became increasingly self-critical. Was he really worthy of this acclaim, was he able to produce something really important, how could he answer the frequent charge that he was wasting his talent and not taking a committed position on the pressing social problems? Chekhov descended into pessimism and self-reproach. He was, he felt, merely at the beginning of his literary career and could not consider himself a major writer. Indeed, he still regarded medicine as his 'legal wife' while literature was a 'mistress' to which he devoted whatever time he could. Even though he had now ceased working for trivial journals and wrote more seriously, he still complained that he had insufficient time to do his serious literary work properly.

Before, Chekhov had known his reason for writing – for money – but this was no longer sufficient motivation, however much he still needed additional income. Given the more elevated demands others, and now Chekhov himself, placed on his work, he spoke of his writing with contempt or with modesty, believing he would be forgotten in five or ten years' time. By 1889 he had reached a fundamental turning-point, even crisis, in in his career. He could no longer carry on as he had, his attempts at a novel or new dramatic forms in *Ivanov* and now *The Wood Demon* (1889), were far from totally successful, while his one-act vaudevilles, however 'fresh', were frankly pot-boilers. At times Chekhov thought of abandoning the whole enterprise. Success and fame bored him, not because he had grown indifferent to it – on the contrary – but because he could not see it leading anywhere. His writing, indeed his life in general, lacked direction or purpose. Chekhov did not quite understand the causes of this disenchantment, but he knew that his attitude to his present and past writing was unsatisfactory. By the end of the year, his disenchantment with his work was complete:

Sketches, feuilletons, vaudevilles, tedious stories, and a great mass of mistakes and absurdities, tons of used-up paper, the Academy Prize, the life of Potemkin — and yet not one line which in my eyes has a serious literary value. There was a mass of forced labour, but not a minute of serious work . . . I want passionately to hide myself somewhere for five years and engage in a serious detailed work . . . I must write with all my conscience, with feeling, with gusto, write not five folios a month, but one folio in five months.[16]

Like the old, defeated doctor at the end of *A Boring Story*, written in this year of profound pessimism, Chekhov lacked any central idea to unite all these 'tons of used-up paper'. At times he positively avoided literature and immersed himself in his other work. But this too no longer sufficed and so he did hide himself, not for five years, but in his expedition to Sakhalin in 1890. This proved to be his salvation as a writer. Neither Chekhov's friends, nor Chekhov himself, were entirely sure why he undertook this long and arduous journey, but one reason does seem to be his quest for a more purposeful direction to his life and writing.

And although he did not immediately transform his art, most of his later stories, which became more serious, less frequent, and above all, more committed reveal a changed approach to literature. *Ward 6* (1892) is perhaps the first work to reveal this greater social awareness which Chekhov learned in the penal colony, and then by way of contrast, in the immensely more civilised world of Western Europe. Korolenko, in particular, perceived this fundamental change in Chekhov's work:[17] all gaiety was finally abandoned, almost as if Chekhov's adoption of a more serious attitude to his art forced him to look seriously at life for the first time. Although Chekhov was never to become an impassioned social critic, he clearly had adopted a much more serious attitude to his writing, both in terms of his approach to reality and in terms of the part it now played in his own life.

At the same time, he realised that writing in itself was insufficient. Practical social work too was needed. Above all, he felt he had to do something socially useful: that is, he now was able to see Russian reality much more clearly and, accordingly, he depicted it critically, but other activities were needed to improve the awful conditions he had seen in Sakhalin and now saw all around him. So, just as he presented the grim conditions of *Ward 6*, or the brutalised life of the peasantry in *The Peasants* (1897) and *In the Ravine* (1900), at the same time he attempted to ameliorate these conditions by his work as a doctor, member of *zemstvo* committees and his other numerous philanthropic activities. Writing now had a direction in his life by being incorporated into a wider sphere of activities.

Doubts, of course, remained. *The Seagull*, for example, had a disastrous first night in 1896 and Chekhov resolved never to write another play, and asked Suvorin not to publish the work. In 1898 he wrote to Lydia Avilova that he experienced a strange 'aversion' whenever he wrote or thought about writing,[18] and in 1900 he regarded *The Three Sisters* as 'dull, verbose and awkward'.[19] Equally, he maintained and even increased his philanthropic work, which at times became more important than his writing. The doubts probably plagued Chekhov to the end, but these uncertainties were as nothing compared to the agonies of the late 1880s, and for the last decade and a half of his life Chekhov was able to work calmly and with increasing confidence, now relatively sure that his writing, augmented by other work, was serving some purpose in society.

Chekhov's theoretical views on the role of art in society follow a similar pattern of development. Before the mid-1880s he expressed few systematic views on art. Only when he began to take his own writing more seriously did he take a more considered view of art in general. Immediately he adopted a serious approach to the artistic enterprise. In 1887, for example, he declared that 'Its [literature's] aim is the truth, unconditional and honest', and the artist 'is a man bound by contract to his sense of duty and to his conscience'.[20] A writer, therefore, should work hard and respect his talent, for he does have the responsibility not to betray his gift. Chekhov rejected in the same year external restrictions on how a writer should use his talent, that is censorship — again he argues, a writer's own *conscience* is the best guide to what and how he should write.

However, in this period, Chekhov was much more concerned with the how rather than the what of literature: in this area he emphasises precisely the same virtues as Pushkin — objectivity, veracity to life, brevity and the absence of clichés.[21] Also, he counselled against undue emphasis on social and political themes. Under attack by the radical critics for his apparent lack of interest in such aspects, he responded angrily to the charges. He deliberately played down their over-emphasis on the social usefulness of art (as he saw it) because he was not even sure whether art had a purpose, whether it could or, more importantly, should be socially useful. Certainly he believed in the late 1880s that art should not strive to solve social problems, and that it should remain impartial from all tendentiousness, from all political stances. Chekhov answered the critics in a number of ways. Why should one, he asked on one occasion, always have to write about corrupt mayors,[22] and elsewhere he rejected the emphasis on ideology in art, which, he believed, imprisoned it.[23] In 1888 he sent to the former Petrashevtsyist and civic poet, Alexei Pleshcheyev, an absolute defence of his lack of political commitment:[24]

> The people I am afraid of are the ones who look for tendentiousness between the lines and are determined to see me as either liberal or conservative. I am neither liberal, nor conservative, nor gradualist, nor monk, nor indifferentist. I would like to be a free artist and nothing else . . . I look upon tags and labels as prejudices. My holy of holies is the human body, intelligence, talent, inspiration, love and the most absolute freedom imaginable, freedom from violence and lies, no matter what form the latter two take. Such is the program I would adhere to if I were a major artist.

The task of the artist, then, is not to push a party line, it is not his role to answer questions, but simply to pose them correctly.[25]

Chekhov did have clear principles as a writer: they were those of Turgenev, to maintain absolute freedom for the artist, and above all his impartial *objectivity*. This was the artistic virtue which Chekhov cherished and defended above all else. Without this quality, he believed, there could be no art. Chekhov, especially in the 1880s, argued against subjectivism in art, as well as partiality. The true artist did not even state his *own* views, let alone those of a political group, but rather attempted to observe, to record, as Turgenev again attempted, 'the changing "body and pressure" of his times'. As early as 1883 he had written: 'Subjectivity is a terrible thing.'[26] But Chekhov went even further than the more poetic Turgenev. In 1887 he wrote, in a fashion that clearly reflects his own scientific training: 'To a chemist there is nothing impure on earth. The writer should be as objective as a chemist; he should liberate himself from everyday subjectivity and acknowledge that manure piles play a highly respectable role in the landscape and that evil passions are every bit as much a part of life as good ones.' The main aim of art, that is, is to record reality as honestly, as impartially, as *coldly*, as possible, however nasty that reality may be. To Suvorin he wrote in 1890, with a tired irony that barely conceals his impatience about the continuing attacks on his objectivity:[27]

> You scold me for my objectivity, calling it indifference to good and evil, lack of ideals and ideas and so on. When I portray horse thieves, you want me to say that stealing horses is an evil. But certainly this has always been obvious without my saying so. Let the jury pass judgement on them; it is my business solely to show them as they are.

However, he came to accept that, in part, his critics were right and more social awareness was required of a good artist, and towards the end of the 1880s there was increase in the social content of his art. However, he still kept politics out: he regarded political affairs as potentially interesting source material, but essentially they were antipathetic to literature. The need for greater social awareness, perhaps even commitment, increased after his trip to Sakhalin, and Chekhov began to disavow *total* objectivity. *Ward 6* again marks someting of a turning-point. Of it, Chekhov wrote that: 'The tendency is liberal',[28] a rather remarkable comment for Chekhov, however brief and possibly ambiguous it is. He now believed that art, like life in general, without a unifying central idea, without an aim and purpose, was pointless, ultimately trivial. Trigorin in *The Seagull*, with his relentless quest for mere descriptive details, clearly reflects Chekhov's dissatisfaction with 'clinical' studies. In the same year as he wrote *Ward 6* he observed in a letter to Suvorin:[29]

> Keep in mind that the writers we call eternal, or simply good, the writers who intoxicate us, have one highly important trait in common: they're moving towards something definite and beckon you to follow, and you feel with your entire

being, not only with your mind, that they have a certain goal.
. . . The best of them are realistic and describe life as it is, but
because each line is saturated with the consciousness of its
goal, you feel life as it should be in addition to life as it is,
and you are captivated by it.

Consistent with his earlier views, though, Chekhov resisted
the utilitarian pull. Art should not, he still maintained, be the
servant of a specific tendency: rather it should follow the loftier
goal of serving truth, and inspiring in the reader the hope and
possibility of a better life. The role of the artist, too, he viewed
with seriousness: hard work, he continued to argue, was necessary as well as talent.[30] Yet Chekhov retained his old ideas
alongside the new: if the artist should try to imply what life
should be like, he should still be as objective as possible: objectivity remained the principal artistic virtue. Tendentiousness he
still considered totally antipathetic to the true nature of good
art, despite his own greater commitment. In 1899 he wrote to
Lidiya Avilova words which echo those to Suvorin nine years
earlier:[31] 'Is it for us to judge in this business? Rather it is the
business of gendarmes, of the police, or of officials especially
destined by fate for this calling. Our business is to write and
only to write.' To the end Chekhov believed that if a writer did
allow judgement to cloud his impartiality then he became not a
liberator, a servant of truth, but a gaoler who imprisoned this
'holy of holies' — complete freedom in art.

Similarly, Chekhov continued to advocate the same stylistic
virtues. He saw the true artist as a highly skilled craftsman who
spoke the truth as clearly as possible and not as a prophet, a
high-priest or a 'citizen'. Chekhov disliked all insincerity, man-
nerism and effects in art: literature, in particular, should be as
simple and comprehensible as possible. He commented to Bunin
for example:[32] 'In one's work one should be truthful and simple to the point of asceticism.' Elsewhere, Chekhov defended
the dark world he had protrayed in *In the Ravine*: he was not
being excessively gloomy, life simply *was* that bad and he had
simply and truthfully depicted it. Equally, Chekhov was frequently attacked by critics of all camps for failing to depict
heroic characters. To this Chekhov would retort that he would
gladly depict them, if they existed in reality. Simplicity and
realism, truth and sincerity are, then, Chekhov's criteria for

good art. They may be traditional and unexceptional, but Chekhov placed unusual emphasis upon them, particularly in an age which saw the flourishing of the esoteric on the one hand and the frankly polemical on the other.

Indeed, Chekhov rejected many prevailing artistic tendencies, as we have already seen with regard to the 'utilitarian' school. Equally, he attacked contemporary bourgeois literature, in particular its theatre. In the 1880s, for example, he advised his brother Alexander to avoid the current bourgeois themes of moralism and marital fidelity, as well as the fondness for positive heroes and hypocritical morality: all of this was false, trite, untrue, conventional – and totally antipathetic to Chekhov's austere realism.[33] Equally, he was generally very scathing about the fashionable Decadents. Occasionally he did speak highly of them,[34] but generally he considered their very 'decadence' a sham, and in particular disliked their mysticism and involvement with religion, as well as their strident, and to his view, artificial tone.[35] Konstantin Treplev's ludicrous play in *The Seagull* is a good example of Chekhov's opinion of such stylistic innovations as the Symbolists cultivated. Dostoevsky, who was as fashionable as the Decadents, and for similar reasons, was just as suspect to Chekhov. In 1889 he commented on his work: 'Good, but very long and indiscreet. Much pretension.'[36] That is, Dostoevsky could not be considered simple and sincere in Chekhov's eyes, and he disliked all the extreme passions and characters, which he did not consider realistic. And, obviously, Dostoevsky's great interest in religion could hardly have appealed to Chekhov. Somewhat more surprisingly, Tolstoy's views of art were criticised by Chekhov – given that they advocated almost exactly the same stylistic virtues. Upon the appearance of an extract from *What is Art?* in *New Times* he commented, rather acidly:[37]

Judging from the extract printed in *New Times,* Lev Nikolayevich's article on art is of no particular interest. Saying that art has grown decrepit and entered a blind ally, that it isn't what it ought to be, and so on and so forth, is like saying that the desire to eat and drink has gone out of date, outlived its usefulness, and is no longer necessary.

That Chekhov does not fully appreciate Tolstoy does not invalidate his basic lack of sympathy for Tolstoy's anti-aestheticism.

For all his advocacy of objectivity on the part of the artist Chekhov did not always observe this principle in practice. One important point can be made immediately. Almost without exception his work was based on what was typical of contemporary Russia. That is, he described only what he knew at first hand, so that he could tell the truth about it, but also so that he could express his own *views* on the subject concerned. This point applies even to his early work. However frivolous his early sketches may appear, from the very beginning, in such anecdotal stories as *Fat and Thin* (1883), his social conscience emerges, in that his satire acts as a defence against the mediocrity – or *poshlost'* – he depicts. Certainly, by the late 1880s one can detect attitudes to the reality Chekhov observes, however impartial or objective he may appear. In *Ivanov*, for example, Chekhov debunks contemporary despair and disillusionment, while the works of that year (1888) onwards, such as *The Name-Day Party* and *A Boring Story*, do become much more explicit in their reproach of what Chekhov considered negative aspects of contemporary Russia, such as the idleness of the intelligentsia or the lack of the ideal.

The last-mentioned story also stands as something of a counter-balance to Chekhov's avowed aims as an artist in that it is unusually *subjective* in its approach[38] – something which Chekhov theoretically rejected in art. One should not overemphasise this point, because *A Boring Story*, as well as being critical and subjective is, for the most part, a *clinical* study in its aloofness on the part of the author, a tendency which was very typical of Chekhov up to about 1892. In this period more than any other, Chekhov approximated his own artistic ideals, and deliberately 'hid' himself as Bunin noted,[39] and let his characters speak for themselves. There are virtually no intrusions on the part of the author, no moralising but simply a clinical probing into the psychology and social situations of the characters involved.

Eykhenbaum continues this medical analogy very appositely.[40] True to his professional training, Chekhov was primarily concerned at this stage with a *diagnosis* of the pathology he saw around him: in Chekhov's own words, he sought to pose the question correctly. But, as his analysis deepened, he was able to suggest some sort of treatment. And this is the important point: after a number of years of diagnosis and particularly after his

more explicitly scientific work in Sakhalin, Chekhov *did* begin
to suggest certain answers to the questions he had posed. His
account of the penal colony is a case in point. The work, while
in some ways continuing the tradition of Radishchev's *A Journey from St Petersburg to Moscow* or Dostoevsky's *Notes from
the House of the Dead* in their attempts to humanise the most
oppressed members of society, stands as a contrast in the presentation of the reality concerned. Indeed, the brutality and
dehumanisation of the penal colony is described in a most
objective way. As in his artistic works Chekhov simply attempts
to be true to life, and at the same time to discover and draw
attention to this truth. But, in contrast to previous works of
this humanitarian tradition, there is a marked absence of
polemic, of sentimentalism, of melodrama or hyperbole. Chekhov avoids explicit tendentiousness and lets the facts speak for
themselves. Nevertheless, the work, beneath its calm surface, is
relatively outspoken and is imbued with a sense of protest
against the inefficiency and cruelty of a society which perp-
etrates such evils against its own members. Without question, the
work is written only with a *message* and does make specific
points.

So, too, in many of his subsequent works he *attacks* contemporary ills quite outspokenly. *Ward 6* again marks a turning-
point, with the character of Doctor Ragin standing as an attack
on Chekhov's own former, Tolstoyan, uncommitted self, while
*My Life* (1896) continues the rejection of Tolstoyanism, as well
as being Chekhov's most outspoken story so far on the mediocrity of Russian provincial life. The two major stories on the
peasantry, *In the Ravine* and *The Peasants*, are equally pointed
and the stories on capitalism such as *A Woman's Kingdom*
(1894) and *A Doctor's Visit* (1898) quite clearly show the
human misery involved for both workers and factory-owners.
Increasingly, Chekhov's views come through to the reader, and
he spares no one in his truthfulness, which now became, as
Gorky notes, *ruthless*.[41] A particular point of attack is the
'arty' intelligentsia with its fine words and lofty emotions, but
singular lack of useful activity. Many of his stories, in particular
*The Grasshopper* (1892), make Chekhov's views on this subject
clear. Again, beneath the objective surface, he is very sharp
about the worthlessness of the self-indulgent, falsely romantic
lives they lead. What is the point of all their soirées and 'intel-

lectual' conversations, Chekhov asks and, significantly, gives no answer.

Chekhov, then, was rarely as 'objective as a chemist'. He may *appear* to be scientific, but in reality his work is infused with sympathy for human suffering, augmented by outrage at human stupidity. Chekhov shows his readers with the underlying force of a satiric, admonitory moralist, that Russian life is dreary and that they cannot carry on living like this. He may seldom *tell* them this specifically, but the implications are clear. Charles du Bois gives an excellent account of the 'quiet, implicit teaching' of Chekhov's mature work:[42]

> They [Chekhov's characters] drift; and where he is unique is that he conveys to us that they cannot do otherwise and, at the same time, without ever stating it, makes us feel that at a given moment, at the start, they might have been different. He seems always to imply — and at the same time: 'It is no longer their fault — and yet it is their fault that it should no longer be their fault'.

That is, Chekov the quiet, almost covert moralist rejected the present in the name of a better future: he increasingly sought, through his writing, to suggest how life might be transformed. Indeed, as early as 1889, he had commented in connection with *A Boring Story* that he had tried to show 'how far life falls short of the ideal life'.[43] Towards the end of his life Chekhov moved even further away from scientific objectivity. A constant motif, principally in such stories as *Lady with the Little Dog* (1899) and *The Betrothed*, is that of *revolt*, a yearning for freedom, the necessity to break out and build a new life. In general, indeed, in these last few years Chekhov himself, in his old quiet way, rebels against contemporary Russian life, in the name of culture and enlightenment. In particular, his last two plays, *Three Sisters* and *The Cherry Orchard*, represent this revolt, in the first against the philistine forces that were dragging down the cultured classes, and in the latter against the weakness and fecklessness of these same classes which allowed this process to continue.[44]

Ultimately, however, and we should note this point well, Chekhov strove to hide his 'message', and his artistic representation of reality remained a fine balance of partiality and objectivity. No one is very obviously to blame for what is happening, except that they are all to blame for being so weak. To the end Chekhov remained faithful to his old artistic virtues and attempted to *show* rather than to persuade. Ehrenburg has summed up his approach well:[45] 'Chekhov's sympathies and antagonisms are clear, but he does not touch up the people he likes and he finds human traits in those he dislikes or even hates.' His avowed aim was objectivity, but beneath that he was clearly a moralist.

In his relationship with existing literary forms Chekhov again differs from most of his predecessors in nineteenth-century Russian literature. In his first years as a writer he was almost entirely out of touch with the main literary traditions and the avenue which he first explored, that of the humorous magazines, was something of a new departure in that these low-brow publications had grown up in response to the demands of a new, urban, middle-class audience for whom the 'landowners' literature' of Turgenev, Tolstoy and Dostoevsky had almost no relevance. However, Chekhov soon gravitated in the direction of more serious literature, in the mid-1880s. But even then, he remained outside the principal traditions of nineteenth-century Russian literature in his choice of genres and in his artistic world. The dominant vehicle of the previous forty years was the novel, with poetry, the drama and the short story being somewhat neglected. All three saw a re-emergence in the last two decades of the century,[46] and it was in the work of Chekhov, in particular, that the short story and drama received a new 'canonisation' as mainstream art forms. Closely connected with this was a deliberate turning away from the apocalypticism of Dostoevsky and Tolstoy and the 'accursed questions' which had actively concerned even the less metaphysical Turgenev. Chekhov is the heir not of the principle 'giants' of the nineteenth century but of Pisemsky and Leskov who had both stood outside the main current in that they dealt with life in the provinces and avoided the 'preaching' elements of their contemporaries.[47]

In technique too, Chekhov sought new methods to reflect the changing currents of his times. His relationship to existing dramatic forms, both Russian and foreign, is particularly striking. He rejected the stock clichés of bourgeois drama, while using the devices of contemporary vaudeville and melodrama in a subtle, even parodic manner. Even more significant was his creation of a new type of stage realism, which surpassed even Strindberg and Ibsen who still had a penchant for the extraordinary and unusual, the obviously dramatic. Chekhov's aim was quite simple: his search for a new mode of presentation was to cut away as many of the conventions as possible, to present life as it really is, and his four major plays show increasing success in this respect.

His contemporaries' confusion about Chekhov's dramatic works and their initial failure indicate the startling quality of his many innovations. There seemed to be no drama, virtually no plot, the plays seemed meaningless in that the dialogue was trivial and nothing seemed to have happened. The crucial point was, of course, Chekhov's use of the *podtekst* (sub-text), the creation of a complex mood where the meaning lies in this mood and in the *indirect* communication between the characters. In *Uncle Vanya*, for example, the end seems to be a precise return to the beginning, in that nothing has happened or changed, whereas in reality, in the emotional lives of the protagonists, everything has changed. Chekhov argued his point in a now famous remark: 'Let everything on stage be just as complex and at the same time just as simple as in life. People dine, just dine, but at that moment their happiness is being made or their life is being smashed.'[48] The 'dull prose' of his plays has the precise intention of reproducing the apparently dull prose of life.

Chekhov's indepence as an artist was also evident in his relationship with the literary world. His first literary association of any consequence was with Leykin, the publisher of *Fragments*, the humorous journal to which Chekhov mainly contributed in the early 1890s. This relationship was almost entirely on a business footing and Chekhov derived little from it, apart from a regular outlet. Within a couple of years strains appeared. Quite apart from Chekov's growing seriousness as a writer, he began to seek publication in other journals, mainly the large daily, *St Petersburg Gazette,* which equally displeased Leykin who, quite correctly, saw that he was losing his monopoly on the highly promising Antosha Chekhonte. By 1885, relations between Chekhov and his publisher had grown very strained, and the following year Chekhov began to publish mainly in *New Times.* However, Chekhov did not sever all links with his first 'patron' and was corresponding with him as late as 1892.

Chekhov had almost no contact with the serious literary world for the first five years of his literary career. In 1885 he made his first entry into this world, travelling with Leykin (who had deliberately kept from Chekhov his growing fame among the celebrated writers of the two capitals) to St Petersburg and Moscow where he met a number of leading writers of older generations, such as Suvorin and Grigorovich, both of whom paid great tribute to Chekhov's promise. He in turn resolved to drag himself out of Grub Street and to become a more serious writer. Over the next few years Grigorovich wrote frequently to Chekhov with praise, criticism and, above all, encouragement. Soon, however, criticism became the keynote. As a long-established, indeed founder, member of the 'natural' school, Grigorovich expected Chekhov to make of himself a more serious, and in particular, *social* writer. As we know, Chekhov neither could do this as yet, nor did he want to and the old lion's reproaches about Chekhov's continuing association with the 'cheap' press led to something of a rift between the two men in 1888.[49]

Meanwhile, however, Chekhov was establishing a literary friendship which was to last almost the rest of his life — with Alexei Suvorin, who more than any of the established world sought to advise and help Chekhov to develop his talents in the proper manner. He, too, saw great promise in Chekhov's early pieces and encouraged him to publish mainly in his own journal, offering him complete artistic freedom. This alone was a great step forward, and so too was his association with *New Times* which, although rather conservative, had the largest circulation of the period.

Like Leykin, Suvorin sought to monopolise Chekhov, offering him 200R per month to publish exclusively for him. Chekhov sensibly refused this offer and continued to publish elsewhere. In fact, as early as 1888 he made a marked step away from *New Times* when he began to publish his larger pieces in the liberal *Northern Herald* and only his shorter works in Suvorin's journal. The liberal and radical writers with whom Chekhov was now acquainted obviously expected him to abandon Suvorin altogether. Again he declined, partly because of his sincere affection for Suvorin, but also because he refused to ally himself with one camp alone. This desire for literary independence caused considerable ill-will.[50]

Chekhov continued his public association with Suvorin, despite all the pressure not to do so, into the 1890s. In 1892 *Ward 6* appeared in a new journal, the liberal *Russian Thought*. Many of his works of the 1890s were to appear there, notably *Sakhalin*, and his association with the journal which was generally antipathetic to Suvorin's own caused a cooling in their relationship. Indeed, from 1893 none of his pieces appeared in *New Times*. Still, however, Chekhov refused to break with his old friend, even if their relationship was now confined to the private arena. It continued more or less on its former basis, with Chekhov continuing to ask Suvorin's help and advice,[51] until 1898, when there was a decided decline in their friendship over the Dreyfus affair. *New Times* took a marked anti-Semitic stance which angered the now more committed and liberal Chekhov. Even though, in private, Suvorin agreed with Chekhov's views,[52] Chekhov could not tolerate the views of his journal, and pointedly told him so. The break was not final. In 1899 he was still writing to Suvorin and maintained a solicitous interest in his affairs and considered publishing his collected works under Suvorin's imprint, although the contract eventually went to Marx. But Chekhov was now wary of trusting his old friend. He may have continued to write to him as if nothing had happened between them but, significantly, he wrote in 1901 to his brother Mikhail, warning him of Suvorin's duplicity.[53] However, maintaining his impartiality and tolerance to almost all opinions to the end, he wrote to Suvorin as late as 1903 – to thank him for an underground journal! It is difficult to imagine many other writers of nineteenth-century Russia taking such a non-partisan approach to their literary confrères and it is indeed a mark of Chekov's determined desire to remain as independent as possible from the 'prison' of ideologies and camps.

When Chekhov was first called upon to break with Suvorin in the late 1880s, the demand came primarily from the radical wing of the literary world. An important point of background should be made. The universities throughout the nineteenth century in Russia were one of the most important centres of radicalism and often politicised those who attended them without prior political affiliation. This tendency was prominent in all institutions of higher education and was increasing in the period covered by the present work.[54] So, too, when Chekhov entered Moscow University in 1879, he was surrounded by radical discussion and activities. Rather surprisingly, for one of such humanitarian sympathies, he took almost no part in these activities, indeed remained rather indifferent to them.[55] He regarded his university education as leading to a medical career, and not to revolution. By the time he encountered the radical writers of the period he was generally much more *au courant* with the leading literary and political movements of his time but still felt no great desire to affiliate himself with the left wing of Russian society.

He met the populist writer Korolenko in 1886 and the latter was very impressed by Chekhov's talent and personality. Chekhov in turn was pleased to have met Korolenko and admired his seriousness in particular, even declaring in 1888 that he was his favourite contemporary author.[56] Various efforts were made to bring Chekhov closer to their circle. Through Korolenko he met Uspensky and Mikhailovsky, and corresponded frequently with the civic poet Pleshcheyev. The efforts proved unavailing. Chekhov refused to break with Suvorin, for which he was strongly criticised, he found himself in conflict with the 'gloomy' Uspensky,[57] and by 1889 had even become disenchanted with Korolenko's art, calling him a 'literary conservative'.[58] In the next few years, Chekhov's dislike of the polemics of the literary world deepened, and it was only in the second quarter of the 1890s that he was able to relate with less defensiveness to the leading liberal and radical wings of contemporary Russian culture. His ties with left-wing writers and intellectuals became closer over the last ten years of his life and he, as Korolenko noted, became quite near to them in spirit. His relationship with Gorky was particularly important. By 1899 they had become close and Chekhov wrote to him with advice on his writing, as well as arranging a charitable reading together.[59] A year earlier Gorky had written with fulsome praise of *Uncle Vanya*, for which Chekhov duly thanked him, and a similar correspondence ensued in 1899 and 1900 over *In the Ravine*, which significantly, was published in the Marxist journal, *Life*.[60] By the end of his life, Chekhov was much more involved with left-wing circles, even if he still remained something of an interested bystander. In 1899 he quarrelled with Suvorin over the latter's criticism of student disturbances, and in 1901 corresponded with the leader of the organisation to aid imprisoned students, as well as with the recent political exiles Amfiteatrov and Sulerzhitsky.[61]

But Chekhov's true affiliation was not with the left wing as such but with *all* forces which he considered to be leading to greater material and spiritual progress in Russia. He was perhaps closest of all to the liberal wing of Russian society, but, above all, maintained his independence from all groups so that he might mix freely with anyone he wanted to. And so, he was on good terms with other progressive elements in Russian society at the turn of the century. In 1895 he visited Tolstoy, who, despite Chekhov's growing critique of Tolstoyanism, produced a powerful impact on him, while Tolstoy's journal *The Intermediary* had already published *The Name-Day Party* (1888), *The Wife* (1892) and *Ward 6*.[62] Chekhov was highly regarded in his own turn by the major *illuminati* of Russian culture. For example, when the relatively disadvantageous terms of his contract with Marx became known, a whole group wrote to the publisher reproaching him for apparently exploiting Chekhov, including such as Shalyapin, Veresaev, Bunin, Andreev and Gorky.[63] He contributed to the liberal journal *The Russian Bulletin*, which Chekhov considered the best of the day, quite apart from his connection with *Life* and other progressive outlets, and in 1902 was corresponding with, amongst others, Balmont, Korolenko, Kuprin and, of course, Gorky — while he still kept in touch with Suvorin.[64] Another notable correspondent was Diaghilev, who in 1903 offered Chekhov the editorship of *The World of Art (Mir Iskusstva)*, the most prominent journal of the Russian Modernist movement. Chekhov rather reluctantly declined. He realised that his rapidly failing health and his consequent residence in Yalta precluded such a venture, but in any case he could not possibly work with Merezhkovsky, whose deep involvement in religion and mysticism Chekhov found most antipathetic.[65]

This last gesture is revealing of Chekhov's position in Russian society. Only with the established and reactionary forces did he feel ill-at-ease and, although he never suffered seriously at their hands, he experienced some difficulties almost from the beginning of his literary career. Chekhov's early pieces were written under a form of self-censorship with a deliberate avoidance of risqué topics or serious themes, but none the less quite a few experienced censorship difficulties.[66] In 1885, for example, *Sergeant Prishibeev* was banned while an edition of *Fragments* was, to use Chekhov's word, subjected to a 'massacre'. Two sketches by Chekhov had been cut while Leykin was told to stop publishing satirical pieces or his journal would be banned altogether.[67] As his work became more serious, so the censorship became increasingly vigilant of him, especially in the mid-1890s. In 1894 *Three Years* was cut, while *The Seagull* also had its problems because of the frank discussion of the sexual relationship between Trigorin and Madame Arkadina.[68] The more overtly social pieces particularly suffered. *My Life* and *The Peasants* with their very gloomy picture of provincial life made the censor very nervous. The former, Chekhov declared, had been made a nonsense of, while a whole page was cut from the latter, and the Literary Association threatened to blackball Chekhov over it. It should be noted, however, that all the cuts were restored when the stories were later republished by the pro-government Suvorin.[69] Not all Chekhov's work, of course, caused problems: *The Cherry Orchard*, for example, with its apolitical tenor, even if the issues concerned are deeply political, was almost untouched by the censor.

Apart from Chekhov's sharp interchanges with Suvorin, he had almost no direct confrontations with conservative forces. The most notable exception was his resignation in 1902 from the Academy over the Gorky affair. Gorky had recently been elected as an honorary member of the literary section of the Imperial Academy of Sciences, despite his police record. When Tsar Nicholas II learned of this he duly expressed his 'profound chagrin' that such an event should have occurred at such a time (it was at the height of the latest wave of student disturbances which had led to the closure of St Petersburg and Kiev Universities). The election was rescinded and subsequently Chekhov, along with Korolenko – and they were the only two – resigned his own membership of the Academy. He was upset to take this step, referring to his action as 'painful and regrettable', but it was the only course he could take.[70]

Chekov's critical reception followed the same general pattern as did his involvement in the literary and political world of his time: we can now turn to an examination of this aspect of his career. His short sketches were noticed in the press as early as 1883, but it was not for two or three years that he was to receive serious critical attention, with the appearance of his *Motley Tales* in 1886. Chekhov wrote to Leykin in 1886 with his usual irony:[71] 'The big magazines are beginning to talk about my book. *New Times* scolds harshly, and calls my stories the ravings of a madman: *Russian Thought* praises them; *The Northern Herald* devotes two pages to my future tragic fate, but finds something in me to praise.' In general, the reaction to this slight collection was favourable, the principal exception being a rather scathing review by the radical critic Skabichevsky – which Chekhov was to remember all his life.[72]

For the next few years, the critical opinion of Chekov's work was to become more and more favourable, though criticisms remained. In particular, he was regarded by many as essentially light-weight. Deeper notes of melancholy were detected by some, but, equally, he was already being attacked for his lack of a clear ideology, as we have seen. *On the Road* created a particularly strong impression and by now critical articles devoted to Chekhov alone were appearing – some of which praised him more highly than Korolenko.[73] The first mark of literary respectability also came soon afterwards with his election, in 1887, to the Literary Fund. The following year, Chekhov's first full-length play, *Ivanov*, was performed. The critical response was decidedly mixed. Leskov in particular liked it and there were some favourable reviews. However, the conservative press attacked its apparent moral cynicism, while the left wing was even less pleased. Mikhailovsy, Uspensky and Korolenko all criticised its lack of social message, while other socialist critics saw the play as positively harmful.[74]

Chekhov, though, stood firm in his own position, and the rest of the decade saw a continuation of the same tendencies – increase in general acclaim, accompanied by a mounting 'campaign' against him by the left, who 'encouraged' Chekhov to adopt a more 'suitable' stance. *The Steppe,* for example, was well received and became Chekhov's first major success in the 'fat' journals: even Korolenko and Mikhailovsky approved of this work, while another radical critic, Garshin, was positively thrilled. Leskov and Shchedrin shared this opinion, and in general the work was regarded as a new contribution to Russian literature, although Chekhov still received the old rebuke of a lack of purpose or central idea in his work.[75] This slightly mixed response was reflected in Chekhov's being awarded the Pushkin Prize for literature in 1888 – but he only received half the normal amount because of his alleged lack of seriousness as a writer.

Critical acclaim continued and in 1889 he was elected a

member of the Society of Russian Drama Writers and Opera Composers. But at the same time the left-wing critics escalated their attacks on his impartial depiction of Russian society and its disillusioned individuals. Chekhov, by some at least, was now regarded as one who was obsessed by the futility of life. As in the critical attacks on Tolstoy and Dostoevsky, Mikhailovsky led those who attempted to point out the 'true' meaning of Chekhov, and the potential danger of praising him too highly. His article primarily discusses *A Boring Story*, but begins with a review of Chekhov's other 'gloomy' pieces of the late 1880s. In the usual style of this school of criticism, Mikhailovsky begins with disarming praise of some of Chekhov's technical achievements. The individual details which Chekhov perceives and describes so acutely are finely sketched in, Mikhailovsky argues, but his stories fail to come alive as a whole. Everything ends up seeming the same, it is all unfocused (that is, lacking an ideological centre), and in the end the impression is almost one of a haphazard collection of isolated, even arbitrary details. In other words, Chekhov's very innovatory skill, his impressionistic creation of a certain psychological or emotional mood were completely misunderstood and misinterpreted by Mikhailovsky, who for ideological reasons expected something altogether more pointed and *argued*.

What is worse, Mikhailovsky argues, Chekhov seems little better than the emotional cripples he depicts. Instead of offering a critique of their defeatism he is uninvolved, cold and aloof. *A Boring Story* receives much the same treatment. Although something of an improvement on the earlier works, the story remains essentially arbitrary, even trivial. Above all, there is no central idea in the story, nor in Chekhov's overall depiction of the world and Mikhailovsky concludes by suggesting that Chekhov would become a much better writer if he found a central idea for his work. Just as Dobrolyubov failed to understand that Turgenev criticised his own contemporary 'superfluous men' in *On the Eve*, so too Mikhailovsky misses Chekhov's own realisation, expressed in the last pages of *A Boring Story*, that life without a central idea was futile and meaningless.[76]

The late 1880s and early 1890s, then, saw something of a decline in Chekhov's critical reputation as he continued to write his 'cold' clinical studies. Other works of the period fared no better. *The Wood Demon* was at first rejected for performance, and then was almost universally condemned. Again, his 'impressionism', his technical innovations and new realism were misunderstood.[77] *The Horse Thieves* received the now familiar criticism for its impartiality, while *The Wife* was also roundly attacked for its lack of positive convictions. Nevertheless, Chekhov was now considered the foremost prose-writer of his day and when *Ward 6* appeared his critical reputation was finally secure, especially as many of the charges of the previous five years no longer seemed appropriate. *Sakhalin* was widely and favourably reviewed, although there was still some disappointment over his 'scientific' approach to such controversial material. But his later prose works stilled all doubts. *The Peasants* caused a great stir and was extremely widely reviewed and generally favourably, although the Populists expressed some disfavour about the depressing view of the peasantry.[78] *In the Ravine* had a similar impact, and Gorky and even Tolstoy were very impressed. Final literary acceptance had, indeed, come the year before with Chekhov's election to the Academy.

If the mid-1890s saw general critical favour for Chekhov's prose works, he had to struggle for some years yet to find acceptance for his dramatic innovations. Initial reactions to *The Seagull* were particularly disastrous. Chekhov's strikingly new, undramatic techniques were almost bound to confuse contemporary critics accustomed to traditional 'well-made' plays. Even Stanislavsky, in fact, found the play undramatic and boring,[79] and the actors completely failed to understand it. The initial critical reactions were almost completely negative, with only Suvorin writing well of it.[80] Chekhov's later plays encountered similar difficulties and lack of understanding when they first appeared. Again the Moscow Arts Theatre, whose symbol was, of course, the seagull of Chekhov's play was just as confused by *Three Sisters* as it had been by *The Seagull* and *Uncle Vanya*. Chekhov did not trust Stanislavsky's excessively naturalistic style to reproduce the true spirit of his play and there were many arguments between the two men during rehearsals. Even when it was first performed in a manner which more or less satisfied Chekhov, the play was not a critical success until its revival in 1901, when the reviews were enthusiastic.[81] The conservative critics had been particularly unhappy about the play, which, because it was associated with the progressive Arts Theatre, was in turn somehow vaguely connected with the student disturbances of the time. On this occasion *New Times* was particularly abusive.[82]

*The Cherry Orchard*, which first appeared in 1904, when Chekhov had fully established himself as the leading writer of his day, was none the less just as poorly received. As in the 1880s, he was attacked on ideological grounds even more than for his new style. In particular the critics disliked his parodic treatment of cherished stereotypes, especially in the characters of Ranevskaya, Lopakhin and Trofimov. He was accused of attacking radicals (in Trofimov), of justifying the capitalist exploitation that Lopakhin represents and of idealising the decadent aristocracy, embodied in the Ranevsky family. Even Korolenko mistook Chekhov's intentions in precisely this fashion. In a manner reminiscent of Mikhailovsky's attacks over a decade earlier, he wrote'[83]

> To my mind, the main defect of the play is its lack of a clearcut artistic design or perhaps of a keynote . . . Ranevskaya is an aristocratic slut, of no use to anyone, who departs with impunity to join her Parisian gigolo. And yet Chekhov has whitewashed her and surrounded her with a sort of sentimental halo. Similarly, that mouldy 'better future' [of which Trofimov talks] is something incomprehensible and unnatural.

And so his basic impartial and objective depiction of reality, as well as his innovatory, 'impressionistic' techniques, received as little critical understanding as they had all along, and reviewers praised only what *they* wished to see in his works. Accordingly, such 'social' works as *Ward 6*, *The Peasants* and *In the Ravine* were widely acclaimed, while his more elusive works, in particular his plays, were largely misunderstood and misinterpreted.

None the less, Chekhov achieved great popularity. His fame as a writer of humorous sketches began to be established about 1883 and the next year his first collection was published, although it did not in itself make his name. Over the next two years, however, he did become more widely known, mainly through publishing in journals other than *Fragments*, in particular in the large daily *The St Petersburg Gazette*. What is particularly striking about Chekhov's popularity in these years is that he was known to a very wide audience, especially the urban middle classes, but he was read by the educated peasantry as well.[84]

Chekhov published under his real name for the first time in 1886 and this signalled a great rise in his popularity. His *Motley Tales* sold quite well and over the second half of the decade his fame increased. His third collection, which appeared in these years, also sold well and by 1888, whenever he visited St Petersburg, he was fêted. In these years Chekhov was considered the rising star in Russian literature,[85] and even if the critics were far from unanimous the reading public was much more unequivocal in its praise. Similarly, *Ivanov* fared much better with the public than with the critics. The first performance of the play in 1887 was a great success, even if none of the actors seemed to know their lines,[86] and the play received many curtain-calls. Immediately there was talk of performing it in St Petersburg (it had opened in Moscow) and when a revival appeared there the following year it was just as successful as it had been in Moscow and the provinces. Chekhov's fame was now secure among the public, and this was enhanced by the great success of his one-act vaudevilles, in particular *The Bear*. Both this and *The Proposal* were perceived as being far above the normally mediocre level of the genre and were particularly appreciated in the provinces.[87]

The rest of his life showed a consolidation of this early success. By the early 1890s, particularly after *Ward 6*, each new work he published was regarded as a major literary event.[88] In 1894 yet another collection appeared and the same year his works began to be published abroad. The only blemish on this increasingly widespread fame was the celebrated débâcle of the first night of *The Seagull*. The circumstances could not have been less propitious. By some curious mix-up, the play was chosen to be performed as the benefit for a popular, but rather untalented middle-aged actress, who was to play the part of Nina. The company, used to conventional dramas and comedies, was at a loss to understand Chekhov's innovations and the audience was totally unsuited for such a new work. The performance was a disaster, a near-fatal blow to his dramatic career.[89] However, the calamity was quickly averted: even by the second and third nights the play was well received, and thenceforth the reception accorded to it surpassed all expectations. It was revived in 1897, Chekhov received masses of congratulatory telegrams and the newly formed Moscow Arts Theatre chose the play as its symbol of a new era in Russian theatre. The play was

most popular among students, who would queue all night for
tickets.[90]

Now Chekhov was acclaimed by all as the leading writer of
the younger generation. Editions of earlier tales had now
reached double figures, news of his illness caused another huge
flood of telegrams. In these years he received many literary
honours and his collected works were published for the first
time. *My Life* and *The Peasants* caused the greatest excitement
in the reading public – not since the appearance of the major
novels of Tolstoy and Dostoevsky had there been such a stir. A
contemporary notes well the impact each new work of Chekhov's had in this period:[91] 'The interest in his work was so great
that conversations about a new story by Chekhov literally occupied all of Russia. . . . A writer of genius conquered his homeland.' For all the hyperbole of this statement, the memoirist
makes an important point. Chekhov was acclaimed, not for
being a 'teacher of life' or the leader of a new party or movement, but simply as a great writer.

Chekhov's last three plays finally confirmed his position
among the educated Russian public. *Uncle Vanya* joined *The
Seagull* in the Arts Theatre's repertory and immediately became
a huge success. Chekhov missed the first performance, but was
kept up all night in Yalta receiving the congratulatory telegrams.
By the third performance all tickets had been sold and the play
was received just as rapturously in the provinces. The theatre
could now hardly survive without a new play by Chekhov and
eagerly asked to stage *Three Sisters*. At its first performance the
acclaim was somewhat less than was now usual, but very quickly
*Three Sisters* followed the other two works and achieved fantastic success wherever it was performed.[92] *The Cherry Orchard*,
the first performance of which Chekhov was able to attend, was
welcomed with ecstatic scenes and cries for the author, who was
now able to acknowledge in person the fame he had struggled so
hard to achieve. As with his previous plays, *The Cherry Orchard*
was also an immediate success in the provinces. Chekhov could
now look back on a distinguished artistic career with great satisfaction. From his lowly origins he had risen to a place at the
very centre of Russian cultural life. At both Melikhovo and then
Yalta he was constantly besieged by visitors. His every birthday
in the last years marked a new influx of congratulatory telegrams, and when he died early in 1904 his body was met in
Russia by huge crowds.[93]

Although this fame did not derive from the solutions Chekhov offered contemporary Russia and even if many modern readers would experience some difficulty in giving an account of his views, none the less, his views on his society and life in general underlie all the preceding discussion and we may suitably conclude the present chapter with a discussion of this aspect of Chekhov's life.

Earlier we noted that one of the major differences between Chekhov and his predecessors was his abandoning of the metaphysical dimension which had so dominated nineteenth-century literature and thought. This new departure signified a completely different approach to the problems of Russian reality. That is, throughout his life, Chekhov sought not grand, all-encompassing solutions, but rather small-scale and, above all, *practical* answers: he was interested in people and their needs, not abstract ideas. But he did not leave man without a moral dimension. For him, unlike Tolstoy and Dostoevsky, the absence of God did not necessarily lead to a decline in morality. Instead, he believed that each *individual* must find the truth for himself and create his own morality. Indeed, Chekhov differed from many of his predecessors in placing an unusual emphasis on a moral and psychological rather than a philosophical or sociological approach to his characters. Even when he did turn to the social problems of Russia in the 1890s, he viewed society in terms of individuals rather than social classes, and in general profoundly distrusted the 'systems' — of whatever ilk — that had sustained intellectual life throughout the nineteenth century.

From the first then, he was not without certain fundamental values. Even in the early 1880s, he had developed a belief in honest hard work as the principal avenue to self-improvement. Perhaps even more important, though, was education, another value which stemmed from his own early experiences. Only through these twin values was he able to rise above his humble beginnings and he extended his experience to the rest of society.

However, once certain demands were placed upon his work and thinking, such relatively 'mundane' values seemed insufficient, and in the second half of the 1880s Chekhov underwent something of a crisis. In particular, he experienced frequent periods of depression, in that his own work, including his medicine, was leading him nowhere, primarily because he had no specific direction to his life. And it was at this time that he began to examine his society more closely, and many of the works of the late 1880s already reflect deeper concern with social issues and problems. His general view of the time was critical and one looks in vain for many positive notes in his artistic works or his letters. *Ivanov* was particularly symptomatic of the grim reality Chekhov saw around him, and he noted that 'disappointment, apathy, frayed nerves and weariness' were typical of his age. The next year, 1889, he added ignorance, of which all were guilty, to this depressing list.[94]

At this time he reproached virtually all sections of Russian society for the world he now depicted. He was not afraid of including himself among the targets for these attacks. Indeed, what most distressed him in these years was his own lack of a positive world-view, the 'central idea' which eludes the old doctor at the end of *A Boring Story*. In 1888 he wrote: 'I still lack a political, religious and philosophical world view'[95] and, while he appreciated the impartiality this position allowed him, he equally felt that it ultimately reduced his life to a meaningless, arbitrary mosaic. Again, in 1888 he wrote to Suvorin: 'A thinking life without a definite outlook is not life, but a burden, a horror.'[96]

For a while, Tolstoyanism, standing midway between the government and the revolutionaries, lent Chekhov some moral direction,[97] but this tendency was bound not to satisfy him fully, coming as it did from outside. He needed to discover his own truth and his visit to the penal colony on the island of Sakhalin served precisely this purpose. Chekhov's reasons for going were not entirely clear, even to himself. In part, it appealed to his developing social conscience, in part he wished to pay back his 'debt' to science, but perhaps primarily he felt that the expedition and his work there would remove the burdensome sense of purposelessness and in this he proved entirely correct. On his return to European Russia he wrote to Suvorin: 'Before my visit, *The Kreutzer Sonata* seemed an event, and now just absurd and ridiculous. Either I have grown up through my journey or I have gone crazy — the devil knows which.'[88]

His published account of Sakhalin stands as a moving testament to his discovery of his way to truth. Chekhov learned there, and in his subsequent travels in Asia and in particular in Western Europe, to see Russian reality anew and now he realised what he had to do and what he felt must be done if his country was to avoid disaster. In accordance with his scientific training and intentions, Chekhov simply records his experiences as calmly and dispassionately as possible. The colony, as Chekhov describes it, is made up of grim, abandoned people, who go around in shackles and rags, who inhabit the most squalid of dwellings. There are elements of serfdom, prostitution and disease of all kinds is rife, the children are listless, hungry and deprived, while the women are bought and sold like chattels. Everything seems arranged to dehumanise the convicts, for whom even escape is an impossibility, so they must drag out their pointless existences without hope or relief. Above all, it is the very conditions on the island which reduce the convicts to this bestial level.

Implicit in the work is a very simple message: if the basic conditions could be improved then the futile exercise in punishment would lose so much of its grim stupidity. The whole Russian system in this microcosm appeared to Chekhov inefficient, corrupt and ultimately inhuman. The underlying point which emerges is one which was to dominate the rest of his work: 'We cannot go on living like this' – and practical reform was viewed by the regenerated Chekhov as absolutely essential.

What was particularly important was his extension of this realisation to the rest of Russia. That is, he saw the penal colony not as an isolated instance but as typical of the whole Russian Empire, even if in an exaggerated form. Thereafter, his sense of purposelessness almost entirely vanished and he devoted the rest of his life to an amelioration of these conditions, through his own work and through his artistic writings. The early 1890s, then, mark a dramatic increase in Chekhov's social awareness, as *Ward 6* clearly shows. Everywhere he saw ignorance, brutality and cruelty and, once his own eyes had been opened to the grimness of contemporary Russia, he set out to eradicate these evils. Central to this enterprise was the necessity for hard, practical work, and Chekhov now took his own medical practice all the more seriously, particularly as he was mainly working in the country areas surrounding his estate at Melikhovo. In the early 1890s he extended his practical philanthropy much further. Chekhov now believed that practical improvements, however small-scale, were the only way to change Russian society, and he was determined to make his own contribution.

And so in these years he widened his range. Not content with depicting the evils of Sakhalin, he attempted to improve the actual conditions there, sending over 2,000 books he had collected. In 1891 and 1892 he worked to relieve the Samara famine and served on the council to relieve a cholera epidemic – all free of charge. However depressed he may have become about the seeming futility of his own efforts, and however incensed he was by the meagre contribution from the rest of society – in particular the wealthy – he worked on. Throughout the first half of the 1890s he was working towards something more definite and, at the least, his positive dislikes became more apparent. In particular, he became ever more critical of the intelligentsia who, for all their fine words, did little to improve the lot of their fellow-men, although he did praise whatever efforts they did make to help the struggle against poverty, disease and ignorance.[99] He remained as distrustful as ever of the socialists, and vowed that he would have nothing but contempt for them if they were to utilise the suffering of the masses during the famine and epidemic for their own propagandistic purposes.

More significantly, these years saw Chekhov break finally with the teachings of Tolstoy, even if he retained a profound respect for the man. In fact, he had never been wholly uncritical of Tolstoy and as early as 1885 had mocked the latter's creed of non-resistance to evil.[100] By 1894 Chekhov had grown very weary of someone who seemed so little concerned with the crying necessities of practical work in the Russian countryside. In a letter of that year he summed up most aptly why he now so disliked Tolstoy's philosophy:[101]

But now something in me protests. Prudence and justice tell me there is more love for mankind in electricity and steam than in chastity and abstinence from meat. War is an evil and the court system is an evil, but it doesn't follow that I should wear bast shoes and sleep on a stove alongside the hired hand and his wife.

And like the radical critics of the same period, Chekhov sought to counteract what he now saw as the potentially pernicious influence of Tolstoy's doctrines, primarily in the peasant stories *In the Ravine* and *The Peasants* and, above all in *My Life*, which illuminates excellently the futility of 'simplification'.

True to his materialist beliefs, Chekhov continued to work patiently through the system, becoming a member of the committees of the local *zemstvo* and charitable hospital, while maintaining his already extensive philanthropic work. As he became ever more closely acquainted with Russian provincial life, Chekhov finally interested himself in specific political questions and his thinking around 1895 takes on a definite political dimension even if he remained suspicious of engaging in political activities. Few aspects of contemporary Russian society escaped his now extremely critical gaze. Thus, for all his beliefs in science and his hopes for future progress through technology, he generally saw capitalism as a great evil. Once more, though, he saw the situation in psychological terms, as such stories as *A Woman's Kingdom* and *A Doctor's Visit* clearly illustrate. In the eerie, gloomy wastelands of the factories, neither the isolated capitalist owners nor the workers can find happiness. As always, Chekhov does not attempt to find an answer to these particular problems: he always depicts as clearly as possible how awful and unbearable are the conditions of all concerned.

This is even more true of his depiction of the peasantry. Most of his practical work in the 1890s was conducted in the countryside and, faced as he was by the intolerable suffering of the peasants, he had little patience with either Tolstoyan or Populist myths about the common people. He knew their lives to be harsh and the people themselves to be brutalised and this was the picture he presented to the world. The peasants were objects of pity, not admiration, and any progress in Russia would have to be preceded by a drastic improvement in their lot. A free Russia involved equal rights for the peasantry, with individual ownership of land.[102] And, in contrast to the preceding generations of Slavophils and Populists, he saw the commune as an irrelevant anachronism in the days of scientific agriculture. It was the source not of some superior wisdom but of ignorance and drunkeness.[103]

As the 1890s wore on, Chekhov's attitude towards the intelligentsia hardened into one of open distrust. When so much needed to be done self-indulgent intellectuals could only horrify the serious doctor, philanthropist and writer that Chekov now was. For him, as for Tolstoy, fashionable 'decadence' was a parasitic disease. By the end of the decade the 'moral' implicit in *The Grasshopper* became brutally clear. In 1899 he wrote: 'I have no faith in our intelligentsia; it is hypocritical, dishonest, hysterical, ill-bred and lazy. I have no faith in it even when it suffers and complains, for its oppressors emerge from its own midst.'[104] Salvation for suffering Russia could no longer be sought from this section of society.

In particular, Chekhov the positivist scientist loathed their immersion in the religious revival which played such a prominent part in Russian intellectual life at the turn of the century. He saw this new tendency as one of the greatest brakes on progress in Russia, as well as one of the most obvious symptoms of the disease of decadence. When refusing Diaghilev's offer of the editorship of *The World of Art*, Chekhov drew particular attention to the religious movement, for which, despite his usual accommodating tone, he clearly had little sympathy:[105]

> You write that we spoke about a serious religious movement in Russia. We were speaking about a movement in the intelligentsia, not in Russia. I can't say anything about Russia as a whole, but, as for the intelligentsia, it is so far only playing at religion, mostly because it has nothing better to do. . . . Present-day culture is the beginning of work, while the religious movement we talked about is a vestige, the end or nearly the end of something that has had its day or is on its way out.

Chekhov disliked such figures as Merezhkovsky most of all for their politics. Towards the end of his life, Chekhov became ever more critical of the most conservative aspects of his society. Whatever the evils of capitalism, the misery of the peasants, or the laziness of the intelligentsia, the true enemies of progress and freedom were the reactionaries — those who inspired the murder of the Jews in Kishinyov, the imprisonment of students or the Gorky affair at the Academy, that is, 'Mr Pobedonostsev and his satanic hosts'.[106]

Although it is true that in the last decade of his life Chekhov's view of the world took on a specifically political tenor, it remains the case that his most frequent reproaches against his fellow-men were of a more psychological and moral nature. He attacked, that is, not political systems which enslaved man, but man himself for the seemingly inevitably tendency within his nature to enslave himself. *A Man in a Case* provides the clearest illustration. Belikov, the principal self-gaoler, with his dark glasses, galoshes and umbrella, represents the sum of all Chekhov came to loathe in mankind, above all, his wilful denial of his own, and others', potential for personal freedom. His whole life is dominated by fear of stepping beyond his normal confines and so malevolent is his influence that the whole town rejoices at his death. The hero of *Gooseberries* similarly encloses himself in a suffocating obsession with owning his own estate where he could grow his own gooseberries. When he finally achieves his dream, his whole life has been wasted and with near-tragic irony, the fruit is sour. . . . *About Love*, in turn, documents the failure of the two protagonists to seize their change of happiness through their own weakness. When they finally declare their love it is too late, and happiness, which had been so near, has disappeared forever. The main theme of Chekhov's work of the later 1890s is this senseless waste of human potential because his characters are too weak and afraid to improve their lot.

Yet Chekhov was equally critical of those who seem to be happy, the smug, complacent and self-satisfied. As for Gogol, *poshlost'*, petty meanness and vulgarity, was perhaps the greatest danger to human freedom and happiness. His last four plays show this tendency most clearly. The only happy characters are those who are smug, self-satisfied or complacent, while the more intelligent, such as Uncle Vanya and Sonya or the three sisters, remain without fulfilment. Chekhov remained, as one of his contemporaries noted,[107] 'the enemy of lies, of replete self-satisfaction, the enemy of deceit and oppression', and the fundamental conflict in his work is between creativity and *poshlost'*, which stifles all that is genuinely human and free.

But how was he, how were his characters and all of Russia to achieve what was genuinely human and free, how was any progress to be achieved in his still benighted country? One can detect certain positive suggestions in his later writings. In political terms, Chekhov was an advocate of liberal gradualism, shading off in many instances to the more left-wing tendencies of his contemporaries. He may not have taken public stands very frequently, but in private he took a sympathetic and active interest in the student disturbances, and in the Marxist press, for example.[108] And his views on the peasantry, the need for the future disappearance of the landowning class, on the pogroms and the treatment of political criminals, were not far from this particular wing of society. He defended the jury system, persuaded a leading industrialist to reduce miners' hours and when in Nice in 1900 commented with evident pleasure on the absence of the police.

A principal condition of a better Russia was freedom of the press, of conscience, assembly and speech,[109] and he was particularly impressed on his visit to the West in 1891 by his freedom to read and say whatever he liked. By the end of the decade, this naive admiration for the 'free' West turned into bitter anger against his own country which he described as 'a backward country where there is no freedom of the press or of conscience, where the government and nine-tenths of society consider journalists their enemies, where life is so oppressive and foul and there is so little hope for better days ahead'.[110] Of prime importance in achieving these essential freedoms was increased education, through the establishment of schools and libraries. It is indeed significant that much of Chekhov's own work was directed towards setting up these particular organs of progress, especially in his home town of Taganrog. Only by spreading enlightenment among the 'dark masses' could there be any hope of progress in Russia, Chekhov believed. He felt particularly concerned that both the government and intelligentsia did so little to tackle a problem of such appalling dimensions, and when he saw that so much needed to be, and could be achieved. The masses, he sometimes observed, might always remain stupid, but the least the cultured classes could do was to alleviate the immense burden of ignorance and illiteracy.

Chekhov also looked to increased industrialisation to drag Russia into the modern, civilised world. Even if they could not hope to raise the people to the level of the cultured elite, they could at least build railways![111] Science, as always, remained his great hope for the future, and now its applied use in technology particularly attracted him. In many ways his very practical beliefs are a throwback to the radical Westernism of Belinsky. Similarly, he shared Belinsky's intense admiration for the first Russian Westerniser, if we might so term him, Peter I: indeed, Chekhov erected a statue to him in Taganrog. For Chekhov, too, the very practical innovations, the looking to the West for material inspiration, was precisely what Russia once again was in dire need of, and the future lay in the building of schools, hospitals, parks and railways, and not in religion, a cult of the people, nor indeed in violent revolution. Chekhov can, in many ways, be best regarded as a belated adherent of Belinskian Westernism.

As we have seen, Chekhov did all he could in his own practical philanthropy to actualise these principles. He undertook all this work not only because he believed, even if not wholeheartedly, in the efficacy of what he was doing, but also as a kind of example to others. For he believed much more in the power of *individuals* to bring about change than in large institutions, parties or systems. Only when individuals improved their own lives and that of their neighbours could Russia really be transformed into that 'better future' of which his characters so frequently dream. Chukovsky sums up well this aspect of Chekhov's beliefs: 'Compassion for the concrete individual was his cult.'[112] But this 'cult' went further than compassion, for Chekhov believed especially in the individual's potential for heroic action within his own life, which would in turn serve as an example. Such heroic individuals were particularly needed in such times. Indeed, in 1888, at the height of his critique of defeatism, he wrote an essay on the explorer N. M. Przheval'sky which stands as a key to much of his later thinking on the subject. 'Such people I love endlessly,' Chekhov observed, and it is significant that he chose as his supreme edifying example a discoverer and explorer, someone who had the courage to overcome real physical hardship and make something of his own life.

Implicit in this essay is the need for the heroic, and this was to remain important. He was, though, fully aware that few would aspire to such heights. But there was still much that the 'concrete individual' could achieve in his own life. First was the absolute necessity to abandon illusion, to realise the truth of one's own life and only then could one even think of worthwhile achievements. For all the gloominess of the endings of *Uncle Vanya* and *Three Sisters* the characters left on stage – Vanya and Sonya and the three sisters – have at least made this crucial first step. Implicit here is the conflict between the false dreams with which people sustain themselves and the hard, prosaic, painful truths of everyday existence. Without a realisation of these truths one cannot even begin to hope. For Chekhov a very genuine form of heroism was to see the world as it is and still love it.[113] And, having realised the truth, one must seek to transform life, whether by striving to achieve one's inner freedom, or by practical work for one's fellow-man. One must never give in, nor give up but continually strive after a better future. Indeed, happiness lies in its quest, and not its achievement. Chekhov could not give any answers, nor did he wish to, but he did at least attempt to point the way by posing his questions correctly.

And so, in both specific political and more general terms, Chekhov attacks a grim present in the name of a better future to which he offered some tentative directions. As Stanislavsky noted,[114] Chekhov's was perhaps the greatest form of idealism in that he genuinely believed in a better future even though he was surrounded by present hopelessness. And, as he sensed his own life drawing to an end he became increasingly optimistic about the future of Russia, which was in turn part of a general upswing in the mood of Russian society. In specific terms, he believed that Russia would have a constitution within ten years,[115] while in the last few years of his life he genuinely believed that a turning-point was imminent, that a new life was about to dawn for Russia.[116] The relative brightness of his last works, especially *The Cherry Orchard* and *The Betrothed*, reflect this growing hopefulness quite clearly.

The great beauty of Chekhov's work is that, for all his increasing anger about Russian society, for all his deep concern for its future, he retained his essential tolerance, his sympathy for all his creations, which he depicted to the end with a fine mixture of idealism and sadness: he allows all a potential for happiness and goodness.[117] He could offer his contemporaries no great solutions. For him life had no transcendent or even immanent meaning and one could only hope to give its arbitrary pattern coherence by one's labours in the cause of humanity. 'One must seek, seek on one's own, all alone with one's conscience'[118] – this was the only faith Chekhov could offer. Yet he could offer the noble example of his own life, his hard work, his Sakhalin exploits, his ceaseless work as a kind of 'wood demon' who cared intensely for the well-being of humanity as well as for the preservation of natural beauty.[119] Perhaps the most autobiographical of all Chekhov's characters is Dr Astrov in *Uncle Vanya*, a man who does all he can to help the sick and to preserve the environment even though he knows all his efforts could well be futile. If Chekhov's central *desideratum* was that one should work ceaselessly for the present and future good of mankind,[120] then Chekhov can be said to have been as true to his ideals as any man.

And Chekhov could offer his own life as a striking example. Born the grandson of a serf, the son of a despotic shopowner, he became one of the most celebrated and, more importantly, most humane of men of nineteenth-century Russia. Chekhov himself was well aware of his own, often painful struggle to overcome his background and described it as early as 1888 in a letter to Suvorin:

> Try to write a story about a young man — the son of a serf, a former grocer, choirboy, schoolboy and university student, raised on respect for rank, kissing the priests' hands, worshipping the ideas of others, and giving thanks for every piece of bread, receiving frequent whippings, making the rounds as tutor without galoshes, brawling, torturing animals, enjoying dinners at the houses of rich relatives, needlessly hypocritical before God and man merely to acknowledge his own insignificance — write about how this young man squeezes the slave out of himself drop by drop and how, on waking up one fine morning, he finds that the blood coursing through his veins is no longer the blood of a slave, but that of a real human being.[12]

In his own life, Chekhov was remarkably successful in this endeavour and he wished simply that others could live, not as he had lived in his childhood, but beautifully. Chekhov did not seek to save man but to improve his material well-being and to call him to realise the 'real human being' within himself. After the prophetic moralists and the political activists who had preceded him, his view may be less apocalyptic, less thrilling. However, not least through his own example, it stood more chance of actually improving the material situation of Russian society.

# Chekhov: Important Biographical Dates

| | |
|---|---|
| 1860 | Born at Taganrog. |
| 1869–79 | Pupil at Taganrog Classical Gymnasium. |
| 1876 | Parents leave Taganrog for Moscow. |
| 1879–84 | Medical studies at Moscow University. |
| 1881–7 | Contributor to humorous journals in Moscow and St Petersburg, in particular Leykin's *Fragments*. |
| 1883 | *Fat and Thin*. |
| 1884 | Commences medical practice. First collection of short stories: *Tales of Melpomene*. |
| 1885 | First visit to St Petersburg. |
| 1886 | Begins contributing to Suvorin's *New Times*. Collection *Motley Tales*. Letter from Grigorovich. *The Requiem. On the Road*. |
| 1887 | Collections *In the Twilight* and *Innocent Talk*. Journey to South Russia. *Ivanov* performed at Korsch Theatre, Moscow. *The Steppe*. |
| 1888 | Contributor to *Northern Herald*. *The Bear* and *The Proposal* performed. Awarded half the Pushkin Prize. Collection *Tales. The Name-Day Party*. |
| 1889 | *Ivanov* performed in St Petersburg. *The Wood Demon. A Boring Story*. |
| 1890 | Journey to Sakhalin. *The Horse Thieves*. |
| 1891 | Travels in Europe. *The Duel*. |
| 1892 | Famine relief work. Buys the estate of Melikhovo. Cholera committee work. Contributor to *Russian Thought. Ward 6. The Grasshopper*. |
| 1893 | *Sakhalin Island*. |
| 1894 | Collection *Tales and Stories. A Woman's Kingdom*. |

| | |
|---|---|
| 1895 | First visit to Tolstoy. |
| | *Three Years.* |
| 1896 | First performance of *The Seagull*. *My Life.* |
| 1897 | Seriously ill with tuberculosis. Holiday at Biarritz and Nice. *The Peasants.* |
| 1898 | Builds house at Yalta. |
| | *The Seagull* at the Moscow Arts Theatre. *The Man in a Case. Gooseberries. About Love. A Doctor's Visit.* |
| 1899 | Sale of copyright to Marx, leading to Collected Works in 14 volumes (1900–1904). Visit of Gorky. *Uncle Vanya* at Moscow Arts Theatre. Melikhovo sold. *Lady with the Little Dog.* |
| 1900 | Elected to Moscow Academy of Sciences. Holiday in Nice. |
| 1901 | *Three Sisters* at Moscow Arts Theatre. Marriage to Olga Knipper. |
| 1903 | *The Betrothed.* |
| 1904 | *The Cherry Orchard* at Moscow Arts Theatre. 2 July: dies at Badenweiler. |

# Conclusion

In conclusion I would like to bring together the strands of discussion in the preceding chapters and point out the important underlying tendencies, concentrating on the areas of investigation suggested in the Introduction.

The background to nineteenth-century Russia contrasts with that of the more advanced, industrialised countries of Western Europe, in that most major writers came from the aristocracy or higher gentry. The century saw a rapid decline in the importance of the aristocracy (particularly after 1861), but their hold on the culture of the period remained strong, even in the period we have covered. One contributory cause of aristocratic dominance was the relative weakness of the class which in the West had become the chief patrons and consumers of art, the bourgeoisie. Only in the last two decades of the century did this class become socially and politically important in Russia, and only then did it begin to play a prominent part in the arts. In turn, most artists of the period were opposed to or uninterested in bourgeois culture, and it finds little reflection in the literature of the period, with the exception of the work of Chekhov.

And so, all the authors who had come to prominence by the middle of the century, such as Dostoevsky, Turgenev and Tolstoy, belonged to the landowning class, even if as is the case of Dostoevsky, some were no longer of the highest rank. After 1861, it is true, the artistocracy's hold on literature declined, and Chekhov's lowly origins did not prevent him from emerging as a major writer. Gorky is an even more striking instance. In the second half of the century, then, the *raznochintsy* became the dominant 'class' of the intelligentsia and of writers. Even so, it should be noted that the 'Silver Age' of Russian literature of the last two decades still had a very marked aristocratic, antibourgeois character, in ideology even if not in actual social origins.

Closely connected with this social background is the education of the writers we have considered. The typical pattern of the first half of the century — expensive private tutors, followed by a period at an exclusive school — was continued in the careers of Turgenev and Tolstoy. Those whose families could not afford such expense suffered intellectually in one way or another. Dostoevsky and Chekhov, whose families were much poorer than those of the higher nobility, both had poor schooling. Even the wealthier writers, however, were somewhat deprived educationally, which is not surprising given the level of pedagogy in the period. In every case, their own reading and contact with their intellectual peers served as the most fruitful source of ideas. Even those who attended universities, such as Turgenev and Tolstoy, derived little from the formal education offered there: Tolstoy even saw it as an obstacle to true education. Chekhov is the significant exception, but even then, he regarded his studies at Moscow University from a practical, scientific point of view.

However, if they suffered from the inadequacies of the official educational system, they gained enormously in terms of the wider influences on them: the ideas which inspired them in their formative period tended, perforce, to be 'unofficial' and very often foreign. By one of the strange paradoxes of the nineteenth century in Russia, the very repression within official channels of learning bred precisely what the authorities tried to suppress — alternative ideas and ways of looking at the world. And so we find in the writers we have covered that in turning elsewhere for intellectual sustenance, they encountered ideas which were generally hostile to the status quo. The tendency was especially important in the 1830s and 1840s. With philosophy severely censored in official academic institutions the intellectuals of the period established their own 'universities', the *kruzhki*, where German Romantic thinkers, in particular Schiller, Schelling and Hegel, were subjected to intense study and examination, to be followed by the even more 'dangerous' French Utopian Socialists. Turgenev and Dostoevsky (as well as many others, such as Herzen, Ogarev and Bakunin) developed their hostility to the reactionary regime in these underground academies. Tolstoy, who was a little younger, took no part in these particular adventures. But in the same way he developed many of his anarchistic ideas from his own reading, again of foreign masters, in this case Montesquieu and especially Rousseau. The pattern continued throughout the rest of the century as each new European influence bypassed official seats of learning to penetrate the men of the underground, who now, of course, also learned from the unofficial ideas of their Russian predecessors. Even Chekhov, mainly from visiting Western Europe, fell in with the established tradition. By driving potentially subversive ideas underground the authorities not only lent them the perverse attraction of the forbidden fruit, but also lost any control they might have had on how these ideas were interpreted. The Tsarist regime in this respect was indeed its own grave-digger from the time Radishchev was arrested in 1790.

The class origin of Russian writers had important consequences in other areas too. For some, such as Tolstoy, high birth was a mixed blessing. After making full use of all the privileges to which the 'nice evil' of serfdom entitled him he came, in the 1860s, more fully to realise the implications of his class position. Like Pushkin, he found himself in conflict with the now much stronger *raznochintsy,* and turned to an examination of his class's role in history to justify his position. But for him his proud affiliation to a doomed class became more of a burden than an advantage: in the last thirty, 'simplified' years his dearest wish was to abandon everything and become a peasant. In ideological terms his origins partially crippled him: for all his anarchism and rejection of contemporary society, he was never able to overcome his class outlook and ignored many of the profound changes in Russian society in these years. Turgenev, though, was able partially to overcome the limitations of his origins. His aristocratic manners and affectations brought him into conflict with the new men and with Dostoevsky, but he strove to go beyond his own class – he was indeed very critical of it in his works – and to understand Russian society as a whole. He was a good friend of Belinsky and later of Lavrov, sympathised with and contributed to the leading radical groups and, while he always remained essentially the grand seigneur in his relations with others, he did at least try to remove the blinkers of his class.

The class dominance of Russian culture makes it hardly surprising that those who came from lower orders found it difficult to enter the inner circles of high culture. Dostoevsky (like Gogol and Belinksy) experienced great humiliations and was accepted with ill-disguised reluctance. Dostoevsky partially compensated for the early insults by affiliating himself with the ideology of the most conservative (and aristocratic) elements of society. But only in part, for he gained positive advantages from his relatively lowly origins in that he had a direct, personal understanding of suffering and was less tied to the status quo, although this spirit of rebellion was countered by a desire to accept, even champion the world of oppression.

When Chekhov came to maturity the cultural world was already much more open to those of non-aristocratic origins and he did not suffer the same difficulties. The struggle against his lowly birth was more personal: he did not have to fight for acceptance and, consequently, experienced none of the traumatic class conflicts that partially vitiated the life of Dostoevsky. However, he felt his serf background to be a burden in a spiritual sense — he loathed the meanness, the drabness and oppressiveness of his own childhood, and strove all his life to 'squeeze the slave' from himself, as well as to inspire others to follow his example.

The main importance, though, of class for all writers in the nineteenth century was financial. Educational standards were low, the reading public limited and literary income alone was insufficient to live on throughout the century. Unless one were wealthy, a literary career was a considerable burden. And so, for Tolstoy and Turgenev a writing career began as a gentlemanly pastime and neither of them, except through excessive gambling or other personal reasons, ever had to worry about money, nor write hastily, nor write at all if they did not so wish. Ironically, and much to Dostoevsky's fury, Turgenev and Tolstoy were not only the wealthiest of Russian writers, they were also the best paid. Each could, moreover, indulge in his own particular causes — Tolstoy could afford to live like a peasant precisely because he was a wealthy aristocrat, while Turgenev was able to contribute generously to radical causes with no personal hardship. Life for the impoverished aristocrats was not so pleasant. Dostoevsky, in particular, was constantly beset by financial problems, which his own proclivities did nothing to alleviate. His life was one of almost perpetual financial crisis. He had no personal fortune, gambled recklessly for long periods and was often literally on the point of starvation. He had to rush his work, meet deadline after deadline, plead with anyone and everyone for money, and only in the last ten years could he write calmly and without

fear of the debtors' prison — and this only because his second
wife, Anna, had taken charge of their financial affairs. In one
sense Chekhov's plight was even worse, but at least by dint of
hard work he was able to survive by his writing. Even so, despite some additional income from his medical practice, and despite being the most popular artistic writer of his age, it was only
in the last four years that Chekhov could afford the luxury of
writing little and writing well.

Most writers of the period took a highly serious attitude to
their profession, especially in their relationship to existing literary forms. Dostoevksy was perhaps the most vocal in proclaim-
ing his 'new word', but all the major writers of nineteenth-century Russia, with the possible exception of Turgenev, followed
the same path of seeking new forms to express new content. By
his own admission, Dostoevsky's principle inspiration was Gogol.
But it was a creative re-interpretation; that is, he attempted to
explain, rationalise and revitalise the world of the dead souls.
Dostoevsky used the contemporary Romantic fiction of his
youth in much the same way. The sentimental, Gothic and fantastic all play a prominent part in Dostoevsky's fiction, even
after his Siberian exile, but these elements are deepened by his
treatment of them, in a much more topical, political and philosophical manner than in the original creations of the 1830s and
1840s.

Dostoevsky added much of his own. His view of man as an irrational and riven being was probably the most original conception in nineteenth-century literature — and not only in Russian
fiction. To convey this new content, this 'higher reality', he
sought new methods. His use of street literature, of newspaper
reports, of intensification, distortion, the grotesque and fantastic were not stylistic effects but were employed as a means of
conveying his highly original insights. The use of dialogue, the
multiple viewpoints embodied in Dostoevsky's novels served the
same goal: of putting an end to the traditional novel, an end to
'landowners' literature'.

Tolstoy and Chekhov in their own ways also regarded existing art forms as inadequate to express their own view of reality.
Tolstoy turned both to foreign models, in particular Stendhal,
and to folk literature and language, while Chekhov revitalised
the neglected genres of the short story and the drama. His
impressionistic, apparently arbitrary presentation of reality, his

use of the sub-text, the creation of a prevailing mood, his indirect, even oblique narrative techniques, all marked a return to what Pushkin had first attempted — the depiction of ordinary, everyday life which to Chekhov seemed to have been buried beneath the epic or apocalyptic works of Tolstoy and Dostoevsky. Chekhov's work reinforces the general theme: each new generation of writers seeks new literary techniques to convey a new view of reality, which in turn, of course, springs from new social conditions.

This prevailing seriousness of attitude is even more true of the writers' theoretical views on artistic practice. For all of them the artist had very elevated responsibilities, even if a variety of interpretations was placed on this basic concept. Dostovesky began his writing career within the prevailing Romantic canon of the 1830s and 1840s wherein art was closely linked to philosophy, was a kind of mystical revelation and creation was intuitive and irrational. During the aesthetic polemics of the 1850s and 1860s he resolutely oppposed the utilitarianism of Chernyshevsky and Dobrolyubov, the successors of Belinsky, but soon developed his own version of the service art could render society. Art was historically linked with man's noblest aspirations and was in essence spiritual, and ultimately Christian. Art was also educative, especially in the aesthetic and spiritual dimensions. Art, particularly when it became identified with the perfect beauty of Christ, could act as spiritual guidance to society, and thereby serve to regenerate the fallen Russian world.

Tolstoy was even more moralistic in his view of art. After some vacillation in the 1850s he developed the view that art without a moral dimension could not be considered art at all. He too rejected the utilitarians' desire for immediate social topicality, and opposed such concerns with a demand that art deal with the eternal, universal themes of man's history. Above all, art should be simple and accessible to all. These views were particularly important for Tolstoy after 1880, but they are implicit in his thinking by the late 1850s. 'Good' art would be comprehensible to everyone, would lose its upper-class bias and serve the teaching of life; it should unite man with man and cause violence to be set aside.

Turgenev and Chekhov were the most 'aesthetic' of nineteenth-century Russian writers (after Pushkin) but even they were 'infected' by Belinsky's tradition. Both put unusual emphasis (for nineteenth-century Russia) on the formal aspects of their art, but even so, there is a covert moralism underlying their work. Indeed, they follow precisely Belinsky's idea of assessing their characters by the degree to which they were useful to Russia's present and future needs. Both, it is true, reasserted Pushkin's emphasis on the need for the utmost objectivity and impartiality, but they could not escape the pull to moralism in their actual depiction of the world.

This tension between objectivity and moralism is one of the principal dilemmas for any artist, and it is certainly extremely characteristic of nineteenth-century Russian literature, as is reflected in the writers's depiction of reality. Turgenev, for example, began his career with a relatively high degree of social commitment, but after the 1840s sought primarily to convey 'the body and pressure of time'. Chekhov partially reversed this path. After many years of cold clinical studies of Russian life, in which his own views would be difficult to detect, he moved in the 1890s to a much more personal involvement with the serious issues that society presented to him. He never became tendentious, but in the works of the last decade one does feel a certain, albeit very implicit, moralism, even judgement of his characters. Dostoevsky proclaimed the need for freedom from utilitarianism in art and he is rightly famous for the 'polyphony' of his novels, that is, the presentation of mutually hostile viewpoints, those of his ideological opponents, as well as his own. None the less, he remained an ideological novelist who judged his characters according to his own norms — their religious beliefs, closeness to the Russian soil and the Russian people, their attitude to suffering and so on. His novels, like almost all novels written in Russia between 1840 and 1880, were *romans à thèse*, which stand as terrible warnings against the dangers inherent in contemporary Russian life.

Representation of reality, and the views implicit therein, were the chief criteria for the critical reception of all writers in nineteenth-century Russia. In the latter half of the nineteenth century, Turgenev was the first casualty of the increasingly ideological criticism adopted by the *Contemporary* group in particular. His early works were generally well received, but by the late 1850s when his split with the *Contemporary* group was imminent, his works began to be attacked on all sides. *On the Eve* was considered by the Left to be a slander on radical Russian youth, while the Right thought that he had portrayed this section of society too positively. His next work, *Fathers and Sons*, aroused these two reactions (as well as praise from other sections of both sides) in a greatly intensified form. A campaign of abuse was levelled at most of his later works: after 1861 Russian literary criticism almost ceased even to consider aesthetic concerns and Turgenev was deeply wounded by the 'ingratitude' his objectivity had caused, and he spent most of the rest of his life abroad.

After 1861 the divisions within Russian society became increasingly evident and art could no longer hope to play a neutral role: ideological criticism now achieved hegemony and Tolstoy and Dostoevsky in turn became objects of sustained assaults from the critics, particularly of the Left. Not all their works were dismissed, of course, but their major novels received rough treatment. The careers of both writers, in terms of critical opinion, followed similar paths. Each began as a potential ally of the radical groups, publishing in *The Contemporary*, and naturally were warmly applauded by this faction. Fairly soon, however, both writers began to develop tendencies which were considered alien to the naturalist tradition — an interest in the fantastic and abnormal in Dostoevsky's case, and a disdain for social topicality in Tolstoy's — and the critics were not so pleased. The next stage was an attempt to 'encourage' both writers to return to the 'correct' line and when this failed, open war was declared. Despite this, both writers achieved immense popularity and it was now that the followers of Chernyshevsky and Dobrolyubov — in particular Mikhailovsky and Korolenko — sought to discredit them in the eyes of the public, by pointing out the 'true' reactionary nature of Dostoevsky, and the false radicalism of Tolstoy.

This type of criticism remained dominant during Chekhov's career: Mikhailovsky and Korolenko attacked him for very similar reasons. In terms of their impact on the general public these attacks proved unavailing, as all the main writers of the latter half of the nineteenth century were extremely popular in their own life-times, at least among certain sections of society, for even at the turn of the century the reading public was not large. Despite this, the writers we have considered all managed to achieve widespread popularity, not only within the literate minority, but also among a much wider public, at least by reputation. The most striking point is that their popularity depended as much upon what the authors stood for as upon their actual literary merits: that is, to the general public as well as to the critics, a writer's ideology was as important as his talent, particularly as the reading public expanded in the second half of the century. Writers *were* acclaimed as much for literary merit as for political reasons, but it was the case that the most successful books were those which were the most controversial and topical – most notably *Fathers and Sons*, *Crime and Punishment* and *The Devils*. All three major novelists of the nineteenth century, Turgenev, Dostoevsky and Tolstoy, while being acclaimed as the greatest writers of their day, achieved greatest popularity for extra-literary reasons. This applies even to the moderate, dispassionate Turgenev. His greatest literary success was in the 1850s when he became the most popular writer of the time, but this reputation declined after the controversies surrounding *Fathers and Sons* and the relative failure of his next two novels. However, the success of the 1850s was far surpassed by the remarkable scenes which witnessed his return to Russia in his *annus mirabilis* of 1879. Significantly he was hailed not only as a great writer but as the champion of the liberal cause and as a sympathiser with the radical cause.

So too with Dostoevsky and Tolstoy. Both were extremely popular in the 1860s and 1870s for their fictional works, particularly the most controversial, such as *The Devils* and *War and Peace*, but this was as nothing compared to the incredible response to Dostoevsky's *Diary of a Writer*, and in particular his *Pushkin Speech* which was greeted by virtual hysteria, or to Tolstoy's publicistics and religious works of the last thirty years of his life. Dostoevsky's funeral procession in 1881 was followed by enormous crowds, while Tolstoy's immense international fame speaks for itself. In them the tendency of prophecy which had always been latent in Russian literature reached its zenith and it was for this, even more than for their artistic works, that they achieved such acclaim.

Although ideological factors were important for all nineteenth-century Russian writers, and, consequently, they can justifiably be termed an alternative government, not all members of the literary fraternity were consistently oppositional: some were *never* hostile to the regime. Only Tolstoy of the present collecttion could really be seen as a subversive member of society.

Dostoevsky soon gave up his early rebellion and taught reconciliation with 'reality'. Turgenev and Chekhov, the two life-long Westernists, would not have been considered at all dangerous in Western Europe — indeed, in Western terms they were very much middle-of-the-road liberals. Despite all this, it is not an over-simplification to see all these writers, and the many other *dramatis personae* of nineteenth-century Russian culture, as a constant alternative voice in society. Their solutions to society's problems and their position within society varied enormously, but it remains true that the consistent themes of compassion and indignation in the face of the immense suffering of their country, which were first enunciated by Radishchev, formed the basis of what we have chosen to call an 'alternative government'.

# Endnotes/References

Publication dates and places, where not mentioned, may be found in the Bibliography.

## 1 TURGENEV

1. For a fuller discussion of this aspect of Turgenev's writing see I. Berlin (1972), p.5.

2. P. V. Annenkov, in *Turgenev v vospominaniyakh sovremennikov (Turgenev in the Reminiscences of his Contemporaries)*, vol. 1, p. 104.

3. H. Granjard, p. 35.

4. See the memoirs of V. N. Zhitova in *Turgenev v vospominaniyakh sovremennikov*, vol. 1.

5. Op. cit., p. 43.

6. Belinsky's career reflects these changes almost exactly.

7. It should be noted, though, that Herzen first encountered the French Utopian Socialists in the early 1830s.

8. For a discussion of the European background, see H. Granjard, pp. 147 ff.

9. For a discussion of the changing attitudes to the peasantry among the intelligentsia, see P. V. Annenkov, *The Remarkable Decade*.

10. It should be noted, on the one hand, that many landowners were opposed to emancipation plans (particularly the more extreme proposals of giving the peasants the land) and on the other, that 'liberation' of the serfs entailed, primarily, the severing of the *legal* tie which made them the material property of the serf-owners, although there were myriad variations and elaborations of this basic principle.

11. For a discussion of the turbulent social background, see H. Granjard, pp. 151 ff. and in particular F. Venturi, *Roots of Revolution*, Chapter 3.

12. Quoted in H. Granjard, p. 111.

13. For a discussion of the various Westernist approaches, see H. Granjard, pp. 163–71.

14. A more detailed account of this incident can be found in Chapter 2 of the present work.

15. See H. Granjard, p. 211.

16. Quoted in I. Berlin (1948), p. 353. I am in general indebted to this article for the present discussion. It should also be noted that Turgenev's own memoirs of the period record very similar impressions.

17. See H. Granjard, pp. 46–9.

18. Ibid., p. 82.

19. Another important influence, at roughly the same time as Stankevich, was the German, Werder: see H. Granjard.

20. For a fuller discussion of Stankevich, see E. Brown, *Stankevich and His Moscow Circle.*

21. See G. Byaly, p. 18.

22. A point made by I. Berlin (1972), p. 11.

23. M. M. Kovalevsky, in *Turgenev v vospominaniyakh sovremennikov,* vol. 2, p. 149.

24. For a discussion of Turgenev's behaviour at this time, see the memoir of A. Ya. Panavea in *Turgenev v vospominaniyakh sovremennikov,* vol. 1.

25. See V. N. Zhitova in *Turgenev v vospominaniyakh sovremennikov,* vol. 1, p. 54 (French in the original).

26. Ibid. p. 64. Turgenev's mother uses the word *popovich* because of the increasing number of *raznochintsy* intellectuals who originated from the clergy, the most prominent of whom were Chernyshevsky and Dobrolyubov.

27. A point made by A. Ya. Panaeva, op. cit.

28. Op. cit., p. 119.

29. Quoted in I. Berlin (1972), p. 49.

30. See D. Magarshack, pp. 125–7.

31. See V. N. Zhitova, *Turgenev v vospominaniyakh sovremennikov,* vol. 1, p. 67.

32. Ibid., p. 111.

33. For fuller discussion of these incidents, see A. Ya. Panaeva, *Turgenev v vospominanivakh sovremennikov,* vol. 1, pp. 128–37.

34. D. Magarshack, p. 132.

35. P. V. Annenkov in *Turgenev v vospominaniyakh sovremennikov,* vol. 1, p. 334.

36. See A. Yarmolinsky, p. 262.

37. See H. Granjard, p. 131.

38. See the memoir of N. A. Tuchkova-Ogareva in *Turgenev v vospominaniyakh sovremennikov,* vol. 1, p. 242.

39. P. V. Annenkov, ibid., p. 288.

40. For a fuller discussion of these views, see my *Writers and Society During the Rise of Russian Realism.*

41. A point made by I. Berlin (1972), pp. 46–7.

42. Turgenev's approach to the peasantry at this stage in his work generally accords with the resurgence of a sentimentalist approach to the lower classes, inaugurated by Gogol's *The Overcoat.*

43. Quoted in D. Magarshack, p. 151.

44. A. Ya. Panaeva, op. cit., p. 157.

45. Quoted in A. Yarmolinksy, p. 266.

46. Quoted in H. James, p. 302.

47. Quoted in R. Freeborn, p. 189.

48. Turgenev's depiction of the peasantry is based very largely on his own direct experiences. In general, Turgenev retained this approach to reality throughout his artistic work, and tried to maintain *direct* contact with Russian life even when living abroad.

49. The eighteenth-century writers Novikov and Radishchev used a similar 'diptych' to point up the iniquities of serfdom, even if neither of them went as far as Turgenev in that neither attacked the system *as such.*

50. A term used by M. Gershenzon, p. 33.

51. Op. cit., p. 11. Pimen is the monk chronicler in Pushkin's *Boris Godunov*.

52. Op. cit., p. 83.

53. As Irving Howe points out (op. cit., p. 137), the only consistent message in Turgenev's writing is the right to indecision.

54. See Turgenev's essay *Hamlet and Don Quixote*.

55. The general remarks apply to Turgenev's major characters, in particular. Some of the minor characters, such as Arkady and Katya in *Fathers and Sons*, do achieve personal happiness, but, then, their aspirations are lower than those of the main heroes.

56. It should be noted that at all times Turgenev took a very *practical* interest in social, political and economic matters. His Westernism was not a fuzzy collection of humane sympathies but consisted of specific proposals for the future of Russia, as his *Memorandum* of 1842 and circular on mass education of 1862 witness.

57. See M. M. Kovalevsky. *Turgenev v vospominaniyakh sovremennikov*, vol. 2, p. 143.

58. There are close parallels between Turgenev's treatment of his generation and that of Lermontov (who was four years Turgenev's senior) in such works as *Meditation* and *The Fatalist*.

59. For a discussion of the political background of this period, see H. Granjard, pp. 257–67.

60. Turgenev's responsiveness to this mood in society was noted later by the populist P. L. Lavrov, who saw *On the Eve* as a prophetic work, which came to be acted out in the 'Going-Into-The-People' movement of the 1870s. (*Turgenev v vospominaniyakh sovremennikov*, vol. 1, pp. 374–5.)

61. D. Magarshack, p. 132.

62. Ibid., pp. 177–89.

63. See P. V. Annenkov in *Turgenev v vospominaniyakh sovremennikov*, vol. 1, pp. 316–19.

64. See A. F. Koni, ibid., vol. 2, p. 125.

65. Op. cit., p. 410.

66. Ibid., p. 419.

67. In an open letter of 1883, ibid., p. 57.

68. See H. Granjard, p. 336.

69. A point made by R. Mathewson, p. 20. Whatever Turgenev's own intentions may have been, it should be noted that he was largely responsible for inaugurating a trend of anti-nihilist novels in the 1860s: see C. Moser, p. 64.

70. P. L. Lavrov, op. cit., p. 410.

71. Quoted in *Turgenev v vospominaniyakh sovremennikov*, vol. 2, p. 38.

72. I. Berlin (1972), p. 44.

73. Quoted in A. Yarmolinsky, p. 224.

74. Op cit., pp. 401 ff.

75. Ibid., vol. 1, pp. 112–13.

76. Quoted by A. A. Fet in *Turgenev v vospominaniyakh sovremennikov*, vol. 1, p. 186.

77. *Turgenev v vospominaniyakh sovremennikov*, vol. 1, p. 510.

78. Ibid., p. 227.

79. See D. Magarshack, pp. 86–7.

80. Ibid., pp. 245–51 and 298.
81. Ibid., p. 123.
82. See A. V. Nikitenko, *Diary*, vol. 1, p. 350.
83. Quoted in M. Lemke, p. 208.
84. Ibid.
85. Quoted in D. Magarshack, p. 143.
86. See A. Yarmolinsky, p. 128.
87. See D. Magarshack, p. 139.
88. See B. Zaytsev, p. 156. Turgenev's ambivalent approach to established authority is very similar to Lermontov's.
89. For a more detailed account of the incident, see H. Granjard, pp. 346–8 and D. Magarshack, pp. 232–4.
90. See B. Zaytsev, p. 146.
91. See N. A. Ostrovskaya in *Turgenev v vospominaniyakh sovremennikov*, vol. 2, p. 79.
92. Quoted in A. Yarmolinsky, p. 208.
93. Ibid., p. 302. (Turgenev was also fond of referring to his troublesome gout as his 'katkovka'.)
94. Ibid., p. 351.
95. See P. L. Lavrov, p. 407. Turgenev was the first Russian writer to become famous outside his own country and enjoyed a huge vogue of popularity in the last three decades of the century, in particular, in England and France. Undoubtedly this helped to save him from government reprisals in 1879 and 1880, but his safe conduct was also a sign of a much weaker position of the government *vis-à-vis* oppositional forces, by comparison with the reign of Nicholas I.
96. See A. Yarmolinsky, pp. 359–60.
97. P. L. Lavrov, op. cit., pp. 416–7.
98. See D. Magarshack, p. 142.
99. N. A. Ostrovskaya in *Turgenev v vospominaniyakh sovremennikov*, vol. 2, p. 90.
100. P. V. Annenkov, ibid., vol. 1, p. 274.
101. Ibid., p. 296.
102. N. Strakhov, p. 4.
103. E. Ardov in *Turgenev v vospominaniyakh sovremennikov*, vol. 2, p. 173.
104. See N. Strakhov, p. 130.
105. See A. Yarmolinsky, p. 304.
106. See Belinsky in *Turgenev v russkoy kritike*, pp. 66–80.
107. See G. Byaly, pp. 48–9.
108. See P. V. Annenkov, op. cit., p. 118.
109. See I. Berlin (1972), pp. 35–6, to whom I am much indebted for the ensuing discussion.
110. Katkov even demanded that Turgenev make some alterations to the novel. For details of these, see I. Berlin (1972), p. 36, n. 47.
111. Ibid., p. 34.
112. See D. Magarshack, p. 219.
113. See I. Berlin (1972), p. 31.
114. The view of C. Moser, op cit., p. 111.
115. I. Berlin (1972), p. 36.

116. N. Strakhov, pp. 4–38.
117. B. Zaytsev (op. cit., p. 146) makes the interesting remark that Tolstoy and Dostoevsky, who were genuinely anti-nihilist and made no concessions to them, were able to ride rough-shod over contemporary criticism, while Turgenev, who was sincerely in sympathy with the radicals, was brutally 'savaged' for all his attempts to appease them.
118. See A. Yarmolinsky, pp. 256–7.
119. Op. cit., pp. 55–67.
120. See H. Granjard, p. 313 and E. Lampert, *Sons Against Fathers*, in particular Chapter 2.
121. Quoted in *Turgenev v vospominaniyakh sovremennikov*, vol. 1, p. 156. 'Seminarist', like *popovich*, refers to the social origins of the *raznochintsy*.
122. See H. Granjard, p. 271 and D. Magarshack, p. 152.
123. For a good, if biased, contemporary account, see A. Ya. Panaeva, op. cit., pp. 155–63.
124. See Chernyshevsky's memoir, ibid., pp. 366–8.
125. P. V. Annenkov, ibid., p. 302.
126. Quoted in H. Granjard, pp. 345–6.
127. Ibid.
128. See E. H. Carr, *The Romantic Exiles*, especially Chapter 12.
129. P. L. Lavrov, *Turgenev v vospominaniyakh sovremennikov*, vol. 1, pp. 423–4.
130. For an account of this, see P. A. Kropotkin's memoir, ibid.

2    DOSTOEVSKY

1. See especially the work of Yu. Tynyanov and D. Fanger.
2. In 1839 Dostoevsky wrote to his brother Mikhail: 'Man is a mystery. It must be solved, and if you spend all your life trying to solve it, you must not say the time was wasted; I occupy myself with this mystery, for I wish to be a man' (J. Coulson, p. 13).
3. For the origins of this remark see E. Lampert in J. L. I. Fennell, p. 237.
4. See *Dostoevsky v vospominaniyakh sovremennikov (Dostoevsky in the Reminiscences of his Contemporaries)*, vol. 1, p. 38.
5. Ibid., vol. 2, p. 37.
6. The term used by K. Mochulsky, p. 16.
7. Certain researchers assess the impact of this last event on Dostoevsky as quite devastating. Freud, in particular, sees the guilt it occasioned as leading directly to his epilepsy. This seems rather unlikely as Dostoevsky's illness did not really emerge until Siberia. Moreover, recent research has thrown considerable doubt as to whether Dostoevsky's father was in fact murdered. (I am indebted to Mr. C. R. Pike for drawing my attention to this point.)
8. *Dostoevsky v vospominaniyakh sovremennikov*, vol. 1, pp. 68–81.
9. Ibid., p. 106.
10. Dostoevsky's behaviour in fact earned him the nickname of Monk Photius; see ibid., p. 97.

11. Quoted in D. Fanger, p. 206.

12. Op. cit., p. 10. I am in general indebted to this work for the ensuing discussion.

13. It should be noted that S. F. Durov, also a nobleman, was well regarded by the other convicts. See *Dostoevsky v vospominaniyakh sovremennikov*, vol. 1, p. 241.

14. For further discussion of this aspect of Dostoevsky's work, see D. Fanger, *passim* and V. Pereverzev, pp. 39 ff.

15. Op. cit., p. 27.

16. See *Dostoevsky v vospominaniyakh sovremennikov*, vol. 1, p. 113.

17. See K. Mochulsky, p. 82.

18. See E. H. Carr, op. cit., pp. 108 ff. Dostoevsky experienced more financial problems on this journey abroad.

19. See *Dostoevsky v vospominaniyakh sovremennikov*, vol. 1, p. 313.

20. Quoted in J. Coulson, p. 132.

21. See E. H. Carr, pp. 138 ff for further details.

22. See the memoirs of Dostoevsky's second wife, Anna, in *Dostoevsky v vospominaniyakh sovremennikov*, vol. 2, pp. 18 ff.

23. See *Letters* (1962), p. 30.

24. In J. Coulson, p. 92.

25. In *Eugene Onegin. A Novel in Verse by Alexander Pushkin*. vol. 3, p. 191.

26. For Dostoevsky's place in the literature of the 1830s and 1840s, see V. Vinogradov's *Evolyutsiya Russkogo Naturalizma (The Evolution of Russian Naturalism)*.

27. For a further discussion see D. Chizhevsky, 'The Theme of the Double in Dostoevsky' in *Dostoevsky: A Collection of Critical Essays*, ed. R. Wellek, pp. 112–29.

28. In *The Romantic Agony*, p. 351. M. Praz also shows how Dostoevsky's belated Romanticism points forward to the Symbolists and Decadents who immediately followed him.

29. Op. cit., pp. 18–25.

30. For further discussion, see Yu. Tynyanov and D. Fanger.

31. Op. cit., p. 107.

32. Op. cit., especially pp. 38 ff (English edition). I am in general much indebted to this work for the ensuing discussion.

33. Op. cit., pp. 185–8.

34. *Diary* (English translation), p. 259.

35. In *Letters* (1962), pp. 166–7.

36. For further discussion, see M. Bakhtin.

37. Ibid., p. 4.

38. Op. cit., p. 210.

39. Quoted in V. Seduro, p. 194.

40. See especially G. Steiner, Chapter III.

41. For further discussion, see the essay by G. Lukács in R. Wellek.

42. See M. Bakhtin, pp. 88ff.

43. Op. cit., p. 312.

44. In *Letters* (1962), pp. 186–7.

45. See K. Mochulsky, pp. 418 and 451.

46. Op, cit., p. 58

47. In *Letters* (1962), p. 42.

48. In *Letters* (1923), p. 71.

49. Quoted in T. Proctor, p. 101.

50. For further discussions see I. Berlin's *Fathers and Children*, and Chapter 1 of the present work.

51. Op. cit., p. 128.

52. In *Dostoevsky v vospominaniyakh sovremennikov*, vol. 2, p. 41.

53. Ibid., vol. 1, p. 271.

54. Quoted in P. V. Annenkov, *The Remarkable Decade*, p. 218.

55. Op. cit., p. 50. I am in general indebted to this work for the present discussion.

56. This assertion is made by P. V. Annenkov in *Dostoevsky v vospomi-maniyakh sovremennikov*, vol. I, p. 139, although D. V. Grigorovich in his memoirs makes no mention of the incident. K. Mochulsky considers the suggestion preposterous, but even if Dostoevsky did *not* make such a demand it is symptomatic of the conflicts that it could even be suggested that he did.

57. A point made by K. Mochulsky, p. 70.

58. Dostoevsky in later years continued to minimise this conflict. See his *Diary*, p. 6.

59. In *Letters* (1962), p. 41.

60. See pp. 6 ff.

61. In *Letters* (1923), p. 91.

62. In *Letters* (1962), p. 221.

63. Op. cit., p. 482.

64. See the memoirs of Dostoevsky's wife in *Dostoevsky v vospominani-yakh sovremennikov*, vol. 2, pp. 259 ff.

65. In his *Diary*, p. 937.

66. The most bitter quarrel between Dostoevsky and a member of the *Contemporary* group was with Turgenev: for an account of this, see Chapter 1.

67. For an account of this period, see ibid.

68. In *Dostoevvsky v vospominaniyakh sovremennikov*, vol. 1, p. 203.

69. To Baron Wrangel, ibid., p. 252.

70. See K. Mochulsky, p. 122.

71. In *Dostoevsky v vospominaniyakh sovremennikov*, vol. 1, p. 313.

72. In J. Billington, p. 84.

73. In *Dostoevsky v vospominaniyakh sovremennikov*, vol. 2, p. 304.

74. Ibid., p. 322.

75. See the memoirs of V. V. Timofeeva, ibid., pp. 127 ff (in particular p. 147).

76. Ibid., p. 176.

77. For further details of this, see the memoirs of Kh. D. Alchevskaya and the radical writers Korolenko and Gleb Uspensky, ibid.

78. See M. Lemke, pp. 197–9, and Chapter 1.

79. Quoted in K. Mochulsky, p. 133.

80. For details, see H. Troyat, pp. 119–28.

81. See *Letters* (1962), pp. 90–5.

82. See K. Mochulsky, p. 223.

83. For details, see *Dostoevsky v vospominaniyakh sovremennikov*, vol. 2, p. 450.

84. For details of the article, see K. Mochulsky, p. 471.
85. In *Letters* (1962), p. 333.
86. In *Letters* (1923), p. 264.
87. See K. Mochulsky, p. 46.
88. See V. Seduro, pp. 11–12.
89. See K. Mochulsky, p.128.
90. Ibid., p. 470.
91. In *Letters* (1923), pp. 164–8.
92. For the texts of the radicals' critiques of Dostoevsky, see *Dostoevsky v russkoy kritike (Dostoevsky in Russian Criticism)*.
93. See J. Billington, p. 51.
94. Op. cit., p. 32.
95. In T. Proctor, p. 179.
96. The remark of S. D. Yanovsky in *Dostoevsky v vospominaniyakh sovremennikov*, vol. 1, p. 155.
97. In *Dostoevsky v russkoy kritike*, pp. 31–4.
98. At least according to A. P. Milyukov, in *Dostoevsky v vospominaniyakh sovremennikov*, vol. 1, p. 196.
99. Ibid., p. 287.
100. For further details see J. Coulson, p. 198.
101. In *Dostoevsky v vospominaniyakh sovremennikov*, vol. 2, pp. 307–8.
102. See *Letters* (1923), pp. 184 and 193.
103. Ibid., p. 219.
104. Ibid., pp. 231 ff.
105. In *Dostoevsky v vospominaniyakh sovremennikov*, vol. 2, p. 341.
106. See, for example, G. Clive, p. 52, and E. Lampert in J. L. I. Fennell, p. 235.
107. See, in particular, the excellent study of this problem in Tolstoy by I. Berlin, *The Hedgehog and the Fox*.
108. In *Letters*, (1962), pp. 70–1.
109. See *Dostoevsky ob Iskusstve (Dostoevsky on Art)*, pp. 50 ff.
110. In *Dostoevsky v vospominaniyakh sovremennikov*, vol. 2, pp. 199–200.
111. For further details of this tendency and Dostoevsky's part in it, see J. Billington, p. 43.
112. In K. Mochulsky, p. 219.
113. See M. Bakhtin, pp. 29 and 51.
114. For an excellent discussion of Dostoevsky's place in European literature as regards his depiction of the city, see D. Fanger, *passim*.
115. K. Mochulsky (op. cit., p. 106) in fact sees the pre-Siberian work *Netochka Nezvanova* as the first exploration of this theme by Dostoevsky.
116. Op. cit., p. 42.
117. It should be remembered, of course, that the alternative title of *Besy (The Devils)* is, in English, *The Possessed*.
118. The fullest discussion of the problem of freedom in Dostoeveky is in N. Berdyaev's monograph.
119. Almost certainly Herzen, whom Dostoevsky met abroad in 1862, had a strong influence on this tendency in Dostoevsky's thinking. See K. Mochulsky, p. 232 and T. Ganzhulevich.
120. In *Letters* (1962), p. 130.
121. In *Letters* (1962), p. 6.

122. See the memoirs of Baron Wrangel in *Dostoevsky v vospominani-yakh sovremennikov*, vol. 1, especially p. 251.

123. In *Diary*, p. 36.

124. Here too Dostoevsky is well within the mainstream of Russian thought. See, in particular, N. Berdyaev, *The Russian Idea*.

125. In *Diary*, p. 203.

126. Ibid., p. 202.

127. In J. Coulson, p. 179.

128. In *Diary*, p. 5.

129. Ibid., p. 105.

## 3   TOLSTOY

1. For a discussion of Tolstoy's early years see H. Troyat, pp. 21 ff. There is, of course, a fictionalised autobiographical account of this period in Tolstoy's own *Childhood*.

2. For a discussion of the origins and application of this term see the work of B. Eykhenbaum and, in particular, *Archaisty i Novatory (Archaicisers and Innovators)* of Yu. Tynyanov.

3. See B. Eykhenbaum (1928), p. 290.

4. Op. cit., p. 293. It is worth pointing out that this often made Tolstoy somewhat myopic in his understanding of the Russia beyond Yasnaya Polyana.

5. See B. Eykhenbaum (1931), p. 108.

6. Pushkin also advanced this view, though he was far from alone.

7. See *Tolstoy v vospominaniyakh sovremennikov (Tolstoy in the Reminiscences of his Contemporaries)*, vol. 1, p. 109.

8. H. Troyat, p. 80.

9. See E. Simmons, pp. 346 and 380.

10. Quoted in H. Troyat, p. 132.

11. Ibid., p. 178.

12. For a discussion of the controversies and conflicts within the *Contemporary* group during the 1850s, see Chapter 1.

13. See *Tolstoy v vospominaniyakh sovremennikov*, vol. 1, p. 71.

14. It is no coincidence that Tolstoy's personal crisis occurred at precisely the same time as one of the turning-points of nineteenth-century Russian history — the Emancipation of the peasantry in 1861.

15. Points made by B. Eykhenbaum (1932), p. 173.

16. Ibid., p. 261.

17. Quoted in H. Troyat, p. 496.

18. For a discussion of this see B. Eykhenbaum (1928), pp. 133 ff.

19. See the essay by B. Eykhenbaum in R. Matlaw, pp. 52-3, and B. Eykhenbaum (1928), p. 144. I am particularly indebted to the latter work for the present discussion.

20. See V. Erlich, *Russian Formalism*, pp. 176-8.

21. It could, of course, be argued that almost all writers are inherently moralistic in that they depict the world from a particular point of view, and that the implications of their plots suggest certain moral imperatives. However, Tolstoy is unusual in that his moralism is much more overt than

in most other writers, and he made little attempt to disguise or diminish it.
22. Quoted in E. Simmons, p. 139.
23. His autobiographical trilogy should, perhaps, be excluded from this general tendency.
24. See J. Bayley's chapter on this particular point.
25. For details of these changes, see the essay by H. Gifford in D. Davie, p. 161.
26. See R. Christian, (1962), p. 255.
27. Ibid., p. 229.
28. Quoted in H. Troyat, p. 268.
29. B. Eykhenbaum, vol. 1, p. 299.
30. Quoted in H. Troyat, p. 307.
31. 'Conversion' is the term usually applied to the severe spiritual crisis undergone by Tolstoy in the years ending 1878. In no way wishing to minimise the importance or intensity of this particular crisis, one should also remember that it was but one of a whole series which had probably begun in the 1840s. Other important critical periods for Tolstoy were at the end of the 1850s and after the completion ot *War and Peace*.
32. The seemingly naive terms 'good' and 'bad' art are used deliberately, as they are the terms employed by the 'simplified' Tolstoy.
33. See *Tolstoy v vospominaniyakh sovremennikov*, vol. 1, p. 345.
34. Ibid., p. 415.
35. Ibid., p. 439.
36. Ibid., vol. 2, p. 39.
37. See the Aylmer Maude translation in World Classics, pp. 128-9.
38. *Tolstoy v vospominaniyakh sovremennikov*, vol. 1, p. 225.
39. *What is Art?* p. 123.
40. Ibid., p. 143.
41. See *Tolstoy v vospominaniyakh sovremennikov*, vol. 2, p. 155.
42. Tolstoy was even less enamoured of contemporary drama, remarking to Chekhov: 'Shakespeare is bad enough, but your plays are even worse!'
43. Other reasons have been advanced for Tolstoy's intense dislike of *King Lear*. George Orwell, for example, argues that Tolstoy felt the depiction of the raging old king was too close a parallel to his own career. See Orwell's essay in H. Gifford.
44. For similar reasons, Tolstoy dismissed other modern playwrights apart from Chekhov. He attacked Ostrovsky's plays for being too 'unrealistic and improbable' while he disliked Ibsen's alleged tendency to write 'mistily, in enigmas': see *Tolstoy v vospominaniyakh sovremennikov*, vol. 2, pp. 41 and 55.
45. Ibid., vol. 1, p. 417.
46. See ibid., p. 545. Tolstoy also admired Lermontov because, like Tolstoy himself, the earlier writer had also disdained to become a professional littérateur.
47. Ibid., pp. 33 and 388.
48. Ibid., vol. 2, p. 78.
49. Ibid., p. 34.
50. See Aylmer Maude's translation, p. 293.
51. Op. cit., pp. 386-7.

52. In. J. L. I. Fennell, p. 272.
53. See R. Poggioli's essay, 'Tolstoy as Alceste' in *The Phoenix and the Spider.*
54. Quoted in H. Troyat, pp. 792–3.
55. See the Aylmer Maude translation, p. 6.
56. For a discussion of this pattern see H. Troyat, pp. 65 ff.
57. For vivid autobiographical versions of this agonising conflict in Tolstoy see the stories of the later period, *Father Sergius, The Kreutzer Sonata* and, in particular, *The Devil.*
58. Quoted in B. Eykhenbaum (1928), p. 309. The primary influence for Tolstoy's early anarchism was Rousseau, reinforced by Herzen and Proudhon, both of whom Tolstoy met abroad in the 1850s and 1860s.
59. For a discussion of this see the essay by I. Berlin in R. Matlaw, pp. 37–8.
60. See H. Troyat, p. 247.
61. See Chapter 1.
62. Quoted in H. Troyat, p. 83.
63. Ibid., p. 158.
64. See B. Eykhenbaum (1928), pp. 349 ff. Again Proudhon's influence is important.
65. See H. Troyat, pp. 198 ff.
66. Ibid., p. 266.
67. See B. Eykhenbaum (1931), pp. 46 ff and 81–95.
68. In *Tolstoy v vospominaniyakh sovremennikov*, vol. 1, p. 118.
69. For a discussion of the importance of this theme in Tolstoy's thought and writing, see E. Lampert in J. L. I. Fennell.
70. See B. Eykhenbaum (1928), p. 374.
71. Tolstoy is extremely unusual in this respect. All the other important writers of the 1860s, in particular Turgenev and Dostoevsky, made contemporary social and political concerns absolutely central to their novels. See Chapter 1 and 2. Even at the end of the 1860s Tolstoy's approach remained essentially the same: we find almost no mention in his writings of the Franco-Prussian War, the Paris Commune or other matters of vital political interest. See H. Troyat, p. 451.
72. See B. Eykhenbaum (1931), pp. 95 ff. I am particularly indebted to this work for the ensuing discussion.
73. For a description of this period of Tolstoy's life see his own *Confession* or the later sections of *Anna Karenina* where Levin experiences almost exactly the same despair as his creator.
74. For elaboration and illustration of these points see Tolstoy's *Confession* and *What I Believe.*
75. For these five commandments see E. Simmons, p. 372.
76. For a discussion of this incident see H. Troyat, p. 588.
77. See ibid., pp. 685–7.
78. See ibid., pp. 741 ff.
79. See *Bethink Yourselves!* in Aylmer Maude's translation in World Classics, p. 246.
80. Op. cit., In Aylmer Maude's translation, p. 205.
81. See *Tolstoy v vospominaniyakh sovremennikov*, vol. 1, p. 412.
82. Ibid., p. 525.

83. See Aylmer Maude's translation, p. 95.
84. The parallels here with Proudhon's famous aphorism 'La propriété — c'est le vol' hardly need emphasising.
85. In R. Matlaw, p. 40.
86. See *Tolstoy v vopominaniyakh sovremennikov*, vol. 2, p. 233.
87. For a discussion of the similarities between Tolstoy and some aspects of Populism see P. S. Kogan, p. 53.
88. See G. Lukács (1964), p. 191.
89. See *Tolstoy v vospominaniyakh sovremennikov*, vol. 2, p. 151.
90. Many writers on Tolstoy have noticed this. See especially T. Mann, p. 155, Plekhanov (in *Tolstoy v Russkoy Kritike*), p. 325. and Gorky (in *Tolstoy v vospominaniykah sovremennikov*, vol. 2), p. 439. Indeed, Tolstoy makes the point himself in his *Confession*, p. 21.
91. In *The Hedgehog and the Fox*, p. 81.
92. See H. Troyat, pp. 182–3.
93. See ibid., p. 187.
94. See B. Eykhenbaum (1928), p.223.
95. For a discussion of this, see B. Eykhenbaum (1931), pp. 249–365.
96. For a discussion of this tendency see C. Moser, *Anti-Nihilism in the Russian Novel of the 1860s*.
97. For a discussion of this see B. Eykhenbaum (1931), pp. 249–365.
98. See B. Eykhenbaum (1974), *passim*.
99. The 1870s also saw a renewed friendship with Turgenev. For an account of their relationship, see Chapter 1.
100. See B. Eykhenbuam (1928), p. 97.
101. See *Tolstoy v Russkoy Kritike*, p. 517.
102. Ibid., pp. 85–98.
103. Ibid., pp. 124 ff.
104. See H. Troyat, p. 139.
105. Ibid., p. 176.
106. See B. Eykhenbaum (1928), pp. 209–210 and 242.
107. See H. Troyat, pp. 221–2.
108. See B. Eykhenbaum (1928), pp. 305 and 317.
109. See *Tolstoy v Russkoy Kritike*, p. 519.
110. Ibid., pp. 105 ff.
111. See H. Troyat, pp. 378–9.
112. See B. Eykhenbaum (1931), pp. 148–50.
113. Quoted in H. Troyat, p. 392.
114. Ibid., pp. 417–18.
115. See *Tolstoy v Russkoy Kritike*, pp. 232 ff.
116. Quoted in H. Troyat, pp. 421–2.
117. Ibid., pp. 417–18.
118. Ibid.,
119. See *Tolstoy v Russkoy Kritike*, pp. 194 ff.
120. Quoted in B. Eykhenbaum (1931), p. 372.
121. See H. Troyat, p. 460.
122. See B. Eykhenbaum (1974), pp. 54–64.
123. In *Tolstoy v Russkoy Kritike*, p. 552.
124. Quoted in H. Troyat, p. 515.
125. In *Tolstoy v Russkoy Kritike*, p. 556.

126. See E. Simmons, p. 596.
127. In *Tolstoy v Russkoy Kritike*, pp. 259–78.
128. Ibid., pp. 326 ff.
129. See H. Troyat, p. 177.
130. In *Tolstoy v Russkoy Kritike*, pp. 517–18.
131. See E. Simmons, p. 252.
132. See H. Troyat, pp. 461–2.
133. See E. Simmons, p. 377 for the text of this letter.
134. Quoted in H. Troyat, p. 563.
135. Quoted ibid., p. 602.
136. See E. Simmons, p. 592.
137. Quoted in H. Troyat, p. 643.
138. See H. Troyat, p. 560.
139. Quoted ibid., p. 691.
140. See *Tolstoy v vospominaniyakh sovremennikov*, vol. 1, p. 511.
141. Quoted in E. Simmons, pp. 499–500.
142. See H. Troyat, pp. 570 ff.
143. Quoted in H. Troyat, pp. 780–1.
144. See E. Simmons, p. 431.
145. See H. Troyat, p. 641.
146. See *Tolstoy v vospominaniyakh sovremennikov*, vol. 2, p. 364.
147. See H. Troyat, p. 831.

## 4    CHEKHOV

1. For details of Chekhov's early life, see E. Simmons, pp. 6 ff.
2. In *Chekhov v vospominaniyakh sovremennikov (Chekhov in the Reminiscences of his Contemporaries)*, p. 27. All references are to the 1954 edition unless otherwise stated.
3. See E. Simmons, p. 26.
4. *Chekhov v vospominaniyakh sovremennikov*, pp. 76–8.
5. See the article by L. Grossman in R. Jackson, pp. 37–47. Maupassant also influenced Chekhov in stylistic terms.
6. In *Letters* (1973), p. 41.
7. See E. Simmons, pp. 58–9.
8. For details of this period, see ibid., pp. 63–87.
9. See E. Simmons, p. 106.
10. Ibid., p. 296.
11. In *Letters* (1926), pp. 207–8.
12. See *Chekhov v vospominaniyakh sovremennikov*, p. 101.
13. See R. Hingley (1950), p. 52.
14. See E. Simmons, pp. 88 ff.
15. In *Letters* (1973), pp. 58–9.
16. In *Letters* (1926), pp. 172–3.
17. See *Chekhov v vospominaniyakh sovremennikov*, p. 106.
18. See, for example, *Letters*, (1965), p. 49.
19. Ibid., p. 136.
20. In *Letters* (1973), p. 62.

21. See *Letters* (1925), p. 78.
22. See *Chekhov v vospominaniyakh sovremennikov* (1960 edition), p. 300.
23. See *Letters* (1973), p. 97.
24. Ibid., p. 109.
25. In a letter to Suvorin of 27 October 1888, Chekhov observed:

> You are right to demand that an author take conscious stock of what he is doing, but you are confusing two concepts: *answering the questions and formulating them correctly*. Only the latter is required of an author. There's not a single question answered in *Anna Karenina* or *Eugene Onegin*, but they are still satisfying works because the questions they raise are all formulated correctly. (In *Letters* (1973), p. 117).

26. In *Letters* (1965), p. 69.
27. In *Letters* (1955), p. 98.
28. In *Letters* (1965), p. 21.
29. In *Letters* (1973), p. 243.
30. See *Chekhov v vospominaniyakh sovremennikov*, p. 542.
31. In E. Simmons, p. 466.
32. In *Chekhov v vospominaniyakh sovremennikov*, p. 473.
33. See *Letters* (1973), pp. 275-6.
34. See, for example, his remarks to Kuprin in *Chekhov v vospominaniyakh sovremennikov*, p. 521.
35. Ibid., p. 576.
36. In *Letters* (1965), p. 234.
37. In *Letters* (1973), p. 312.
38. A point made by E. Simmons, op. cit., p. 193.
39. In *Chekhov v vospominaniyakh sovremennikov*, p. 475.
40. See his article in R. Jackson, pp. 21-31.
41. In *Chekhov v vospominaniyakh sovremennikov*, p. 154.
42. In R. Jackson, p. 189.
43. See *Letters* (1965), p. 15.
44. For an excellent discussion of Chekhov's last two plays in these terms, see R. Brustein, pp. 148 ff.
45. In *Chekhov v vospominaniyakh sovremennikov*, p. 41.
46. For a discussion of the poetry of this period see R. Poggioli, *The Poets of Russia 1890-1930* (Cambridge, Mass., 1960).
47. Points made by B. Eykhenbaum, in R. Jackson, p. 22.
48. In R. Jackson, p. 73.
49. See E. Simmons, p. 163.
50. Ibid., p. 237.
51. See, for example, *Letters* (1973), p. 263.
52. Ibid., p. 306.
53. Ibid., p. 395.
54. See the monograph *Plekhanov* by Samuel T. Barron (London, 1963).
55. See E. Simmons, pp. 38-9.
56. See *Letters* (1973), p. 95.

57. See *Chekhov v vospominaniyakh sovremennikov*, pp. 106–8.
58. See *Letters* (1925), p. 163.
59. See E. Simmons, p. 464.
60. See *Letters* (1973), pp. 371 and 381.
61. See E. Simmons, p. 561.
62. See *Chekhov v vospominankyakh sovremennikov* (1960 edition), p. 365.
63. See *Chekhov v vospominaniyakh sovremennikov*, p. 449.
64. Another important association at this time was, of course, that with the newly-formed Moscow Arts Theatre. For details of this, see the memoirs of Stanislavsky and Nemirovich-Danchenko.
65. See *Letters* (1973), p. 453.
66. See E. Simmons, p. 68.
67. See *Letters* (1955), p. 6.
68. See E. Simmons, p. 365.
69. See *Letters* (1973), p. 291.
70. For further discussion of this, see ibid., p. 418 and pp. 425–6.
71. In *Letters* (1965), p. 39.
72. See E. Simmons, p. 107.
73. Ibid., p. 117.
74. See *Letters* (1925), p. 150.
75. See E. Simmons, pp. 144–9.
76. Tolstoy, who was the object of critical rejection from the radical press at this time, also attacked the lack of an explicit philosophy in Chekhov's work. See W. Gerhardi, p. 73.
77. See E. Simmons, pp. 199–200.
78. See R. Hingley (1950), p. 109 and *Letters* (1973), pp. 291–2.
79. Op. cit., p. 321.
80. See E. Simmons, p. 376.
81. See M. Valency, pp. 209–11 and 252.
82. See E. Simmons, p. 527.
83. In *Letters* (1973), p. 443.
84. See K. Chukovsky, p. 13.
85. See *Chekhov v vospominaniyakh sovremennikov*, especially the memoirs by V. I. Nemirovich-Danchenko, N. D. Teleshov, V. G. Korolenko and A. S. Lazarov-Gruzinsky.
86. See *Letters* (1973), p. 72.
87. See *Chekhov v vospominaniyakh sovremennikov*, pp. 150–1.
88. Ibid., p. 396.
89. See ibid., pp. 157 ff.
90. Ibid., p. 327.
91. In *Chekhov v vospominaniyakh sovremennikov* (1960 edition), p. 301.
92. See E. Simmons, p. 542.
93. See *Chekhov v vospominaniyakh sovremennikov*, p. 454.
94. In *Letters* (1925), p. 171.
95. In *Letters* (1973), p. 115.
96. In *Letters* (1925), p. 133.
97. For a discussion of this, see E. Simmons, p. 126.
98. In *Letters* (1925), p. 185.

99. See *Letters* (1973), p. 240.
100. A point made by M. Shotton, op. cit., p. 320.
101. In *Letters* (1973), pp. 261–2.
102. See *Chekhov v vospominaniyakh sovremennikov* (1960 edition), p. 449.
103. See *Letters* (1955), p. 231 (a letter of 1899).
104. In *Letters* (1973), p. 341.
105. In ibid., pp. 435–6.
106. Ibid., p. 296.
107. In *Chekhov v vospominaniyakh sovremennikov*, p. 537.
108. See E. Simmons, pp. 466–7.
109. See *Chekov v vospominaniyakh sovremennikov* (1960 edition), p. 449.
110. In *Letters* (1973), p. 353.
111. A point made by F. L. Lucas, p. 131.
112. Op. cit., p. 30.
113. A point made by L. Grossman in Jackson, p. 48.
114. Op. cit., p. 348.
115. See *Chekhov v vospominaniyakh sovremennikov*, p. 431.
116. Ibid., p. 572.
117. Natasha in *Three Sisters* is a rare exception to Chekhov's humanistic portrayal of mankind: see Brustein. It should be noted that some critics consider Chekhov to be rather less positive in his depiction of humanity. L. Shestov, for example, asserts: 'Chekhov, too, was a "treasure-digger", a sorcerer, a necromancer, an adept in the black art; and this explains his singular infatuation for death, decay and hopelessness' (op. cit., p. 23). Such a view seems far from the truth, particularly if one considers the evidence of Chekhov's letters and, especially, the memoirs of his contemporaries.
118. In *Letters* (1973), p. 414. This is a remark of 1901.
119. See K. Chukovsky, pp. 19–21. The destruction of trees was a very potent symbol in Chekhov's work, usually signalling the passing of a beautiful, if ineffectual old order. See, in particular, *Uncle Vanya, Three Sisters,* and *The Cherry Orchard.*
120. M. Valency sums up this aspect of Chekhov's work and thought very well (op. cit., pp. 80–1): 'Life was painful, and it was senseless; that much was evident. But it was also evident that it is our duty as humans to work towards the improvement of life. . . . A lifetime of service to the cause of humanity was, in Chekhov's eyes, the only rational solution to the problem of existence.'
121. In *Letters* (1973), p. 85.

# General Bibliography

Works consulted on Russian History and the social and cultural background to Russian literature.

P. Annenkov, *The Remarkable Decade* (Ann Arbor, 1968).

N. Berdyaev, *The Russian Idea* (Boston, 1962).

I. Berlin, 'Russia and 1848', *Slavonic and East European Review* (April 1948).

V. Bill, *The Forgotten Class. The Russian Bourgeoisie from the Earliest Beginnings to 1900* (New York, 1959).

J. Billington, *Mikhailovsky and Russian Populism* (Oxford, 1958).

——, *The Icon and the Axe* (London, 1966).

J. Blum, *Lord and Peasant in Russia from the 9th to the 19th century* (New York, 1968).

E. Crankshaw, *The Shadow of the Winter Palace. The Drift to Revolution 1825–1917* (London, 1976).

R. Hare, *Pioneers of Russian Social Thought* (London, 1951).

N. Has, *Russian Educational Policy 1701–1917* (London, 1931).

A. Herzen, *My Past and Thoughts*, 2 vols. (London, 1924).

R. Hingley, *Russian Writers and Society* (London, 1967).

E. Lampert, *Studies in Rebellion* (London, 1957).

——, *Sons against Fathers* (Oxford, 1965).

M. Lemke, *Nikolayevskiye Zhandarmy i Literatura 1826–1855 gg* (The Hague, 1965; originally St Petersburg, 1909).

M. Malia, *Alexander Herzen and the Birth of Russian Socialism* (Harvard, 1965).

J. Masaryk, *The Spirit of Russia* (London, 1919).

R. W. Mathewson, *The Positive Hero in Russian Literature* (New York, 1958).

J. Maynard, *The Russian Peasant and other Studies* (London, 1942).

D. Mirsky, *A History of Russian Literature* (London, 1949).

S. Monas, *The Third Section* (Cambridge, Mass., 1961).

A. V. Nikitenko, *Dnevnik*, 3 vols. (Leningrad, 1955–6).
D. Ovsyanniko-Kulikovsky, *Istoria Russkoy Intelligentsii* (Moscow, 1908).
R. Pipes, *Russia under the Old Regime* (London, 1974).
N. Riasanovsky, *A History of Russia* (New York, 1963).
A. M. Skabichevsky, *Ocherki istorii Russkoy Tsenzury* (The Hague, 1965; originally St Petersburg, 1892).
M. Slonim, *The Epic of Russian Literature* (New York, 1964).
P. S. Squire, *The Third Department* (Cambridge, 1968).
H. Troyat, *Daily Life under the Last Tsar* (London, 1961).
F. Venturi, *The Roots of Revolution* (London, 1960).

Works consulted on the theory and sociology of literature and culture.

J. Berger, *Art and Revolution* (Harmondsworth, 1969).
M. Bowra, *Politics and Poetry 1900–1960* (Cambridge, 1966).
A. Camus, *The Rebel* (London, 1971).
J. Duvignaud, *The Sociology of Art* (London, 1972).
V. Erlich, *Russian Formalism*, 3rd ed. (The Hague, 1969).
R. Escarpit, *Sociology of Literature,* 2nd ed. (London, 1971).
E. Fromm, *The Fear of Freedom* (London, 1963).
L. Goldmann, *The Hidden God* (London, 1964).
I. Howe, *Politics and the Novel* (London, 1961).
C. G. Jung, *Modern Man in Search of a Soul* (London, 1941).
F. R. Leavis, *The Common Pursuit* (London, 1952).
G. Lichteim, *Lukács* (London, 1970).
G. Lukács, *The Theory of the Novel* (London, 1971).
K. Mannheim, *Essays on the Sociology of Culture* (London, 1956).
J. P. Sartre, *What is Literature?* (London, 1950).
G. Steiner, *Language and Silence* (London, 1967).
A. Swingewood and D. Laurenson, *The Sociology of Literature* (London, 1972).
L. Trotsky, *Art and Revolution* (Ann Arbor, 1960).
I. Watt, *The Rise of the Novel* (Harmondsworth, 1968).
R. Wellek and A. Warren, *Theory of Literature* 3rd ed. (Harmondsworth, 1968).
R. Williams, *The Long Revolution* (London, 1961).

# 1. BIBLIOGRAPHY

V. Belinsky, *Polnoye Sobraniye sochineniy*, vols. 7 and 10 (Moscow, 1953-9).

I. Berlin, *Fathers and Children* (Oxford, 1972).

——, 'Russia and 1848' in *Slavonic and East European Review*, vol. XXVI (April 1848), pp. 341-60.

G. Byaly, *Turgenev i Russkiy Realizm* (Moscow-Leningrad, 1962).

N. Chernyshevsky, 'Russkiy chelovek na rendezvous (1858)' in *Polnoe sobraniye sochineny*, vol. 5 (Moscow, 1939-53).

J. Conrad, 'Turgenev (1917)' in *Notes on Life and Letters* (London, 1926).

N. Dobrolyubov, 'Kogda zhe pridet nastoyashchiy den'? (1860)' in *Sobraniye Sochineny*, vol. 6 (Moscow, 1961-4).

R. Freeborn, *Turgenev: The Novelist's Novelist. A Study* (London, 1960).

E. Garnett, *Turgenev. A Study* (London, 1927).

M. Gershenzon, *Mechta i Mysl' I. S. Turgeneva* (Moscow, 1919).

H. Gifford, 'Turgenev' in J. L. I. Fennell (ed.), *Nineteenth-Century Russian Literature* (London, 1973).

H. Granjard, *Ivan Tourguénev et les courants politiques et sociaux de son temps*, 2nd ed. (Paris, 1966).

H. Hershkowitz, *Democratic Ideas in Turgenev's Work* (New York, 1932).

Irving Howe, *Politics and the Novel* (London, 1961).

Henry James, 'Ivan Turgénieff (1818-1883) (1897)' in *Russian Literature and Modern English Fiction* (Chicago and London, 1965).

M. Ledkovsky, *The Other Turgenev: from Romanticism to Symbolism* (Würzburg, 1973).

M. Lemke, *Nikolayevskiye zhandarmy i Literatura 1826-1855*, (The Hague, 1965; originally published St Petersburg, 1909).

D. Magarshack, *Turgenev: A Life* (London, 1954).

R. Mathewson, *The Positive Hero in Russian Literature* (New York, 1958).

C. Moser, *Antinihilism in the Russian Novel of the 1860s* (The Hague, 1964).

G. Phelps, *The Russian Novel in English Fiction* (London, 1956).

D. Pisarev, 'Bazarov' (1862) in *Sochineniya*, vol. 2 (Moscow, 1955).

V. S. Pritchett, *The Russian Day. The Living Novel* (London, 1946).

——, *The Gentle Barbarian; the Life and Work of Turgenev* (London, 1977).

P. Pustovoyt, *Roman I. S. Turgeneva 'Ottsy i deti' i ideynaya bor'ba 60-kh godov XIX veka* (Moscow, 1965).

L. B. Schapiro, *Turgenev: His Life and Times* (Oxford, 1978).

N. Strakhov, *Kriticheskiye Stat'i ob I. S. Turgeneve i L. N. Tolstom (1862–1885)* (Kiev, 1901).

I. S. Turgenev, *Polnoe Sobraniye sochineny i pisem.* Sochineniya (Moscow–Leningrad, 1960–8).

——, *Turgenev v russkoy kritike, Sbornik Statey,* K. Bonestsky (ed.) (Moscow, 1953).

——, *Turgenev v vospominaniyakh sovremennikov,* V. V. Grigerenko and others (eds) (Moscow, 1969).

——, *Turgenev's Literary Reminiscences and Autobiographical Fragments,* D. Magarshack (trans.) (London, 1959).

A. Walicki, 'Turgenev and Schopenhauer' in *Oxford Slavonic Papers* vol. X (1962), pp. 1–17.

Virginia Woolf, 'The Novels of Turgenev' in *The Captain's Death-bed and Other Essays* (London, 1950).

A. Yarmolinsky, *Turgenev: The Man, His Art and His Age* (New York, 1959).

B. Zaytsev, *Zhizn' Turgeneva* (Paris, 1949).

## 2. BIBLIOGRAPHY

M. Bakhtin, *Prolemy poetiki Dostoevskogo* (Moscow, 1963). (Translation *The Problems of Dostoevsky's Poetics* (Ardis, 1973).)

A. Bely, *Tragediya Tvorchestva: Dostoevsky i Tolstoy* (Prideaux Press, 1973).

N. Berdyaev, *Mirosozertsanie Dostoevskogo* (Paris, 1923). (Translation: *Dostoevsky* (London, 1957).)

J. Billington, *Mikhailovsky and Russian Populism* (Oxford, 1958).

E. H. Carr, *Dostoevsky (1821–1881). A New Biography* (London, 1930).

G. Clive, *The Broken Icon: Intuitive Existentialism in Classical Russian Fiction* (New York and London, 1973).

J. Coulson, *Dostoevsky: A Self-Portrait* (London, 1962).

D. Davie (ed.), *Russian Literature and Modern English Fiction* (Chicago and London, 1965).

F. M. Dostoevsky, *Sobraniye Sochineny*. L. Grossman and others (eds.), 10 vols. (Moscow, 1956-8).

——, *Polnoe sobraniye sochineny*. V. Bazanov, G. Fridlender and others (eds.), 30 vols. (Leningrad, 1972-   ).

——, *F. M. Dostoevsky ob iskusstve* (Moscow, 1973).

——, *The Diary of a Writer*, translated by B. Brasol (London, 1949).

——, *Letters and Reminiscences*, translated by S. S. Koteliansky and J. Middleton Murry (London, 1923).

——, *Letters to his Family and Friends*, translated by E. C. Mayne (London, 1962).

——, *F. M. Dostoevsky v Russkoy Kritike*, A. Belkin (ed.) (Moscow, 1956).

——, *F. M. Dostoevsky v vospominaniyakh sovremennikov*. 2 vols., V. V. Grigerenko and others (eds.), (Moscow, 1964).

——, *Dostoevsky: ego Vremya*, V. G. Bazanov and others (eds.), (Leningrad, 1971).

D. Fanger, *Dostoevsky and Romantic Realism. A Study of Dostoevsky in Relation to Balzac, Dickens and Gogol* (Cambridge, 1965).

J. Frank, *Dostoevsky; The Seeds of Revolt 1821–1849* (Princeton, 1976).

T. Ganzhulevich, *Dostoevsky i Gertzen v istorii Russkogo samosoznaniya* (High Wycombe, 1971; originally, St Petersburg, 1907).

A. Gide, *Dostoevsky* (London, 1962).

R. Hingley, *The Undiscovered Dostoevsky* (London, 1962).

V. Ivanov, *Freedom and the Tragic Life. A Study of Dostoevsky* (London, 1916).

R. L. Jackson, *Dostoevsky's Quest for Form* (New Haven, 1966).

——, *Dostoevsky's Underground Man in Russian Literature* (The Hague, 1958).

M. V. Jones, *Dostoevsky. The Novel of Discord* (London, 1976).

A. de Jonge, *Dostoevsky and the Age of Intensity* (London, 1975).

G. C. Kabat, *Ideology and Imagination; the Image of Society in Dostoevsky* (New York, Columbia, 1978).

E. Lampert, 'Dostoevsky' in J. L. I. Fennell (ed.), *Nineteenth-Century Russian Literature* (London, 1973).

M. Lemke, *Nikolayevskiye Zhandarmy i Literatura 1826–1855 gg* (The Hague, 1965; originally published, St Petersburg, 1909).

R. Mathewson, *The Positive Hero in Russian Literature* (New York, 1958).

D. S. Merezhovsky, *Tolstoy i Dostoevsky. Zhizn' i tvorchestvo*, 4th ed. (St Petersburg, 1909).

K. Mochulsky, *Dostoevky. Zhizn' i tvorchestvo* (Paris, 1947; English translation, Princeton, 1967).

C. Moser, *Antinihilism in the Russian Novel of the 1860s* (The Hague, 1964).

C. Passage, *The Russian Hoffmannists* (The Hague, 1963).

R. Peace, *Dostoevsky; An Examination of the Major Novels* (Cambridge, 1970).

V. Peververzev, *F. M. Dostoevsky* (Moscow-Leningrad, 1925).

R. Poggioli, *The Phoenix and the Spider* (Cambridge, Mass, 1957).

M. Praz, *The Romantic Agony* (Oxford, 1970).

T. Proctor, *Dostoevskij and the Belinskij School of Literary Criticism* (The Hague, 1969).

V. Rozanov, *Legenda o Velikom Inkvizitore F. M. Dostoevskogo* (St Petersburg, 1906).

V. Seduro, *Dostoevsky in Russian Criticism* (Columbia–Oxford, 1957).

E. J. Simmons, *Feodor Dostoevsky* (New York and London, 1969).

A. Steinberg, *Dostoevsky* (London, 1966).

G. Steiner, *Tolstoy or Dostoevsky. An Essay in Contrast* (London, 1959).

H. Troyat, *Firebrand: The Life of Dostoevsky* (English translation), (London, 1946).

Yu. Tynyanov, *Arkhaisty i Novatory* (Leningrad, 1929).

R. Wellek (ed.) *Dostoevsky. A Collection of Critical Essays* (New Jersey, 1962).

## 3. BIBLIOGRAPHY

J. Bayley, *Tolstoy and the Novel* (London, 1966).

I. Berlin, *The Hedgehog and the Fox* (London, 1953).

A. Bely, *Tragediya Tvorchestya. Dostoevsky i Tolstoy* (Prideaux Press, 1973; originally Moscow, 1911).

R. Christian, *Tolstoy's 'War and Peace'* (Oxford, 1962).

——, *L. Tolstoy* (Cambridge, 1969).

G. Clive, *The Broken Icon: Intuitive Existentialism in Classical Russian Fiction* (New York and London, 1973).

D. Davie (ed.), *Russian Literature and Modern English Fiction. A Collection of Critical Essays* (Chicago, 1965).

B. Eykhenbaum, *Lev Tolstoy*, vol. 1 (Leningrad, 1928).

——. *Lev Tolstoy*, vol. 2 (Moscow, 1931).

——, *Lev Tolstoy. Semidesyatye Gody* (Leningrad, 1974).

G. Gibian, *Tolstoy and Shakespeare* (The Hague, 1957).

H. Gifford (ed.), *Leo Tolstoy. A Critical Anthology* (Penguin Books, 1971).

M. Gorky, *Reminiscences of Tolstoy, Chekhov and Andreev* (London, 1934).

M. V. Jones (ed.), *New Essays on Tolstoy* (Cambridge, 1978).

A. V. Knowles (ed.), *Tolstoy; The Critical Heritage* (London, 1978).

P. S. Kogan, *Lev Tolstoy i Marksistskaya Kritika* (Moscow, 1928).

E. Lampert, 'Tolstoy' in J. L. I. Fennell (ed.), *Nineteenth-Century Russian Literature* (London, 1973).

J. Lavrin, *Tolstoy. An Approach* (London, 1944).

F. R. Leavis, *'Anna Karenina' and Other Essays* (London, 1967).

V. I. Lenin, *O Tolstom. Literaturno-kritichesky sbornik* (Moscow–Leningrad, 1928).

P. Lubbock, *The Craft of Fiction* (London, 1965).

G. Lukács, *Studies in European Realism* (London, 1964).

——, *The Historical Novel* (London, 1962).

T. Mann, *Essays of Three Decades* (New York, 1947).

R. Matlaw (ed.), *Tolstoy. A Collection of Critical Essays* (New Jersey, 1947).

D. Merezhkovsky, *Tolstoy i Dostoevsky. Zhizn' i tvorchestvo* (St Petersburg, 1909).

R. Poggioli, *The Phoenix and the Spider* (Cambridge, Mass., 1957).

T. Redpath, *Tolstoy* (London, 1960).

R. V. Sampson, *Tolstoy. The Discovery of Peace* (London, 1973).

E. Simmons, *Leo Tolstoy* (London, 1949).

G. Steiner, *Tolstoy or Dostoevsky. An Essay in Contrast* (London, 1959).

L. N. Tolstoy, *Polnoye Sobraniye Sochineny* (Jubilee Edition), 90 vols. (Moscow, 1928–58).

——, *Sobraniye Sochineny*, 20 vols. (Moscow, 1960–5).

——, *L. N. Tolstoy v Russkoy Kritike*, S. Bychkov (ed.), (Moscow, 1949).

——, *L. N. Tolstoy v vospominaniyakh sovremennikov*, S. N. Golubov and others (eds), 2 vols (Moscow, 1960).

——, *Tolstoy's Letters*, selected, edited and translated by R. F. Christian (London, 1978).

H. Troyat, *Tolstoy* (Harmondsworth, 1970).

E. Wasiolek, *Tolstoy's Major Fiction* (Chicago, 1978).

G. Woodcock, *Anarchism. A History of Libertarian Ideas and Movements* (Harmondsworth, 1963).

S. Zweig, *Adepts in Self-Portraiture* (English translation), (London, 1952).

## 4. BIBLIOGRAPHY

W. H. Bruford, *Chekhov and his Russia. A sociological study* (London, 1947).

——, *Anton Chekhov* (London, 1957).

R. Brustein, *The Theatre of Revolt* (London, 1965).

A. P. Chekhov, *Polnoye Sobraniye sochineny i pisem A. P. Chekhova.* 20 vols. (Moscow, 1944–51).

——, *Letters of Anton Chekhov*, translated by M. H. Heim and Simon Karlinksy (London, 1973).

——, *The Selected Letters of Chekhov*, Lillian Hellman (ed.), (London, 1955).

——, *Letters of Anton Chekhov on the short story, the drama and the other literary topics*, selected and edited by L. S. Friedland (London, 1965).

——, *The Life and Letters of Anton Tchekhov*, translated and edited by S. S. Koteliansky and Philip Tomlinson (London, 1925).

——, *Chekhov v vospominaniyakh sovremennikov*, A. Kotova (ed.), (Moscow, 1954). (2nd edition 1960).

——, *Chekhov: ego Vremya*, L. D. Opulskaya and others (eds.), (Moscow, 1977).

R. Corrigan, 'The Drama of Anton Chekhov', in *Modern Drama: Essays in Criticism*, ed. T. Bogard and W. Oliver (New York, 1965).

D. Davie (ed.), *Russian Literature and Modern English Fiction* (Chicago, 1965).

I. Ehrenburg, *Chekhov, Stendhal and other Essays* (London, 1962).

O. Elton, *Chekhov. The Taylorian Lecture* (Oxford, 1929).

F. Fergusson, *The Idea of a Theater* (Princeton, 1949).

W. Gerhardi, *Anton Chekhov* (London, 1923).

M. Gorky, *Literary Portraits* (Moscow, 1959).

B. Hahn, *Chekhov; A Study of the Major Stories and Plays* (Cambridge, 1977).

R. Hingley, *Chekhov. A Biographical and Critical Study* (London, 1950).

——, *A New Life of Anton Chekhov* (London, 1976).

R. Jackson (ed.), *Chekhov. A Collection of Critical Essays* (New Jersey, 1967).

F. L. Lucas, *The Drama of Chekhov, Synge, Yeats and Pirandello* (London, 1963).

D. Magarshack, *Chekhov: A Life* (London, 1952).

——, *Chekhov the Dramatist* (London, 1952).

T. Mann, *Last Essays* (London, 1959).

N. V. Mikhailovsky, 'Ob otsakh i detyakh i og. Chekhove' in *'Literaturnye Stat'i* (Moscow, 1957).

V. Nemirovich-Danchenko, *My Life in the Russian Theatre* (London, 1937).

R. Peacock, *The Poet in the Theatre* (London, 1961).

D. Rayfield, *Chekhov: the Evolution of his Art* (London, 1975).

L. Shestov, *Chekov and other Essays* (Ann Arbor, 1966).

M. Shotton, 'Chekhov' in J. L. I. Fennell (ed.), *Nineteenth-Century Russian Literature* (London, 1973).

E.J. Simmons, *Chekhov: A Biography* (Boston, 1962).

K. Stanislavsky, *My Life in Art* (London, 1924).

J. Styan, *The Dark Comedy* (Cambridge, 1962).

, *The Elements of Drama* (Cambridge, 1960).

M. Valency, *The Breaking String. The Plays of Anton Chekhov* (New York, 1966).

R. Williams, *Drama from Ibsen to Eliot* (Harmondsworth, 1964).

T. Winner, *Chekhov and his Prose* (New York, 1966).

# Index

For all works, whether artistic or critical, see under relevant author; e.g.
*Anna Karenina* is listed under Tolstoy, *Fathers and Sons* under Turgenev.